The Weeping Time

In 1859, at the largest recorded slave auction in American history, more than 400 men, women, and children were sold by the Butler Plantation estates. This book is one of the first to analyze the operation of this auction and trace the lives of slaves before, during, and after their sale. Immersing herself in the personal papers of the Butlers, accounts from journalists who witnessed the auction, genealogical records, and oral histories, Anne C. Bailey weaves together a narrative that brings the auction to life. Demonstrating the resilience of African American families, she includes interviews from the living descendants of slaves sold on the auction block, showing how the memories of slavery have shaped people's lives today. Using the auction as the focal point, *The Weeping Time* is a compelling and nuanced narrative of one of the most pivotal eras in American history, and how its legacy persists today.

Anne C. Bailey is an Associate Professor of History and Africana Studies at Binghamton University, State University of New York.

The Weeping Time

Memory and the Largest Slave Auction in American History

ANNE C. BAILEY

Binghamton University, State University of New York

CAMBRIDGE
UNIVERSITY PRESS

CAMBRIDGE
UNIVERSITY PRESS

One Liberty Plaza, 20th Floor, New York, NY 10006, USA

Cambridge University Press is part of the University of Cambridge.

It furthers the University's mission by disseminating knowledge in the pursuit of
education, learning, and research at the highest international levels of excellence.

www.cambridge.org
Information on this title: www.cambridge.org/9781316643488
DOI: 10.1017/9781108140393

First published 2017
8th printing 2020

Printed in the United Kingdom by TJ International Ltd. Padstow Cornwall

A catalogue record for this publication is available from the British Library.

Library of Congress Cataloging-in-Publication Data
Names: Bailey, Anne C. (Anne Caroline), author.
Title: The weeping time: memory and the largest slave auction
in American history / Anne C. Bailey.
Description: New York, NY: Cambridge University Press, [2017] |
Includes bibliographical references and index.
Identifiers: LCCN 2017023930 | ISBN 9781107193055 (hardback) |
ISBN 9781316643488 (paperback)
Subjects: LCSH: Slave trade – Georgia. | Slavery – Georgia – History – 19th century. |
Butler, Pierce, Jr. 1807–1867. | Butler family. | Slaves – Georgia – Biography. |
Plantation life – Georgia. | Plantations – Georgia – History – 19th century. |
Collective memory – United States.
Classification: LCC E442. B19 2018 | DDC 306.3/6209758–dc23
LC record available at https://lccn.loc.gov/2017023930

ISBN 978-1-107-19305-5 Hardback
ISBN 978-1-316-64348-8 Paperback

*To the memory of James Alan McPherson, writer
and descendant of Congressman Robert Smalls,
the Gullah Statesman, and my grandparents,
David and Sarah Ramsay.*

Contents

Figures

Acknowledgments

When you write a book, you want an editor who both believes in the book and believes in you. That is what I found in my editor, Debbie Gershenowitz of Cambridge University Press.

I am thankful for her knowledge of the subject and her craft, her commitment to getting it just right, and her desire to see this project come to life. Any errors are mine, not hers.

That said, there is a long list of people to thank. At the top of that list is Dr. Mary Frances Berry. Her support over the last twenty-five years is nothing short of extraordinary. I am most grateful for her unflinching critiques of my work over the years – at every stage exhorting me to achieve my fullest potential. She is the consummate historian and the consummate teacher. I also thank my other former teachers: Dr. Robert Engs, Dr. Lee Cassanelli, Dr. Sandra Barnes – all of University of Pennsylvania. Since then, scholars like Dr. Michael West, Dr. Bernice DeGannes Scott, Dr. Isidore Okpewho, Dr. Donald Quataert, Dr. Tom Dublin, Dr. Kathryn Sklar, Dr. Kathryn Geurts, Dr. Vincent McDonald, Dr. Thelma Thompson, Dr. Omowunmi Sadik, Dr. Sharon Bryant, Dr. Michael Gomez, Dr. Betty Wambui, Dr. Yasmin Hurd, Dr. Jacqueline Copeland Carson, Dr. Barbara Sertig, Dr. Hilary Robertston Hickling, Dr. Particia Lespinasse, Dr. Heather Dehaan, Dr. Doug Bradburn, and Dr. Learotha Williams Jr. have greatly influenced and supported this work.

I am also grateful for those men and women who provided much-needed support behind the scenes in a variety of ways: Michael Turner, Edwin Coleman, Johni Cerny, Lynette Stoudt, Thomas Lisanti, Allison Hudgins, Steve Engerrand, Barry and Lisa Mensah Ford, Gloria Mensah, Scott and Michelle Otey, Abigail and Darren Winslow, Carol Bennett, Iberkys Dalmasi, Carla Yanez, Mark Devoux, Muriel Walters, and my mother, brother, and son, Daphne, Anthony, and Mickias Bailey. When I think of their assistance and support, the African proverb "I am because we are" comes to mind.

In this regard as well, I am indebted to those involved in the production of the book. Joshua Penney, Kristina Deusch, Newgen Knowledge Works Pvt Ltd, and others on the production team helped me to the finish line in the last leg of this marathon effort.

Last but by no means least, I could not have written this book without the help of the descendants of the Weeping Time auction: Annette Holmes, Griffin Lotson, Tiffany Shea Young, and Mabel Thompson Hewlin. This is their story, and I am thankful that they shared their experience and personal history with me. I feel a great sense of connection to the Gullah Geechee community and know that that connection will long outlive this project.

Finally, I am indebted to many influential writers and thinkers whose work has been invaluable to me: James Alan McPherson, Gloria Naylor, Toni Morrison, Dr. Beverly Guy-Sheftall, Dr. Henry Louis Gates Jr., and W. E. B. Dubois. Dubois began *The Souls of Black Folk* the way I would like to begin here:

Gentle Reader, I pray you then, receive my little book in all charity, studying my words with me, forgiving mistake and foible for the sake of the faith and passion that is in me, and seeking the grain of truth hidden there.

PART I

THE BREACH

I

The Weeping Time

On March 2 and 3, 1859, Pierce Mease Butler of the Butler Plantation estates in the Georgia Sea Islands sold 436 men, women, and children, including 30 babies, to buyers and speculators from New York to Louisiana. It was the largest recorded slave auction in US history, advertised for weeks in newspapers and magazines across the country. The venue was the Savannah Tenbroeck Racetrack, three miles shy of the city. Eager potential buyers filled every hotel in Savannah. The two-day auction netted $303,850 for the debt-ridden Butler, a phenomenal sum. On the eve of the Civil War, this unprecedented sale was noteworthy not only for its size but because Butler Plantation slaves were generally not sold on the open market before; many lived their entire lives on Butler's estates. Surely, these lives were difficult and burdensome, but together they formed a community with its own norms, values, and customs – often informed by their shared African heritage. Now they were displaced from their "home" and separated from their families. It is for this reason the slaves called the auction "The Weeping Time."

A new chapter of their families' stories began after the auction, and then again after Emancipation in 1863, when some of these newly freed slaves set out toward plantations all over the South searching earnestly for their loved ones. It is likely that the only lingering connections to their relatives were memories of their last meeting – on the auction block. They pursued every avenue in search of those whom they had lost. In some very special cases, they found each other. Others remained in the communities of their masters, bought property, worked the land, and built new lives for themselves.

This is their story.[1]

At exactly 11:55 a.m. on March 3, 1859, Dorcas, chattel number 278, was sold away from her first love, Jeffrey, a twenty-three-year-old "prime cotton hand." She stood on the auction block motionless – emptied of words, emptied of tears. She spent the greater part of that cold and rainy Thursday morning contemplating their final separation. Now the moment came and she stood as still as a bronze cast, her head covered with a beaded gray shawl. She stared vacantly at the auctioneer who, with one stroke of his gavel, declared a death knell on her future.

"SOLD! Young Negro wench and a family of 4 to the fine gentleman from South Carolina at 11:55 am!" bellowed auctioneer William Walsh, as he pulled out his watch to check the time. He had a grandfatherly look, with a soft, pearl-gray beard that jutted out above his slightly protruding chest. He wore a double-vested black suit with several well-appointed pockets, one of which contained a shiny silver stopwatch that hung from a short chain. Dorcas might have expected a monster of a man, with blood-red eyes and a cold, cobbled face. Then she might have surmised, unreasonably, how a man with one stroke of the gavel and the stop of a watch could separate her from the man she loved.

Jeffrey, a tall, strapping field hand with soft eyes, who was sold earlier for $1,310 to another master, pulled off his hat, dropped to his knees, and wept. Just the day before, he had cherished high hopes. As soon as he was sold to a rice plantation owner of the Great Swamp, he spent the rest of the day begging and pleading with him to purchase Dorcas:

I loves Dorcas, young Mas'r; I loves her well an' true; she says she loves me, and I know she does; de good Lord knows I loves her better than I loves any one in de wide world – never can love another woman half as well. Please buy Dorcas, Mas'r. We're be good sarvants to you long as we live. We're be married right soon, young Mas'r, and de chillun will be healthy and strong, Mas'r, and dey'll be good sarvants, too. Please buy Dorcas, young Mas'r. We loves each other a heap – do, really true, Mas'r.[2]

When his new master seemed deaf to his pleas, he came up with another strategy:

"Young Mas'r," he said in an almost businesslike manner,

Dorcas prime woman – A1 woman, sa. Tall gal, sir; long arms, strong, healthy, and can do a heap of work in a day. She is one of de best rice hands on de whole plantation; worth $1,200 easy, Mas'r, an' fus'rate bargain at that.[3]

These words seemed to move his new master, who looked at him obligingly and indicated he would consider his proposal. He approached Dorcas with white-gloved hands and first opened her lips to check her age. He turned her around, as if spinning a top, and bade her take off her turban. As she turned, his white-gloved hand would alternately brush against her back and breasts. He examined her limbs one by one and put his hands around her ample waist. Yes, these hips might be worth something. They might, in fact, breed a few children, all to his profit. He nodded approvingly at Jeffrey and agreed to bid on her the next day, providing the price was right.

This was all the hope that Jeffrey needed. They would be together, he and his Dorcas; they would be far from home and family but at least they would be together. They would be married, and they would create a new family.

But when that hour came, Jeffrey's master did not comply. Had she been sold alone, he said, he would have raised his paddle for a bid. But Dorcas was not to be sold alone. At the last minute, Mr. Walsh had added her to a family of four to be sold as one lot to a South Carolina plantation. Perhaps it was because she was a rice hand herself (as opposed to a cotton hand like Jeffrey) that she was sold with Chattel no. 277, Eli, a thirty-five-year-old rice hand and his three small children, Celia, Rose, and Eliza (Chattel nos 279–281), ranging in age from six months to ten years. Rice was a premium in South Carolina and experienced rice hands were always in demand.

The thread that connected Jeffrey and Dorcas was undone. Dorcas was led away, and Jeffrey, who by this time was inconsolable, was joined by his friends. They stood in a circle around him expressing no emotion but standing guard of his.

Dorcas and Jeffrey were not the first slaves up for bid on those fateful days of March 2 and 3, 1859; George, Sue, and their young children, George and Harry, held that distinction. Cotton and rice planters respectively, each member of the family was originally sold for $600 each, but the buyer did not take the family that first day because of a dispute about the bidding process. As such, although George and his family were the first up to bid, their fate was not settled until the second day of the sale, when they were bought for $620 each, for a grand total of $2,480.[4]

Chattels

1. George, age 27, 1832, Prime Cotton Planter
2. Sue, age 26, 1833, Prime Rice Planter
3. George Jr., age 4, 1855, Boy Child
4. Harry, age 2, 1857, Boy Child

How did these slaves end up in this smoke-filled stable? All their lives, they heard it said about the Butler Island Negroes:

"We're Geechees. We don't get sold up river like no common cattle." Overseer Roswell King Jr. reiterated this in his boasts that Butler Island negroes weren't bought and sold like slaves on the mainland plantations. "And there isn't a dirt eater among them," he declared, meaning that they were well fed and housed by their masters.[5] Even the mainland residents of Darien who came to market would comment that the Butler negroes were a race apart. In fact, many noted that they had their own dialect that only they could understand, and it was not until after the Civil war that they mixed with other black populations in the area.

None of the Butler slaves have ever been sold before, but have been on these two plantations since they were born. Here they have lived their humble lives, and loved their simple loves; here were they born and here have many of them had children born unto them; here had their parents lived before them, and now are resting in quiet graves on old plantations that these unhappy ones *are to see no more forever*;[6]

Such was the account of a certain reporter, Mortimer Thomson, nick-named "Doesticks," who was disguised as a buyer at the two-day auction. Doesticks was a man of the North and a writer for the *New York Tribune* who, during the auction, mingled among the buyers while carefully hiding his abolitionist sympathies. He recorded every word of their conversations with interest; no doubt with the intent to show how cruel an institution slavery indeed was.

Just as their parents and grandparents before them, the Butler slaves made Butler Island and St. Simon's their home. Now they would have to leave it behind – relatives resting in gravesites on the estates and a thousand memories in the place they called home.

Butler Island Plantation and the St. Simon's estate called Hampton Point had been in the Butler family for over four generations. Located off the coast of Georgia, between the Altamaha River and the Atlantic Ocean, these islands were worlds to themselves. The river, as the slaves liked to say, was like a prison wall. Only the slave boatmen, who skillfully navigated its many twists and bends, viewed the river differently. The field hands were obliged to work in gangs according to tasks. The overseers and the slave drivers watched their every move. But these boatmen who carried goods, people, and produce on their hand-carved canoes from the islands to the mainland enjoyed a semblance of freedom.[7] If the slaves were prisoners, they were prisoners of hope whose songs of freedom heralded a better time to come.

Many a day they could be heard singing the hymn: "I want to climb up Jacob's ladder," or even the more subversive freedom song:

Oh brudders, let us leave
Dis buckra land for Hayti
Dah we be receive
Grand as Lafayetty.
Make a mighty show
When we land from steamship,
Youu'll be like Monro,
Me like Lewis Philip ...
No more our son cry sweep
No more he play de lackey
No more our daughters weep
'Kasedey call demblacy
No more dey servants be
No more dey scrub and cook-y
But ebbry day we'll see
Dem read de novel book-y[8]

With the wind at their backs, how they dared to sing songs of freedom in a land of slavery; how they dared to sing of Haiti who had fought for its freedom in 1791. The boatmen and other slaves likely heard about the Haitian revolution from none other than the Butlers themselves and their slave-owning neighbors. Those were days filled with fear and anxiety about the possibility that such an uprising could take place in their backyard.[9]

Major Pierce Butler, the patriarch who came from South Carolina by way of Ireland, was the master of Butler Island at the time. He was famous for having been one of the signers of the United States Constitution. Since 1774, he had made a fortune cultivating rice along the marshy shores of the Altamaha Delta on the Butler estate and growing thousands of acres of Sea Island cotton on St. Simon's island.

He had a reputation for being controlling and curiously cut his own children out of his will but left all of his properties to his grandsons Pierce Mease and John. As a result, Pierce Mease Butler lived a very comfortable life in an expensive town home in Philadelphia. He ran his plantation estates from afar through overseers who, in turn, employed a number of slave drivers. But Pierce Mease Butler, who inherited the Butler plantation estate with his brother John, was careless with his finances. His divorce in 1848 from the famed Shakespearean actress Fanny Kemble was costly and, moreover, he gambled much of his inheritance away.[10]

Slaves were long used to pay off the debts of their masters. If a master lost a wager in a poker game, his slaves would go to the winner. If he defaulted on a bank loan, slaves would be added to the bank's balance sheet. It was also not unusual for them to be given as wedding gifts or for individual family members to be willed to different parties. In 1859, this was not a new practice.[11]

The auction was years in the making. Butler's 440 slaves – his half of his grandfather's inheritance – had to be sold because, by 1856, Butler had gambled away much of his fortune on the stock market.[12] His grand home in the heart of Philadelphia was to be sold in lots and his "hereditary negroes" were to be sold on the auction block. The stock market crash of 1857 that caused a run on many of the major banks only served to worsen his situation. As his friend George Fisher lamented at the time, this crisis may not have happened had people not been so reckless:

A prudent people will make prudent banks. A wild and reckless people will make rash and headlong banks, and we are a wild and reckless people. We like to make money fast, because the circumstances of the country tempt us to make money fast by offering unprecedented facilities for doing so. This creates a demand for capital beyond the supply and therefore fictitious capital is created. So long as confidence is maintained, all is well, but a failure at length must occur and then the fiction becomes apparent.[13]

Here, he very well could have been describing the dapper Pierce Mease Butler, whose "hereditary fortune of $700,000 (was) lost by sheer folly and infactuation … Such is the end of folly."[14]

By 1856, Butler's situation worsened to the degree that Tom James and Henry and George Cadwalader of Philadelphia were appointed trustees over his estate and that of Gabriella Butler, the wife of his deceased brother, John Butler.[15] Along with Butler, they decide to sell his half of the plantation slaves, pay off his debts, and regain a large income.

On February 16, 1859, Trustee Thomas C. James was authorized by Gabriella Butler, the widow of Pierce's brother John, to represent her in the "agreement made the following day appointing Thomas M. Foreman, James Hamilton Couper and Thomas Pinckney Huger to appraise and divide the slaves." This appraisal only listed those slaves as Share A, who were to remain on the plantation as part of Butler estate.[16] Slaves like Frank, the driver, and his wife Betty were at the top of the list of those who would remain on the estate. Frank was listed as age 61 and, under the REMARKS category, he was said to be "bedridden superannuated." Betty, his wife, was listed as 58 years old and, under REMARKS, was listed as a "poultry minder." She was valued at $100 but there was ironically no value listed for Frank, who was once second only to the overseer in terms of authority on the plantation. This is likely because he was now 61, sick and bedridden, well past his usefulness to the Butlers or anyone else.[17]

The other 440 were to be sold on March 2 and 3.

In the same month, Joseph Bryan, a well-known slave dealer and former serviceman and chief of police of Savannah was commissioned to manage this major slave sale. Savannah was the perfect choice because of its proximity to the Butler estate in Darien County as well as the fact that it was one of the South's largest centers for the trade in slaves.[18] Bryan was one of the largest slave brokers in the South, with both an office and a slave pen on the corner of Johnson Square. He was a highly regarded US Navy veteran and city official. Upon his death, *The Savannah Republican* would record: "He was one whom a large number of the young selected as their guide and example in life."

In the early months of 1859, Bryan anticipated this slave sale to be a major boon to his business. He was not to be disappointed. Records show that he made a handsome sum of $8,000 in commissions on the sale. His slave pen was located next to the site that was eventually to be the location of the First African Baptist Church, founded by George Leile, Savannah's oldest black church and said to be the oldest black church in North America (and eventually pastored by an ex-slave preacher named Andrew Bryan[19]). The slave-holding pen itself later became a schoolhouse after the Civil War, a black underground school called the Savannah Educational Association. All that remains today is "418 Bryan St." marked above the door and the remains of a two-story building whose decrepit walls alone know the whole story of the shattered lives that passed through those doors.

In 1859, Bryan's slave mart was thriving. He put ads in papers all over the country announcing the sale in *The Savannah Republican, The Savannah Daily Morning News, The Charleston Courier, Christian Index, Albany Patriot, Augusta Constitutionalist, Mobile Register, New Orleans Picayune, Memphis Appeal, Vicksburg Southern* and the *Richmond Whig*, announcing:

FOR SALE

Long Cotton and Rice Negroes!
A gang of 440
Accustomed to the culture of Rice and Provisions, among them are a
    no of good mechanics and house servants
Will be sold on 2nd and 3rd day of March at Savannah
by J Bryan

SALE OF 440 NEGROES!

Persons desiring to inspect these Negroes will find
Them at the Tenbroeck Race Course[20]

It was to this race course, surrounded by dense woods, just three miles
shy of Savannah, that all of Pierce Butler's slaves were taken. From the
late eighteenth century, this racetrack was said to be one of the finest of
its kind and was host to the Savannah Jockey Club's racing season from
1857 onwards. The mile-long track with its "fineinclosure (sic), halls, sta-
bles for other large gatherings" was one of the playgrounds of Savannah's
elite.[21]

But on this sad occasion, it housed those on the opposite end of the
spectrum: those without property, much less horses; those who were

FIGURE 1.1 Savannah's Tenbroeck Racetrack, site of the largest slave auction in
US history.
Courtesy of Georgia Historical Society. Scholar Kwesi DeGraft-Hanson has
recently recreated the racetrack as it would have looked at the time in "Unearthing
the Weeping Time: Savannah's Ten Broeck Race Course and 1859 Slave Sale,"
Southern Spaces (2010); he also documented that space as currently occupied
by Bradley Plywood Corporation, southernspaces.org/2010/unearthing-weeping-
time-savannahs-ten-broeck-race-course-and-1859-slave-sale#sthash.X9uYsOJI
.dpuf, accessed November 2, 2016.

considered property themselves and treated no better than the animals whose sheds they temporarily occupied. Most of the slaves arrived at the racetrack via railroad cars from the Darien town center on the coast that was minutes from the Butler estate. Some also traveled by steamboat.

They were herded into sheds that normally housed the horses and the carriages of the gentlemen attending the races. In the continuous, pouring rain in the days before the sale, broker after broker, speculator after speculator arrived at the race course to examine and inspect the slaves. The buyers paraded them and made them dance. They opened their clothing to check for wounds; they pinched their limbs and flexed their muscles. They searched earnestly for scars, since scars were said to be evidence of a rebellious nature. When they finished their inspections, they posed questions regarding their abilities and their willingness to work. They were to be sold in families in the narrowest sense of the word: married couples and mothers and young children, not brothers or sisters or older parents.[22]

They were the talk of Savannah that spring of 1859. Negro buyers and brokers, slave breakers and drivers from North and South Carolina, Virginia, Alabama, Georgia, and Louisiana eagerly came to put in their bids. The office of Joseph Bryan, the Negro broker who superintended the sale, was flooded with inquiries from those in other parts of the country who could not come but wanted to send proxies to ensure that their bids would be considered.

The buyers were a rowdy lot. They were like a group of hard-playing, top-of-the-lungs-swearing poker players in a smoke-filled game. The best-dressed "fine" Southern gentlemen with long white gloves mixed amongst these hard-nosed and often unkempt Negro buyers, who attended at least two auctions a week and were as callous as their business. They did not stand on ceremony or assume any of the genteel etiquette associated with the Old South. They did not wear suits and jackets, and instead ambled around the market in their shirtsleeves in tall, weather-beaten leather boots. At a glance, they looked like hunters, and of course they were hunters of a sort: of the human species.[23]

But it was business, just business, and many of the buyers jostled with one another at numerous auctions. They swore and carried on like sailors on a slave ship. A thick gray smoke emanating from their continually lit pipes wafted through the long room adjoining the race course that was appointed for the sale. Now and again, one could hear them almost groan with delight at the prospect of purchasing a nice Negro wench for their more upscale clients.

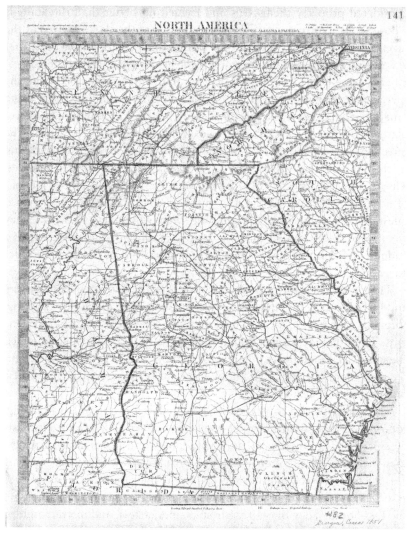

FIGURE 1.2 Gullah Geechee region.
Courtesy of Georgia Historical Society.

"Well, Colonel, I seen you looking sharp at Shoemaker Bill's Sally. Going to buy her?"

"Well, Major, I think not. Sally's a good, big, strapping gal, and can do a heap o'work; but it's five years since she had any children. *She's done breeding, I reckon.*"[24]

Just then, Anson and Violet, a couple who looked older than their fifty years, Chattel nos 111 and 112, were brought to the stage. Each carried a bundle under their arms that seemed almost to dwarf their small, tender frames. Violet's hair was silver-gray but Anson's was salt and pepper. Both were infirm. Violet had an irrepressible cough and Anson was listed in the catalog as "ruptured and as having one eye." Their deeply lined faces told their own stories – much like the stories they and others told on the Butler plantation. In the legend of the Butler slaves who could fly, for example, brave slaves walked into the waters to their death rather than face a life under the lash. They flew back to Africa, the old folks said; they flew away and now they were free.[25] Maybe those tales were of some comfort now. Maybe only those stories – the idea that there would be freedom someday, even if only in death – kept them from falling onto that stage in the face of the raucous taunts of the buyers and brokers.

"250 going once, going twice; SOLD! To the good man from Georgia," said Walsh scarcely containing his laughter as Anson and Violet were led off the stage.

"Cheap gal, that, Major!" said one of the buyers to another.

"Don't think so. They may talk about her being sick; it's no easy sickness she's got. She's got consumption, and the man that buys her will have to be a doctrin' her all the time, and she'll die in less than three months. I won't have anything to do with her – don't want any half dead niggers about me."[26]

For their part, Anson and Violet stepped down from the stage without even looking in the direction of their new owner. At the last moment, Anson might have turned a glance at the jeering crowd, his well-worn eyes concealing his anger and his pain. Like many a slave spouse before and after him, he had probably learned the art of self-restraint.[27] He had learned to bite his tongue in order to save his family from certain death. He, himself, could take the taunts and ridicule of the crowd, but he could not protect the wife he loved. He could not protect her on the plantation from the overseer's lash, he could not protect her from sexual abuse, nor could he protect her on the auction block from this open scorn. A quiet sense of misplaced shame likely hovered above him as he descended the stage.[28]

The next group up for sale, however, reacted altogether differently.

Chattels

  99. John, aged 31, prime rice hand
100. Betsey, aged 29, rice hand, unsound
101. Kate, aged 6
102. Violet, aged 3 months

Chattel nos 99–102 (John and Betsey, husband and wife, holding their two children – Kate, six years old, and baby Violet, three months old), from the beginning, struck a decidedly defiant pose. Betsey, in particular, a young twenty-nine-year-old rice hand, who was barely four feet tall with old woman hands, was the kind of woman who was not going to go complacently. She was long known for having a fiery temper, perhaps the reason she was listed in the catalog as "unsound."[29] Rebellious slave women who defied their masters were often called unsound. Those were the women who attempted to poison their slave owners at dinnertime or who feigned mental or physical illness to deprive them of their labor. In their own way, they were fearsome and commanded a certain respect from slave and free alike.[30]

Now here stood this "unsound" Betsey before her would be buyers – belligerent and unafraid. She stared into their eyes. With one look, she indicted them. Indicted them for their cruelty, indicted them for their indifference. When she and her family were finally sold to a Mr. Archibald W. Baird of Louisiana for $510 apiece, her determination was even more evident. She would not let them see her cry. The slaves were already calling these fateful days "the weeping time," but her tears would not flow. She and her husband John and their children, named after their respective mothers, would turn their backs and walk to the stalls in quietude and dignity.

Chattel nos 138–143 should have been up next to bid, since they were listed in the auction catalog, but their lots were withdrawn.

138. Doctor George, age 39, born 1820.
139. Margaret, age 38, born 1821
140. Maria, age 11, born 1848
141. Lena, age 6, born 1853
142. Mary Ann, age 3, born 1856
143. Infant, boy, born February 16, 1859

Apparently through circumstances that could not be fully ascertained, Margaret's baby, having been born on February 16, was only four days old at the time that the slaves were to begin their long, arduous journey from Butler Island to the point of sale in Savannah. As such, she asked Mr. Butler if she and her family could remain on the plantation and Mr. Butler surprisingly "uttered no reproach," even though he stood to lose the handsome sum of $4000 – their value on the auction block since they were a family of six.[31]

Unfortunately, though the circumstances were similar, there was to be no such reprieve for Primus, Chattel no. 72, and Daphney, Chattel no. 73, and their young children, Dido, Chattel no. 74, a girl of three years, and a baby, Chattel no. 75, only one month old, that Daphney was holding protectively in her arms beneath a large shawl. This simple act of maternal love provoked the most boisterous remarks:

"What do you keep your nigger covered up for? Pull off her blanket."

"What's the matter with that gal?" said another. "Has she got a headache?"

"Who's going to bid on that nigger if you keep her covered up?" asked still another without any regard for her newborn that had been born on Valentine's Day. "Let's see her face!"[32]

Auctioneer Walsh had to repeatedly assure the boisterous buyers that there was no attempt at subterfuge: she was not an ill slave that they were trying to palm off as a healthy one but that Daphney had given birth only fifteen days before. For that, she was entitled to the "slight indulgence" of a shawl to wrap around her and her newborn baby to ward off the cold and the rain. With these assurances made, the bidding began and in the end, Primus, who was a plantation carpenter, and Daphney, a rice hand, were both sold for $635. Their two small children, including the infant born on Valentine's Day, were also sold for the sum of $635 each.[33]

As the day progressed, other slaves were sold, including brothers Noble and James, Chattel nos 256 and 260, who were sold with their families for the sum of $1,236 each.

Chattels

255. Sally Walker, age 44, born 1815, Cotton Hand, $1,236
256. Noble, age 22, born 1837, Cotton, Prime Man, $1,236
257. Sophy, age 20, born 1839, Cotton, Prime Woman, $1,236
258. Malsey, age 17, born 1842, Cotton, Prime Young Woman, $1,236
259. Chaney, age 13, born 1846, Cotton, Prime Girl, $1,236
260. James, age 9, born 1850, $1,236

Wiseman, age nineteen, described as a prime cotton hand, was also sold with his family, as was the family of Ned and Lena (also known as Scena) – Chattel nos 127 and 128 – who had seven children: Bess, Mary, Flanders, Molsie, Hannah, Thomas, and Ezekiel. Little Brister, at age 5, son of Matty, a twenty-seven-year-old rice hand described as in her prime, was among the many young people sold; he and his mother were sold for $855 each.[34]

Chattels

225. Kit, age 38, born 1821
226. Matilda, age 38, born 1821
227. Wiseman, age 19, born 1840
228. Hannah, age 12, born 1847
229. William, age 11, born 1848
230. Matilda, age 6, born 1853
231. Kit, age 1, born 1858

Chattels

127. Ned, age 56, born 1803
128. Lena, age 50, born 1809
209. Matty, age 27, born 1832
211. Brister, age 5, born 1854[35]

"Gentlemen!" called out Mr. Walsh. "This is a good time for a break. I encourage you to see the attractions of our bar to your right. May I also remind you of the terms of the sale for when you return:

"One-third cash, the remainder payable in two equal annual installments, bearing interest from the day of sale, to be secured by approved mortgage and personal security, or approved acceptances in Savannah, Ga., or Charleston, S. C. Purchasers to pay for papers," he said all in one breath.

"As a reminder, we have carpenters, mechanics, we have blacksmiths, we have shoemakers, we have coopers – and prime, prime rice and cotton hands ... Pure blooded negroes ..."[36]

Indeed, there were many skilled tradesmen, like Joe and his son Robert, Chattel nos 9 and 15, who were considered prime plantation carpenters. Robert was the product of Joe's first marriage to a slave called Psyche, sometimes known as Sack, who died years before the auction. In many cases, a certain trade had become like the family business – a skill that was passed from father to son. In the best of times, this skill could earn a slave and his family a little extra money, but in the worst of times, such as these, it meant fetching a higher price and even the possibility of being separated from one's family if it suited either buyer or seller.

With that, the Negro buyers, speculators as they were called at the time retreated to the bar, puffing away on their cigars and cigarettes. The room was putrid with smoke. They ordered their drinks and gathered together in small parties of four and five. Some were eyeing the auction catalogue, looking at the next slaves who were up for bid.[37]

Chattels

103. Wooster, age 45, hand, and fair mason.
104. Mary, age 40, cotton hand.
105. Commodore Bob, aged, rice hand.
106. Kate, aged, cotton.
107. Linda, age 19, cotton, prime young woman.
108. Joe, age 13, rice, prime boy.
109. Bob, age 30, rice.
110. Mary, age 25, rice, prime woman.
120. Pompey, Jr., age 10, prime boy.
121. John, age 7.

Others were heartily engaged in conversation about the best methods to control a "refractory nigger." All the while, Doesticks, the reporter in disguise, was recording their conversation. He overheard them discussing all the known methods, with agreement that the crack of a whip and the brand of an iron were most effective. As for pure-blooded negroes, they were much to be preferred to mulattoes with a little white blood.

"A little white blood and they don't respond to the lash in the same way …" one hoary-voiced slave driver said above the din of voices.

Others engaged in more political discussions. The year, after all, was 1859 and tensions were rising to a boiling point between North and South. The reopening of the Atlantic slave trade was a subject foremost on their minds. Doesticks reported as much:

The discussion of the reopening of the slave trade was commenced and the opinion seemed to generally prevail that its reestablishment is a consummation devoutly to be wished, and one red faced Major or General or Corporal clenched his remarks with the emphatic assertion that "We'll have all the niggers in Africa over here in 3 years – we won't leave enough for seed.[38]

Meanwhile, Dembo, age twenty, and Frances, age nineteen, Chattel nos 322 and 404, were eagerly awaiting their turn at the hammer. They stood huddled together with their small bundles of cloth and tin gourds – all the possessions they owned in the world. They were eager for the sale to resume for one reason only. They hoped to bring a little plan of their own to fruition.

The night before, they had found a minister among those attending the sale. They begged him to join them in holy matrimony. As a result, they would now be sold as one lot if all went as planned.[39]

Mr. Walsh called Dembo and Frances to the stage. With a little help from a few of the more boisterous buyers, he then proceeded to poke fun at the couple.

An Alabama buyer with an exposed revolver at his side came up to examine Frances. He did not use white gloves. With his bare hands, cracked with dirt, he checked her teeth, hips, and other assets. Frances looked straight ahead. She displayed no emotion, no embarrassment, and no anger. She kept her focus on their little plan and, within moments, a deal was struck. Dembo and Frances were sold together for $1,320 apiece.

And off they went, smiling broadly. They could hardly contain their joy. They would build a life together on a cotton plantation in Alabama.

But there was to be no such ending for Jeffrey and Dorcas. Jeffrey was going to North Carolina and Dorcas to South Carolina. When last seen, Jeffrey was sitting alone on the ground, crying into his hands, as Dorcas was led away by her new master. She sat in the back of his carriage – emptied of words, emptied of tears.

At the end of the auction, as the final separations were taking place, the *New York Tribune* correspondent witnessed the following scene:

Leaving the Race buildings, where the scenes we have described took place, a crowd of negroes were seen gathered eagerly about a white man. That man was Pierce M. Butler, of the free City of Philadelphia, who was solacing the wounded hearts of the people he had sold from their firesides and their homes, by doling out to them small change at the rate of a dollar a-head. To every negro he had sold, who presented his claim for the paltry pittance, he gave the munificent stipend of one whole dollar, in specie; he being provided with two canvas bags of 25 cent pieces, fresh from the mint, to give an additional glitter to his generosity.[40]

It was still raining violently, as if the sky was both weeping and protesting the day's proceedings.

Notes

1 Mortimer "Doesticks" Thomson, "What Became of the Slaves on a Georgia Plantation," *African American Perspectives: Pamphlets from Daniel A. P. Murray Collection*, 1818–1907, Library of Congress.

   The following account of the auction incorporates some poetic license only in some of the physical descriptions of the individuals involved; the account is based on the above contemporary account of Northern newspaperman Mortimer Thomson also known as Doesticks. Thomson posed as a buyer to write the story for the *New York Tribune*. The quotes from the buyers and the slaves are exactly as recorded by Doesticks including his attempt to capture the dialect.

2 Ibid., p. 16.

3 Ibid., p. 17.

4 Ibid., p. 11.

5 Roswell King, "On the Management of the Butler Estate," *Southern Agriculturalist* (December 1828). According to King, dirt eating by slaves was an "incurable propensity produced from a morbid state of the stomach from the want of a proper quantity of wholesome food, and a proper time." The term Gullah/Geechee here and elsewhere in the book refers to west and central-African peoples, traditions, and language of coastal islands and areas of South Carolina, Georgia, North Carolina, and Florida; the population is composed of many different African ethnic groups, including Gola, Kissi, Mende, Temne, Twi, and Vai.

6 Thomson, p. 5.

7 Malcolm Bell, *Major Butler's Legacy: Five Generations of a Slaveowning family* (Athens, GA: University of Georgia Press, 1987), p. 148–149, p. 281–283.

8 Frances Butler Leigh, *Ten Years on a Georgia Plantation Since the War* (London: Richard Bentley and Son, 1883) p. 229. "This delightful song was composed somewhere about 1840, at the time of one of the Haytian revolutions, when the negroes, imagining that they would have no more work to do, but all be ladies and gentlemen, took the most absurd airs, and went about calling themselves by all the different distinguished names they had ever heard," *Documenting the American South*, docsouth.unc.edu/fpn/leigh/leigh.html, accessed October 2, 2016.

9 The revolt began in 1791. It was several years later before freedom was actually won by the formerly enslaved people, and later still before the new republic was declared the independent state of Haiti in 1804.

10 Thomson, p. 3, and Bell.

11 See also classic works by Walter Johnson, *Soul by Soul: Life inside the Antebellum Slave Market* (Cambridge, MA: Harvard University Press, 1999), p. 26 and Frederic Bancroft, *Slave Trading in the Old South* (New York: Frederick Ungar Publishing, 1959).

12 Nicholas B. Wainwright, ed., *A Philadelphia Perspective: The Diary of Sidney George Fisher Covering the Years, 1834–1871* (Philadelphia: Historical Society of Pennsylvania, 1967), p. 257.

13 Ibid., p. 279.

14 Ibid., p. 277–278.

15 William Dusinberre. *Them Dark Days: Slavery in the American Rice Swamps* (New York: Oxford University Press, 1996) p. 214–215 and Sidney George Fisher and Nicholas Wainwright, *A Philadelphia Perspective: The Diary of Sidney George Fisher covering the years 1834–1871*, (Philadelphia: Historical Society of Pennsylvania, 1967), p. 317.

16 Bell, p. 326.

17 Documents pertaining to division and appraisal of slaves in Superior Ct, Chatham County, Savannah Deed Book 3-S, p. 247–255 and in Glynn Cty, Brunswick deed book No. 52–71.

18 Walter Fraser, *Savannah in the Old South* (Athens, GA: University of Georgia Press, 2003) p. 310 and Martha Kleber, Georgia Historical Society marker application program, March 1, 2007.

19 First Avenue Baptist Church website, firstafricanbc.com/history.asp.

20 Bell, p. 328–329.
21 Martha Kleber, "Sale of Pierce M. Butler's Slaves." Georgia Historical Society Application, March 1, 2007.
22 Thomson, p. 5.
23 Ibid., p. 13.
24 Ibid., p. 9.
25 Bell, p. 132.
26 Thomson, p. 18. The word "nigger" here and elsewhere in the text is used in direct quotes from the contemporary newspaper account.
27 Thomson, p. 19.
28 See also Jacqueline Jones, *Labor of Love, Labor of Sorrow: Black Women, Labor and Family from Slavery to the Present*, (New York: Basic Books, 2010) regarding enslaved men who preferred to marry women on other plantations since they could not prevent exploitation of their wives. See also the seminal slave narrative by Harriet Jacobs, *Incidents in the Life of a Slave Girl written by herself* (1861), p. 231–233. Here she recounts the abuse of not only women but also in some cases of men. See also Thomas A. Foster, "The Sexual Abuse of Black Men under slavery," *Journal of the History of Sexuality*, Vol. 20 no. 3, 445–464. Web, September 3, 2011, also details little-known incidents of abuse of males.
29 Thomson, p. 11–12, Interview #2 with Annette Holmes, descendant of John Butler (2006).
30 See Lucy Mair, *The Rebel Woman*, (Jamaica: Institute of Jamaica Publications Ltd., 1975).
31 Thomson, p. 15.
32 Ibid.
33 Thomson, p. 14–15.
34 Reprinted from the Auction Catalogue, Historical Society of Pennsylvania, www.glynngen.com/slaverec/butler.htm.
35 Ibid.
36 Thomson, p. 11 and Bell, p. 328–329.
37 Thomson, p. 12–13.
38 Ibid., p. 9.
39 Ibid., p. 18–19.
40 Ibid., p. 20.

2

The Auction and American History

It is true they were sold "in families;" but let us see: a man and his wife were called a "family," their parents and kindred were not taken into account; the man and wife might be sold to the pinewoods of North Carolina, their brothers and sisters scattered through the cotton fields of Alabama and the rice swamps of Louisiana, while the parents might be left on the old plantation to wear out their weary lives in heavy grief, and lay their heads in far-oft graves, over which their children might never weep. And no account could be taken of loves that were as yet unconsummated by marriage; and how many aching hearts have been divorced by this summary proceeding no man can ever know.[1]

Mortimer "Doesticks" Thomson

Why study the Weeping Time? Fundamentally, the Butler auction and others like it represent a traumatic breach in family bonds not only between those separated on the auction block but also between present and future generations. The auction gives us a glimpse of the enormity of the impact of slavery on both individuals and entire generations of slaves. Moreover, and importantly, it reveals that the auction in particular and slavery in general had equally profound effects on White families.

To tell the story of the auction, its pre-history, and its legacy underscores four key themes in American history and the history of the African Diaspora: slave labor, emancipation from slavery, the reconciliation of lives and loved ones in the era of Reconstruction, and historical and contemporary notions of the Black family. These topics reveal that the fates of Black and White families were linked from the start, yet ran parallel to one another. From the nation's founding, these two groups have informed each other's histories, experiences, and memories, sharing experiences but with very different outcomes.

Yet, for all that was shared by Blacks and Whites over the course of American history, the auction represents a massive breach in historical memory. In antebellum America, there were hundreds if not thousands of auctions; they were essential to the nation's economic life and its expansion, yet most readers would be hard-pressed to name one. Moreover, our story is about a breach in the very ideals that birthed the United States, in that the auction marked the destruction of the ideals and values encoded in the Declaration of Independence and the American Constitution. Principles such as the primacy of equality, freedom, and democracy were set aside in favor of economic interest. Profit took precedence over people, despite the fact that those are the very tenets that make the United States unique and an inspiration to immigrants, refugees, minority groups, and other populations worldwide.[2]

Historians and other scholars like Eric Foner, Michael Gomez, David Blight, Mary Frances Berry, Evelyn Higginbotham, Diana Ramey Berry, Annette Gordon Reed, Walter Johnson, Catherine Clinton, Kenneth M. Stampp, Eric Williams, John Blassingame, Herbert Gutman, Deborah Gray White, and writers such as Alex Haley have produced impressive accounts and analyses of this period, returning people of African descent to the history books.[3] Notwithstanding their groundbreaking work, the auction block remains all but forgotten in American memory.

In using the auction block as an anchor in this book, we obtain a lens through which we can better understand the parallel lives, yet linked fates, of Black and White families during slavery – and the denial of these links – as a legacy of slavery.[4] The auction and its retelling illustrates the value and importance of slave work for both masters and slaves, reaping huge profits and ensuring a rich life for the former, but honoring and regenerating the skills and traditions of the latter's forebears learned on the African continent. Slave work was omnipresent in the lives of both groups, yet the outcomes and meanings of this work were very different for each. We see further evidence of Black and White parallel lives with linked fates in the migration of African culture to the culture of slavery in the Americas when we examine foodways, musical traditions, and religion. Finally, and perhaps most important in the era under investigation in this book, the Civil War brings the parallel lives and linked fates of Black and White communities into sharp relief. Though the North and South went to war for different reasons, both sides experienced devastating tolls in the same battles. At the same time, war – during and after – brought significant gains for former slaves.

This book adds to the historiography on slavery, emancipation, and especially Reconstruction – when former slaves began to heal the breach. For African Americans, Reconstruction was first and foremost about the recovery of family members lost to auctions such as the Butler sale and other tragic events. Then and now, recovery remains a constant theme in African American history, as we shall see in the noble efforts of modern-day descendants from the victims of the Butler auction to restore the pieces of their fragmented past. Their voices – which have never been heard until now – make this story unique.

The Black Family and Its Resilience

The auction and its aftermath also speak to contemporary perceptions of the Black family by providing it with a historical context. Then and now, policymakers and many others are wont to observe that the African American family is in a state of crisis. Senator Daniel Moynihan's famous report on the Black family, "The Negro Family: The Case for National Action," did little to alleviate concerns about the state of the Black family in 1965.[5] He mistakenly blamed the Black female "matriarch" for its breakdown, while others who wrote after him placed the blame more squarely on the institution of slavery and its subsequent legacy of racial discrimination and exclusion. As Congress of Racial Equality (CORE) activist and psychologist William Ryan said in reaction to the report in an article in *The Nation* in 1965, "The problem is discrimination;" we ought not, then, "blame the victim."[6] Or, as historian Dylan Pennigroth says eloquently: "rather than a source of continuing dysfunction, proponents of this view argue, that the Black family, the Black community and Black traditions of property ownership have been the only things keeping Black people from total annihilation."[7] This book affirms the view that the Black family is a resilient institution.

The statistics of the second decade of the twenty-first century are no better than those from 1965 and, according to the Urban Institute's 50th anniversary report on the Moynihan Report, they are in fact worse, and not just for Black families.[8] Even with a Black family in the White House from 2008–2016, and a much larger Black middle class than ever before, little can be said to have changed for a persistent underclass. Sociologist William Julius Wilson points the finger at the loss of manufacturing jobs, "the suburbanization" of employment, and structural racism. It is the high rate of joblessness, he asserts, that leads to crime and other negative impacts on Black family life and communities.[9] The Urban Institute additionally identifies disparities in education and the need for reform of the criminal justice system as major contributing factors, particularly with respect to Black men.

With the ongoing debate about "dysfunction" stemming from the breakdown of the Black family, it is perhaps not surprising that Black students in my classes on slavery often try to draw a straight line from slavery to modern times when attempting to make sense of the Black family. "Is this why the Black family is in the state that it is in today?" they often ask, while reading historical texts. I continually have to remind them that there is not, and has never been, a straight line that can be drawn between slavery and contemporary times.

In fact, what this account of the Weeping Time may tell us, if nothing else, is just how Black families struggled to stay together in spite of the odds during and after slavery. The auction itself is a stark reminder of the structural attacks with which Black families have had to contend throughout American history, the series of disruptions they have endured from Africa to America's shores, and then again and again as slaves were sold to different locations across the country. So while the line may not be straight, there is definitely continuity in terms of the themes of struggle and resilience.

The Weeping Time strives to show how critical it was for slave families to restore the breach after emancipation, and the importance of family ties – more crucial than money, jobs, and education. Many of these newly freed slaves set out on foot to plantations all over the South in search for their loved ones. They took with them a lock of hair, a swath of clothing – small mementos that they saved prior to the auction. They pursued every avenue in search of those whom they had lost. They found their way to African American churches and other gathering places to look for their loved ones. They searched from town to town, and in some cases from state to state, attempting to reassemble the broken fragments that the auction, among other experiences in slavery, brought about.[10] So the story of the Weeping Time is not just about the breach caused by the auction itself, but about restoring the breach of kinship ties in spite of the odds. It is a story of resilience, or what I call here "the gift of resilience."[11]

In spite of the seemingly dire statistics regarding African American families, the picture is not completely bleak. In this book's Epilogue, I consider the central role that memory plays in building hope. While much has been written and lamented about Black family "dysfunction," not enough has been said about the modern-day surge of Black interest in genealogy, the Black Family Reunion movement, and the love in and amongst many African American families exemplified in their fierce determination to stay together just as they did during and after slavery.

A sizeable number of African American families are exploring genealogical websites like Afrigeneas.com and using available DNA technology to make sense of incredible loss. Some DNA services, for example, offer families the opportunity to trace either their paternal or maternal lines. Some also enable families to determine the region of Africa that was their point of origin. I myself used the service African DNA and traced my maternal line, sending in samples of my DNA from cotton swabs. The results were fascinating.[12]

I was born in Jamaica, a part of the African Diaspora with strong ties to West and Central Africa. Though African-descended Jamaicans hail from a number of different ethnic groups in these regions, the ethnic groups of Ghana have long been strongly associated with the island's population. In fact, one of our national heroes, Nanny, was of Akan/Ashanti origin – one of the main ethnic groups of Ghana. Nanny was a female maroon chief who led the maroons to victory against the British in the eighteenth century. She was known for using her strong cultural ties to her Akan/Ashanti heritage to secure and establish a 500-acre maroon settlement then called Nanny town. Oral history in my family, particularly from my elder uncle and family historian, Mr. Eardley Ramsay, also points to an African woman named Amanda Carr, who was believed to have been of Ashanti origin (see Fig. 2.1 below). This Ashanti woman, at the tender age of sixteen, was the common-law wife of a Scottish overseer named Ramsay. He was the de facto master of the Craigie Plantation in the parish of St. Elizabeth in eighteenth-century Jamaica.[13]

The DNA test results, however, appear to tell another story, suggesting that my origins on my mother's side are further north and west – more towards Sierra Leone and neighboring countries. This discovery alone puts me close to the region and people under investigation in this book, as the Low Country region is closely associated with Sierra Leone and its neighbors. It is also interesting to note that the Gullah Geechee language spoken in the Low Country region, with its strong African retentions, is reminiscent of Jamaican patois. Though much more research would have to be done to draw stronger conclusions, the fact that I, as a native of Jamaica, may have an ancestral link to the people of this study is both fascinating and rewarding.

FIGURE 2.1 Mr. Eardley George Ramsay.
Photo Credit: Alison Ramsay.

In addition to genealogical services, Black families draw on reunions to reconstruct and connect with their relatives, forebears, and histories. For generations many Black American families held reunions, often in the South, as opportunities to pool resources, share genealogical discoveries, and to celebrate their achievements. Much of this activity has been taking place under the radar, but Black families with family names proudly emblazoned on brightly colored t-shirts and other memorabilia are making their mark by staying connected.

As we shall see later in the book, anthropologist Dr. Jacqueline Copeland Carson and her cousin, Ms. Antoinette Stanley, who share the Gullah heritage of the families of the Weeping Time, have organized several family reunions over the years and are a good example of the growing Black Family Reunion movement.

On an anecdotal level, there are many situations in which parents (married or not) are doing their best to express their love to their children and keep the connection with their families, albeit often in material ways. It may be that the shopkeeper who buys her son $150 Nike sneakers is not just a shameless consumer but someone trying to express her love ironically in the way that our society often emphasizes the most – material things. The salesperson on a minimum-wage salary brags that, when her daughter graduates from high school, her father will buy her a new car. He is not another deadbeat Black dad, she proffers, though she is not asked the question. They may not be married, but their daughter's graduation in a sea of negative statistics on Black drop-out rates is cause for celebration. Then there is the five-year-old whose mother of humble means gives a lavish "Hollywood-style" birthday party befitting a movie star's daughter, complete with red carpet and professional photos. Her child's birthday, she reasons, is cause for celebration. No one asks regarding her dad's absence. He could be dead. He could be in prison. He could simply be unable to attend. In the Black community, we learn not to ask regarding parentage. We learn to celebrate with those who celebrate and mourn with those who mourn.

From my academic and memory-obsessed perspective, I used to think that all these gestures were misguided. After all, books, books, and more books were what we needed as a people. Or, as Thomas Jefferson himself said: "I cannot live without books." But then one day I looked closer and realized that what I was witnessing was love. This was their way of giving them what, in their minds, was the very best.

Genealogy, family reunions, and other initiatives go far in filling the gaps created by historical breaches, yet they cannot fully bridge the chasm of loss and displacement of identity and name. Nothing – no car, no pair of sneakers, no video game – can take the place of forefathers forever unknown, ancestral places never visited, and of artifacts, heirlooms, and memories never inherited.

This book attempts to put the Black family crisis in historical perspective. It shows that the Black family has proven itself to be incredibly resilient. Out of the ashes of the Weeping Time and slavery, many are putting these fragments of historical memory back together, piece by piece, block by block, and brick by brick with faith, fortitude, and hope that these missing pieces will represent a surer foundation than any material thing ever could.

In this vein, the Weeping time is also about recovery and restoration. Out of the ashes of this experience, there is beauty. The beauty is in the restoration: restoration of African American families who were torn asunder; restoration of historical memory, particularly evident in the noble efforts of modern-day African American descendants attempting to restore the pieces of their fragmented past; and restoration of the memory of men and women of conscience like Englishwoman Fanny Kemble, who sacrificed much for her stance on the evil of slavery. Her brave actions, like the actions of John Brown, ironically in the same year of the auction, 1859, make this a story of restoration and redemption. Furthermore, we shall see that there is beauty too in the rich cultural heritage of the enslaved informed by their African background that miraculously survived the experience of slavery. These cultural assets include music, faith, work, family, and kinship ties. This is how they managed to survive and in some cases thrive in spite of enormous challenges.

The Journey to the Weeping Time

Of my previous book, *African Voices of the Atlantic Slave Trade: Beyond the Silence and the Shame*, I said the following: "it could be said that this may very well be *Roots* in reverse – in the sense that instead of trying to plug all the gaps, the gaps, ironically are the story. The fragments, the broken pieces of history and narrative that periodically but not consistently break the overwhelming silence on this period of slavery are at the center of this work."[14] This notion has been beautifully captured by The Taylor Architectural company of Jamaica in their 2013 submission to the competition for a permanent memorial on slavery at the United Nations Headquarters, "Fragments of a Tragedy." *The Weeping Time* is also a story of fragments.

This is perhaps why the auction seemed so significant to me when I first stumbled upon the topic in 2006 while perusing the website for Thomas Jefferson's Monticello. I noted the updates about Jefferson's slave mistress, Sally Hemings, as well as other attempts by the Foundation to include and highlight the slave experience. Then I read a portion of the short biography of Jefferson on the website and the last lines jumped off the page. After his death, when Jefferson's will was opened in 1826, he freed Madison and Eston, the children of Sally Hemings. There was no mention that Madison and Eston were thought to be his children, just as there was no mention of Jefferson's paternity in his will. The 2014 version of the site mentions that his other two surviving children from his liaison with Sally Hemings – Harriet and Beverly – were allowed to move away from the plantation in 1822 when Jefferson was still alive, and were thus informally granted their freedom.[15] It is worth noting that, according to Virginia law at the time, freed slaves would be required to leave the state, which meant that Harriet and Beverly and others like them would have to endure yet another separation.

"As for the rest of his slaves – 140 men, women and children because Jefferson was heavily indebted, they were to put up for auction."[16]

Auction. It was not a word that I was searching for as I was more interested in seeing the latest updates on the Hemings family, but the word took center stage. A word that captures the essence of the objectification of slavery because only objects are auctioned, not people. The word auction reminds us that there was a time when people had a price.

This one word in a single line of Jefferson's will may have meant little more than that – the disposal of property whose labor was no longer needed or whose value was now required to pay his debts – but for all of African descent in America since the seventeenth century, when slavery was institutionalized, "auction" was feared as much as death itself. In fact, it was considered a kind of death since separation from loved ones was most often permanent. Loved ones, family, kinship ties – all this was treasured from the African experience as it migrated across the Atlantic, yet those ties could vanish at the stroke of an auctioneer's hammer.

The auction block is all but forgotten in American memory, yet the average American slave could be sold as many as six times in a lifetime and not because he or she did not do all in his or her power to prevent these sales from taking place. We know that for all the Nat Turners and Denmark Veseys who resisted their enslavement, there might have been many more had the specter of the auction not hung over them and their families like a dilapidated roof. How many more uprisings, big and small, might have taken place had this one word – auction – not caused dread in even the most fearless African warrior? Or conversely, how many revolts were set in motion precisely because of the threat of the auction block?[17]

Fixated on this term, I decided to bring this fragment of the African American experience front and center. Even those African Americans that live in a state of denial about slavery and its impact tend to be jolted back to this part of their history with the word "auction." But this story is not just about the past. It is also about the ongoing attempts to restore and recover pieces of the past.

Roadmap of *The Weeping Time*

As we saw in Chapter 1, the auction – a story of the slaves and slave owners of the Butler plantation on the Sea Islands of Georgia that was a footnote in history but now takes center stage – is the entry point to a larger story of breach and recovery in American history and in American historical memory, and the parallel-yet-linked lives of the nation's Black and White communities. We begin not at the beginning, but *in medias res* – in the middle of things. In keeping with a book as much about an isolated incident as it is about its memory, much that follows will seem like flashbacks to life on the Butler plantations. In the book's final section, we come full-circle to the present day, with stories of contemporary descendants of the slave auction who are putting together the disparate pieces of their history. First coined by the Roman poet Horace, the term *in medias res* advises writers to go straight to the heart of the story instead of beginning at the beginning, and in this spirit, via the account of the auction detailed in Chapter 1, we go straight to the heart of the African American experience. It is that experience that guides the entire story from beginning to end. The auction account is largely based on a contemporary account of the Northern newspaper man Doesticks, who posed as a buyer to write this story for the *New York Tribune*. Each subsequent chapter begins with a memento from the auction, which reflects the main theme of the chapter.

The text is divided into three main parts: The Breach, Linked Fates, and Healing of the Breach. The first part, as we saw in Chapter 1, is about the breaking up of these families through the auction – a site of fear, negotiation, and separation. At the same time, it represents the constant scattering of African peoples in the last 500 years or the constant making of diasporas big and small, on the African continent and again in the Americas, a throwback to African families left behind on the continent and now again in the Americas splitting and scattering to the four winds. It thus attempts a contribution to the field of African Diaspora Studies. This section contributes to our historical knowledge about auctions, following up on the great work of Frederic Bancroft and Walter Johnson.

The second part of the book returns to events that led up to the auction and is driven by the book's core theme of the linked fates of Blacks and Whites. The auction was not only momentous for the Black families who endured separation and displacement from home and community, but also for the master and mistress that regarded them as property. The sale and subsequent breakup of these African American families mirrored the breakup of the White family that owned them. Butler and his wife, Fanny Kemble, had long debated about the morality of owning slaves. She was an abolitionist, and he was a staunch slaveholder. Their relationship, which began as a fairytale, did not end like one. The sale would cement the demise of their relationship that culminated in divorce and division in their family.

In this manner, this book seeks to add to the literature on family histories that tell the story of antebellum America history in Black and White, such as the Ball, Hairston, and Hemings families. Their chroniclers, Edward Ball, Henry Wiencek, and Annette Gordon-Reed, make good use of oral history, as does this work, and all reflect a growing acceptance of oral history as an integral source for scholars of African American

FIGURE 2.2 Slave Memorial at George Washington's Mt. Vernon estate including three steps marked "Faith," "Hope," and "Love" to represent values that sustained African Americans during bondage.
© Dennis K. Johnson / Collection: Lonely Planet Images / Getty Images.

history in particular and American history in general. Finally, chapters in this section make a small contribution to historical analyses of the Gullah/Geechee region of the southern United States produced by Edda Fields and others.[18]

The third section of the book addresses the restoration and reconstruction of Black family life and historic memory, especially as it pertains to attempts to rebuild important ties after the Civil War. If the auction is an accurate symbol of the attack on Black family life that was the institution of slavery, then the attempts of Black families then and now to reconstruct their past is a symbol of hope. That hope is beautifully captured in the slave memorial at George Washington's Mt. Vernon's estate as shown in Figure 2.2.

In this section of the book, as sources permit, we meet Annette Holmes, Tiffany Young, and Mabel T. Hewlin and their families – descendants of those sold on the auction block, fifteen percent of the original total: Bram and Joan Butler, Primus and Daphne Wilson, the Ferguson family, Ned and Scena Bleach, Matty and Brister Mcintosh, and George and Sue Broughton – the first family sold in the 1859 auction. Together they represent ten families and fifty-nine men, women, and children who were sold at the Weeping Time. The story of these families did not end on the auction block, just as the story of the other four million American slaves did not end when the clock struck midnight, January 1, 1863 and they were declared free. Instead, a new and more hopeful chapter of their lives began.

For now, we return to the memory of the auction block. Those 436 men women and children who were sold: how did they get there? What led up to this epic event?

Notes

1   Thomson, p. 5–6.
2   See also the 1964 Civil Rights Act and other 1960s legislation such as the 1965 Voting Rights Act. For more discussion, see also Epilogue. See Rhonda Y. Williams et al., *Teaching the American Civil Rights movement: Freedom's Bittersweet Song* (London: Routledge, 2002).
3   See *Forever Free: The Story of Emancipation and Reconstruction* (2006) and *Voices of Freedom* (2013) and *Gateway to Freedom* (2015) by Eric Foner, *Exchanging Our Country Marks: The Transformation of African Identities in Colonial and Antebellum South* (1998) by Michael Gomez, *Race and Reunion* (2009) and *Frederick Douglass' Civil War: Keeping Faith in Jubilee* (1991) by David Blight, *The Long Memory: The Black Experience in America* (1982) and *My Face is Black Is True: Callie House and the Struggle for Ex-Slave Reparations* (2009) by Mary Frances Berry, Catherine Clinton's *Harriet Tubman: The Road to Freedom* and *Tara Revisited: Women War and the Plantation Legend* (1997), Kenneth Stampp's *The Peculiar Institution* (1984), Diana Ramey Berry, *The Price of Their Pound of Flesh*, (2016), Ana Lucia-Araujo's *Public Memory of Slavery* (2010), Sven Beckert's *Slavery's Capitalism: A New History of American Economic Development* (2016), Eric Williams' *Capitalism and Slavery* (1944), John Blassingame's *The Slave Community: Plantation Life in the Antebellum South* (1979), Deborah Gray White's *Arn't I A Woman: Female Slaves in the Plantation South* (1999), Herbert Gutman's The *Black Family in Slavery and Freedom 1750–1925* (1976), Alex Haley's *Roots* (1976 and 2007). Walter Johnson's *Soul by Soul: Life inside the Antebellum Slave Market* (1999) is one of the few books to focus on auctions. Likewise, Frederic Bancroft's seminal *Slave Trading in the Old South* (1964) looks at the domestic slave market, including some auctions. See also more recent works, such as Sylviane Diouf's *Dreams of Africa in Alabama* (2009) Annette Gordon-Reed's *Thomas Jefferson and Sally Hemings: An American Controversy* (1999) and *The Hemingses of Monticello: An American Family* (2009), Evelyn Higginbotham and John Hope Franklin's *From Slavery to Freedom* (2010) and Edward Baptist's *The Half Has Never been Told: Slavery and the Making of American Capitalism* (2016).

4   Prominent historians in the 1990s and early 2000s particularly pursued this notion of the inextricable link between masters and slaves, including Eugene Genovese, Elizabeth Fox-Genovese, and Drew Gilpin Faust, among others. Fox-Genovese's *Within the Plantation Household: Black and White Women of the Old South* (2000) is a good example.

5   Daniel Patrick Moynihan, "The Negro Family: The Case for National Action," Office of Policy Planning and Research, US Department of Labor, March 1965.

6   Kay Hymowitz, "The Black Family: 40 years of lies," *City Journal*, Summer 2005, www.city-journal.org/html/15_3_black_family.html, accessed November 2, 2016.

7   Edward Baptist and Stephanie Camp, *New Studies in the History of American Slavery* (Athens, GA: University of Georgia Press, 2006), 173.

8   Gregory Acs, Kenneth Braswell, Elaine Sorensen, *Moynihan Report Revisited* (Washington, DC: Urban Institute, June 13, 2013).

9   William Julius Wilson, *Truly Disadvantaged* (Chicago: University of Chicago Press, 1987) 17.

10   Herbert Gutman, *The Black Family in Slavery and In Freedom 1750–1925* (New York: Vintage Press, 1976)

11   See more in the last chapter on memory.

12   See African DNA, https://www.africandna.com/, accessed June 21, 2017.

13   Anne Bailey, Interview #10 with Eardley Ramsay, August 2006.

14   Anne Bailey, *African Voices of the Atlantic Slave Trade* (Boston: Beacon Press, 2005) p. 22.

15   "Thomas Jefferson and Sally Hemings: A Brief Account,", www.monticello .org/site/plantation-and-slavery/thomas-jefferson-and-sally-hemings-brief-account, accessed August 14, 2016.

16   This was the account on the website in 2014; the 2017 website suggests there were 200 slaves sold, www.monticello.org/site/plantation-and-slavery/slaves-who-gained-freedom.

17   Dr. Michael West, email message to author providing this last question, July 2016.

18   See Annette Gordon-Reed's *Thomas Jefferson and Sally Hemings: An American Controversy* (Charlottesville: University of Virginia Press, 1999) and *The Hemingses of Monticello: An American Family* (New York: W.W. Norton and Co., 2009), Edda Fields's, *Deep Roots: Rice Farmers in West Africa and in the African Diaspora* (Bloomington: Indiana University Press, 2008), Henry Wiencek's, *The Hairstons: An American Family in Black and White* (New York: St. Martin's Griffin 1999), Edward Ball's, *Slaves in the Family*, (New York: Ballantine Books, 1998).

PART II

LINKED FATES

3

Pierce Butler and His Grandfather's Legacy

Leaving the Race buildings, where the scenes we have described took place,
a crowd of negroes were seen gathered about a white man. That man was
Pierce Butler, of the free city of Philadelphia who was solacing the wounded
hearts of the people he had sold from their firesides and their homes by
doling out to them small change of a dollar a head.[1]

Mortimer "Doesticks" Thomson

Bequeathing Denial

Doesticks describes the unfortunate ending of the two-day sale when
Pierce Mease Butler sold the slaves he inherited from his grandfather,
Major Pierce Butler Sr., on March 2–3, 1859. The income from the
estates on which they had labored without recompense had enabled
him to live in fine style in the free city of Philadelphia, but this was
not his only inheritance. Pierce Mease Butler also inherited the denial
that characterized his grandfather's public and private life. For Major
Butler, famously one of the signers of the US Constitution and a founding father, was like many of his counterparts who publicly advocated for
the highest ideals of freedom while privately maintaining the institution
of slavery. This denial is particularly evident in the auction scene illustrated by Doesticks.

For all their toil, they were rewarded one silver coin. It is noteworthy
that they lined up "eagerly" before Butler, and those with hats tipped
them in respect. Something about these words and the scene in general
evokes the familiarity between the slaves and Butler. After all, they were a
kind of family. They considered the Butler estates their home and, though

slaves, had connections with their masters as human beings; one of the greatest ironies of the master – slave hierarchy. The Constitution considered a slave three-fifths of a person, viewed more as chattel that could be bought and sold and less as humans. But they were indeed human, and relationships did develop between masters and slaves. Butler, focused on paying his debts and, more importantly, regaining for himself the substantial income that he wasted, denied that connection in selling these human beings. He had to deny it in order to sever his ties with them and their ties with each other. To maintain his luxurious public life, he had to privately deny his ties to this slave community. He tried to rationalize his actions in giving them a dollar apiece as they were auctioned off; in so doing, he denied the linked fates of slaves and masters.

This denial was as much a legacy of the Butlers as were the people, land, and things they possessed. The legacy began with Major Pierce Butler, the maternal grandfather of Pierce Mease Butler. Major Butler was born in Ireland, the third son of Sir Richard and Lady Henrietta Percy Butler of Garryhunden. Sir Richard was a baronet of Cloughrenan and a member of Parliament from County Carlow. As Sir Richard's third son, Major Butler could not inherit his father's title; that privilege went to his eldest brother, Thomas. As a result, he embarked on a distinguished military career. In fact, he became the youngest captain "without purchase in His Majesty's 29th regiment."[2] Butler became a major in 1766, and in 1767, as tensions were rising on the North American continent between the colonies and Great Britain, he and officers of his regiment, were sent to Philadelphia. On his own, he traveled for the first time that year to Charleston South Carolina, where he would later return in 1771 and marry Mary Middleton, the heiress to the Middleton rice plantation fortune.[3] The Middleton rice plantation was prosperous and was well known to be the home of a number of slaves who came originally from Barbados and Jamaica. In effect, he chose to make South Carolina his home only ten years before the state was officially constituted in 1776.

In marrying Mary Middleton, Butler made a critical decision. He would surrender his military commission in His Majesty's army and assume the role of rice planter and manager of the estates that his wife inherited from her grandmother within a year of their marriage. Butler, with his formidable and forthright personality, would also help administer the estate and affairs of her father and brother, Thomas and William Middleton. Both were slave merchants involved in the business of importing and dealing in slaves on the domestic and international markets. They died leaving a mountain of debts and holdings, like the slave ship *Middleton,* which had to be settled.

While Butler came into this marriage with no title and little money, he did have a military commission, which he sold by 1774, using the resulting funds to buy 1,700 acres on St. Simon's Island off the coast of Georgia. The plantation was known as Hampton Point and was later to become the home of some of the slaves auctioned in 1859. Hampton Point, as a contemporary historical marker shows, was a major cotton plantation in its heyday.

These properties would become Pierce Mease Butler's physical inheritance (along with his brother John) and were located on Butler Island and St. Simon's Island off the coast of Georgia. Butler Island was a 1,500-acre tidewater island that the patriarch, Major Pierce Butler, named after himself soon after he acquired it in 1793. One mile from the mainland, it had the look and feel of an isolated place. It was more swamp than sand, whereas St. Simon's was more sand than swamp. Each was suited to different crops. The twice-daily tides on Butler Island made it possible to flood the rice fields, while the fresh water from the Altamaha River would protect the crops from salt water. The sounds of migrating songbirds like yellow throat, indigo bunting, and swamp sparrow could always be heard, but in the background – much like the music of the slaves. Malaria-carrying mosquitoes were a constant menace. By contrast, the sweet smell of yellow jasmine hung pleasantly in the air, and the wooded areas were replete with towering magnolias and stately oak trees.

And so, five years before the onset of the American Revolution, Major Butler effectively switched sides, with his marriage to a stakeholder from an important colony. With these new acquisitions, he was now more invested in life in the New World than the Old. Ironically, 1771, the year of his marriage and his adoption of the status of colonist, was the same year that his brother in Ireland inherited from his father the title of Baronet and became the sixth Baronet of Cloughrenan. They had completely different fates.

Major Butler did not simply adopt a new status as a colonist and was not fated to be an anonymous figure in the historic events that were to envelop the country and the world. He was destined instead to be a very prominent actor in the American Revolution: one of America's founding fathers, notwithstanding the fact that he is perhaps less remembered for this tremendous feat and more remembered for his slaveholding estate.

On his wife's father's side, he acquired great property and wealth. On her mother's side, the Bull family, he married into a slew of political connections. These relatives included her sister Sarah Middleton, who married Benjamin Guerard – who was to become governor of South Carolina in 1783. Prior to that, other relatives had held the title of Lt. Governor. Most remarkably, however, another cousin's wife would marry Edward Rutledge, a South Carolina politician who, at twenty-six, was the youngest signatory of the Declaration of Independence.[4]

Two Parallel Worlds: Public and Private Lives

Major Butler's public life from his entry into the South Carolina social and political scene was markedly different from his private life. By 1775, the war had come to South Carolina and, in 1776, the British attempted unsuccessfully to recapture Charleston. Though Butler's actual role in the war effort was a minimal one, he was now a Patriot and his sympathies were clear. He and his family (the Bull Middletons) lost property and profits when the British reopened their Southern campaign in 1778 and burned and looted their estates.[5]

After the war was over, he worked at restoring his properties and engaged in public service. In 1787, he was designated by the South Carolina legislature to be one of the delegates sent to the Constitutional Convention in Philadelphia. At forty-three, he was one of the four delegates sent to Philadelphia to represent South Carolina. There, he and the other fifty-four delegates, including George Washington, Ben Franklin, and James Madison, came together initially to remedy the supposed defects of the Articles of Confederation. There were a variety of issues on the table but many centered on trade, commerce, and taxation. A uniform policy was needed to facilitate domestic and foreign trade. States with more access to ports had distinct advantages over those without.

Butler made quite an impression at the Convention and was described as a man "of noble birth and inordinately vain of it, had served America as an officer in the British army. He was a man of fortune and having sold his commission and settled in this country, he had become very popular."[6] Freedom and independence were key themes espoused by the individual states. States were protective of their territory and their rights. Tensions between small and large states were palpable because each state wanted to be sure that the newly constituted confederated republic would neither shortchange them nor infringe on their liberties.

Their discussions may have started as a result of conflicts regarding trade and taxation, but they also touched on many other subjects important to the nation. It soon became clear that they were not simply revising the Articles of Confederation, but were creating an altogether new document. There would be three branches of government as well as specific term limits and policies to adopt new states in the future. The most contentious issue was that of representation and rules of suffrage. Would wealth and property be used to determine the issue of representation? How would the slaves be counted in the Southern states – as equal to the free population in terms of numbers, or would the 3/5 ratio be used? This was not the first time that this ratio was used. It had been recommended by Congress for use in 1783.[7]

The end result was what historians now call "The Great Compromise." In the upper house, each state would have equal voting rights (thus, one-man-one-vote prevailed). The lower house, however, would operate under the principle of proportional representation: the free white population would be counted along with 3/5 of the slaves.[8]

Direct taxation was to be in proportion to that representation.[9] So, after much debate, the United States Constitution was developed. By the time they finished their deliberations, Jefferson would declare that "with all the imperfections of our present government, it is without comparison the best existing or that did exist."[10]

But where did this document and the Revolution that preceded it leave the enslaved population, and what was Major Butler's role in their future? If freedom and independence of the colonies and eventually the states were key themes during and after the war, the opposite was true for the Black enslaved population. The war itself at first signified *the promise* of freedom due to several factors. First, a major turning point in the war was the Dunmore Proclamation, promulgated by John Murray, Earl of Dunmore, the last Royal Governor of Virginia. Dunmore made an offer of freedom in November 1775 to Black slaves who enlisted to serve with the British forces. To White Virginians, he became one of the first villains of the American Revolution, but to Blacks he was a liberator.

This represented something of a breakthrough for a certain number of Blacks who left plantations in order to gain their freedom. In total, approximately 100,000 Blacks were said to have deserted their owners during and after the war (similar to what happened during the US Civil war). It is said that as many as 800 joined the Loyalist cause and became known as Dunmore's Ethiopian Regiment. They wore shirts declaring "Liberty for Slaves" and served as guards and laborers in the war effort.[11] At the same time, prominent property owners like the Randolphs of Colonial Williamsburg were extremely anxious about the possibility of losing their slaves to the British forces. This proclamation became a major bone of contention and point of division between White and Black residents of Virginia, even though only a relatively small number of Black slaves joined the British cause.

George Washington did not initially attempt to enlist Blacks and, in fact, had earlier in the war effort issued an order excluding Blacks from enlistment. But, by early 1777, there was a manpower shortage, at which time he permitted the enlistment of a number of Black and interracial units. Black Patriots were said to have been about 5,000 in number.[12] They too were promised freedom for serving. In fact, it is likely that it was their brave and loyal service that helped to change Washington's views of Blacks in general. It was their service that started him on a journey to seriously consider the emancipation of the slaves, though he did so only as a result of his last will and testament.[13]

Still others presented in colonial courts "freedom petitions" in an attempt to break free of their masters by legal means. As one petition on behalf of Boston's Black enslaved residents boldly affirmed:

We acknowledge our obligations to you for what you have already done, but as the people of this province seem to be actuated by the principles of equity and justice, we cannot but expect your house will again take our deplorable case into serious consideration, and give us ample relief which, as men, we have a natural right to.

This particular petition was made to the courts on behalf of "fellow slaves in this province" by Peter Bestes, Sambo Freeman, Felix Holbrook, and Chester Joie.[14]

The slaves did not need an exterior stimulus to seek their freedom, but events of the day did much to encourage and provide them with opportunities to further struggle for their freedom. Social unrest and talk of freedom in the colonies like Virginia, as well as the groundbreaking Somerset court case in 1773, moved many of them to take their petitions to the courts. In the Somerset case, a slave who had been brought to England by his master sued for his freedom and the judge, Lord Mansfield, in making his decision, declared: "slavery is so odious, nothing can be done to support it but positive law." He then ruled that slavery was to be outlawed in England, though not in its colonies.[15]

And so, eventually there were Blacks fighting on both sides of the Revolutionary War for their promised freedom – a promise that was largely not kept. Of the hundreds who served the Patriot cause on behalf of Virginia, only eight were freed by the Virginia legislature after the war.[16] On a third front, the British evacuated upwards of 20,000 Blacks at the end of the war, most of whom were either sent to Nova Scotia, Sierra Leone, or sold in the West Indies.[17] In a retaliatory effort, the British further refused to return those who had been enslaved and did not take into account the Dunmore Proclamation, which would have granted their freedom.

As such, the quest for Black freedom was largely not achievable as a result of the American Revolution. The same was true of the Constitutional Convention of 1787, where delegates jointly developed the US Constitution. Delegates talked around the subject of slavery, even going as far as to use obtuse terminology to refer to the Black population. For example, it was agreed that a Census should be taken regularly "of the free white inhabitants and 3/5 of those of other descriptions." In all the discussion regarding representation from each state, the slave population was the elephant in the room. During the course of the debates, John Dickinson, a delegate representing Delaware, said that the US Constitution represented the triumph of experience over reason.[18] The men who came together to form this new government relied heavily on their experience – what they had seen and done in their home states.[19] And, for the majority of the delegates, this experience was slave ownership. It is logical, then, that their connections to slavery had an impact on their decisions, yet there was relative silence on exactly how their experiences pertained to slavery.

Ironically, Butler and the others in the South Carolina and Georgia delegations wanted Blacks to be counted as equals but only for the purpose of representation. They were, however, outvoted eight states against two.[20] Blacks could be equal to Whites as long as they enhanced White power bases in their individual states on the federal level. Otherwise, they were to be denied equality, denied personhood, denied the right to vote.

A Costly Procrastination

The delegates sidestepped this issue, yet it was to influence the course of American History deeply from that moment onwards. Some chalk it up to the fact that slavery in 1787 "was not the important moral question it later became."[21] But again, that is precisely the point. The delegates were preoccupied with the organization of the new government and ignored this issue to their detriment – not only from the standpoint of morality, but also of practicality.

It was to be a costly procrastination. They left this question to future generations, and it took a Civil War to make them deal with the unfinished business of the American Revolution and the Constitutional Convention. Later, because of the backlash from the Civil War, it took the Civil Rights movement of the twentieth century, particularly the 1950s and 1960s, to address the issue of equality and freedom for all in America.

Black slaves were not the only population overlooked in the development of the Constitution. The Native American population and so-called Department of Indian Affairs did not feature prominently in the republic's new document. Prior to the 1787 debates in Philadelphia, the thirteen colonies had developed a policy of dealing with Native American groups as sovereign states.

"The new Congress also sent diplomatic representatives to the tribes and promised friendship and peace, and ultimately it signed eight treaties with Indian tribes between 1781–1789, including treaties with the Iroquois Confederacy, the Cherokee Tribe, the Shawnee Tribe and numerous other tribes."[22] But individual states continued to meddle in Indian Affairs. As a result, the delegates of 1787 declared in the Constitution that Congress alone would have the right to make treaties and to manage Indian affairs.

In Article I, the United States Constitution accomplishes the goal of excluding states and individuals from Indian affairs by stating that only Congress has the power "To regulate Commerce with foreign Nations, and among the several States, and with the Indian Tribes." Furthermore, though Blacks were considered at 3/5 ratio, Native Americans would not be considered citizens of the US but rather of their "sovereign" states unless they paid taxes. This would continue until 1924, when they were granted US citizenship.[23]

But as far as Butler was concerned, at the time of the Convention, there would be no reconciliation between his public and private lives, just as there was to be no reconciliation between the high ideals of the newly formed United States republic and its practice of slavery. The very slaves from whom his family had extracted wealth were the basis of his prominence and stature in America, yet he acted to deny their freedom at every turn. His main contribution, ironically, was to propose the Fugitive Slave Law (US Const. Sec. 2 Article 4). In his public life, he fought for freedom and independence, embracing the Patriot cause fully, and in his private life he was dependent on the deprivation of the freedom of others.

This is the legacy that Major Butler bequeathed to his grandson, Pierce Mease Butler. It was a dual legacy, as he bequeathed both his estates and his denial to Pierce Mease. In this way, his inheritance was both literal and figurative. This dual legacy laid the foundation for what took place on the auction block of 1859. Major Butler passed on the denial of Black citizenship and Black rights to his grandson and, in so doing, the denial of the Black contribution to their lives as well.

Notes

1 Thomson, p. 20.
2 Bell, p. 1–2.
3 Ibid., p. 5–6.
4 Bell, p. 19–20.
5 Ibid, p. 28.
6 Max Farrand, *The Framing of the Constitution* (New Haven: Yale University Press, 1913) 31.
7 Ibid., p. 34.
8 Ibid., p. 35.
9 Ibid., p. 106.
10 Ibid., p. 43.
11 James Corbett David, *Dunmore's New World: The Extraordinary Life of a Royal Governor in Revolutionary America* (Charlottesville: University of Virginia Press, 2013) Introduction, and Benjamin Quarles, "Lord Dunmore as Liberator," *The William and Mary Quarterly*, Vol. 15, no. 4 (October 1958), p. 494–507. Numbers vary according to sources.
12 Robert Selig, "The Revolution's Black Soldiers," www.americanrevolution.org/blk.html, accessed November 3, 2016.
13 Henry Wiencek, *An Imperfect God: George Washington, His Slaves and the Creation of America* (New York: Farrar Strauss and Giroux, 2003) 4.
14 Ibid., p. 253, and Gary B. Nash, *Race and Revolution*, (Madison, WI: Madison House, 1990), p. 171–176.
15 Selig, "African Americans During the American Revolution," Colonial Williamsburg Foundation, 2006, www.history.org/history/teaching/enewsletter/volume5/images/reference_sheet.pdf, accessed November 2, 2016.
16 Wiencek 2003, p. 248.
17 Bell, p. 37–41.
18 Farrand, p. 204.
19 Ibid., p. 203.
20 Ibid., p 101–104.
21 Ibid., p. 110.
22 Robert Miller, "American Indians and the US Constitution," *Native America Discovered and Conquered*, www.flashpointmag.com/amindus.htm, accessed November 2, 2016.
23 Ibid.

4

Mr. and Mrs. Butler

"The slaves in whom I then had an unfortunate interest were sold some years ago." [1]

– Fanny Kemble

Thus said the former wife of Pierce Mease Butler in the preface to her 1863 publication, *Journal of a Residence on a Georgian Plantation, 1838–39.* As we learned in Chapter 3, Major Butler bequeathed to his grandson Pierce a legacy of denial regarding the linked fate of Blacks and Whites under the institution of slavery, which he accepted without question. Fanny Kemble, by contrast, did not accept this legacy, especially after she met some of the slaves on her visit to the plantations in the late 1830s; the very slaves that would eventually be sold on the auction block years later. As her quote above captures with the words "unfortunate interest," she had at least a partial understanding that her fate was linked to that of the slaves, but found no comfort in such a link.

It is no wonder that Fanny and Pierce's marriage, in spite of their exhilarating courtship, ended in a bitter divorce, chiefly because they were on the opposing sides on the question of slavery. If Pierce Butler was able to deny the humanity of the slaves he inherited, Fanny was not. The "problem" of slavery became *their* problem. Furthermore, their break up and the dissolution of their marriage mirrors and foreshadows the dissolution of the slave families on the auction block in 1859. Notwithstanding Fanny's struggle against slavery in her very household, she was not immune to denial herself. When it came to confronting England's involvement in the slave trade and slavery in the West Indies, she was oblivious to this aspect of English history. Eighteenth-century

England gave liberty to any slave that graced its shores. At the same time, slavery in its colonies in the West Indies was allowed to thrive till well into the nineteenth century.

How did Butler and Fanny come together in the first place, especially given their differing ideas and personalities? Pierce Butler had few responsibilities since his properties were worked by slaves and managed by overseers. He lived in an elegant town home in the Philadelphia on the income the properties generated and in effect ran the plantation by proxy. For those with no direct knowledge of his Southern possessions, he was simply a wealthy Philadelphia businessman. With few cares, he indulged himself in every way. He gambled, he played the stock market, and he frequented the arts, particularly the theater. That was the mutual passion that brought them together.

It was at one of the many performances he attended where he met Frances (Fanny) Kemble, a Shakespearean actress and writer of London fame. Fanny was from a family of artists who had performed on the London stage for generations. Her father, Charles Kemble, had a stake in Convent Garden theater.[2] Along with the prestige and popularity of this old theater, there were, however, longstanding debts and financial difficulties. The theater burned to the ground in 1808, and the resulting rebuilding process was costly to the family.

Fanny's aunt and Charles' sister, Sarah Siddons, known as "The Tragic Muse," were very famous on the London stage, and Fanny followed suit with her debut in *Romeo and Juliet* in 1829. She was held up to be the next generation of Kembles that would command the British stage and, indeed, the critics and high society were in complete agreement.[3] In spite of her popularity, however, the Kembles still had debts stemming from the management of the theater. It is for this reason that Charles Kemble organized a two-year theatrical tour of America, starting in 1832.[4]

Pierce Mease Butler was in the audience on the day of her Philadelphia debut, October 12, 1832. He was so captivated by her performance and personality that he followed Kemble from city to city on her American tour for over a year. Tall with a lean, angular face and straight black hair, he had the look of a stern headmaster but was also a very dapper dresser who could make quite a first impression. Butler spared no expense on his wardrobe. As noted by his friend George Fisher on one visit to his home in Philadelphia 1846, Butler wore "a very rich velvet dress of an English nobleman of a former century covered with lace and embroidery."[5]

Fanny Kemble was also physically quite striking. As can be seen in Figure 4.1, her features were pronounced, and she had a face reminiscent

FIGURE 4.1 Fanny Kemble.
Courtesy of Georgia Historical Society.

of the Mona Lisa, save for a bevy of brown curls pulled back in a bun. Young ladies all over the Northeast adopted the style that came to be known as "Fanny Kemble curls." In terms of personality, having grown up in the theater, Fanny had a flair for the theatrical on and off the stage. She was known for having passionate opinions and was not shy to share them.

Kemble had many suitors, but none was as persistent as Butler. From the time she first set foot on American soil, men like Edward John Trelawney, known as a friend to the literary giants Shelley and Byron, entertained her with wit and affection. She undoubtedly found all this attention flattering. Butler, however, designed dates and outings in keeping with her tastes; he indulged her love of horseback riding, and they enjoyed elaborate picnics in Niagara Falls with fine silverware and flowing wine.

All the while, Fanny assumed that Butler was simply a wealthy American, an urbane gentleman who lived in a stately town home in Philadelphia. There were only passing and unspecific references to land he would inherit from his grandfather in the South but his life was in Philadelphia. As far as she was concerned, he was not unlike many of his class and station who lived off trust funds or remittances from businesses elsewhere and who indulged themselves in the varied pleasures of the city. He was a lover of the arts and so was she. That was their common bond.

There was no talk about his Southern properties in any detail. Kemble may have even assumed that he, hailing from the urban North, shared her abolitionist sympathies, as did a number of people in Philadelphia and elsewhere in the region. In effect, Kemble, during their courtship, did not know that Butler's income was a direct result of slave labor. She did not know that he would become a slave master in only a few short years, when his grandfather's will went into full effect.

In their brief courtship, Butler seemed not to notice her abolitionist leanings or simply was so captivated by her charms that he chose to ignore them. As he was to make clear in his 1850 autobiography, he was a very traditional man who expected that a future wife would submit to him in every way. He expected no less of this passionate actress when he married her.[6]

Perhaps Butler was too preoccupied in overcoming his considerable competition, since, in courting Fanny, he had to contend with her many admirers. But Butler had social standing and promised income.[7] Fanny was to say later that she initially found him not to be a man of great stature but, in appearance, a "pretty spoken genteel youth." She concluded: "He has it seems a great fortune; consequently, I suppose, a great man."[8] She equated greatness with wealth.

If not a man of great stature, he was a man of grand gestures. After calling on Fanny after her stage debut in Philadelphia, he was relentless in his attempt to impress both Fanny and her father while at the same time trying to help her forget his rivals. Their tour continued to meet with great success. Fanny and her father Charles were particularly well received in Washington, DC and Boston. Throughout, Butler was a constant companion. He even played the flute in the orchestra pit.[9]

So when he eventually proposed, she accepted. In the end, she was a woman of the Victorian era; she did not expect to be on stage forever.

She assumed, like many women of her station, that she would marry (hopefully well), have children, and cease working to look after her family. Although she had already transcended the traditional female role by working on stage from an early age, she still accepted that the Victorian norm would be her life. And besides, Butler was financially secure. Given the financial insecurities that her theatrical family endured for most of her life, this probably seemed ideal to Fanny at the time.

Fanny consented to marry Butler in spite of the trepidations of her father and brother John. John was most passionate about his objections and begged his sister to reconsider: "do let me know, dearest Fan when this terrible affair of marriage is to be … much righteous indignation has been excited that when you have a house and nursery to look after, you will leave off writing plays."[10] They knew her all too well and wondered if a life of quiet domesticity to a wealthy American truly suited her. They wondered if she could give up the stage so easily and if her temperament was compatible with the life she was assuming, for Fanny had a tendency to be headstrong. In many ways, she was a woman not completely suited to the times. Off stage, she was expected to be less outspoken and opinionated. Fanny was neither quiet nor demure and was not likely to be subservient to anyone, least of all a husband. Her family appreciated her strong will, but knew that others might hold a different view.[11]

True to her strong-willed nature, Fanny ignored their reservations and married Butler at Christ Church in Philadelphia on June 7, 1834. They quickly settled down in Branchtown, Pennsylvania at Butler Place – a 300-acre estate, six miles from Philadelphia.[12] Initially, she embraced her new life with the joyful exuberance of any new bride. The plan was that they would live in the mansion at Branchtown, and she would run their household with the aid of hired servants. At first, Fanny seemed happy to be married and preoccupied with family matters. Pierce, for his part, was anxious to have children, and thus produce heirs to his fortune.

In April 1836, Butler's Aunt Frances died and John and Pierce became the holders of the second-largest holding of slaves in Georgia.[13] Around the same time, Fanny begged Butler to spend the winter in London, where she could visit with family that she had not seen in four years.[14] There she became reacquainted with debates about the slave trade and slavery, so it was not surprising that on her return to Philadelphia, Kemble was drawn to abolitionist circles. While she never became an official member of either Philadelphia's Anti-Slavery Society or the American Anti-Slavery Society, she nevertheless came to share their sentiments.[15]

Long a center for abolitionist thought and action, Philadelphia's abolitionists were strongly influenced by Quakers such as Pennsylvania's founder William Penn, who believed that "there is that of God in every man." The Religious Society of Friends were also prominent in the city's abolitionist community, and were most effective in their protection of runaways from slave catchers and assistance in the Underground Railroad.[16] In fact, they are said to have made one of the world's first declarations against slavery in Germantown, Philadelphia in 1688:

"There is a liberty of conscience here which is right and reasonable, and there ought to be likewise a liberty of the body, except for evil doers, which is another case. But to bring men hither, or to rob and sell them against their will, we stand against."[17]

It was a bold stance, though it was not until 1784 that the last Quakers emancipated their slaves.[18] Still, before and after this period, many of their number, including most notably the tailor-turned minister John Woolman of New Jersey, called in his *Journal* for slavery's end and a general emancipation of slaves, as well as peace with the Native American population.[19] He was to greatly influence generations of Quakers and others all over the Northeast.

The Underground Railroad was also in full operation by the early nineteenth century. An organized system of secret sites for escaped slaves heading north, the Railroad was manned predominantly by Blacks but also sympathetic Whites, including Quakers. "Conductors" like the famous Harriet Tubman shepherded thousands to safety. In Pennsylvania, William Still was a well-known conductor who kept a record of all those whom he helped. That group of runaways included Henry Box Brown, as seen in Figure 4.2, who escaped from slavery in 1849 in Richmond Virginia by having himself boxed up and forwarded to Philadelphia by an express train. The box was addressed to James A. Smith, a shoe dealer, and would eventually make its way to the City's Anti-Slavery office. William Still records: "The witnesses will never forget that moment. Saw and hatchet quickly had the five hickory hoops cut and the lid off, and the marvelous resurrection of Brown ensued. Rising up in the box, he reached out his hand, saying, "How do you do, gentlemen?" Then he sang the Psalm: "I waited patiently for the Lord and He heard my prayer."[20]

Though this particular incident took place approximately ten years after Fanny's time in the Philadelphia area, there were hundreds more stories, perhaps less dramatic, but no less important to the abolitionist cause. Fanny no doubt would have heard of some of these stories from her abolitionist friends with whom she found common cause.

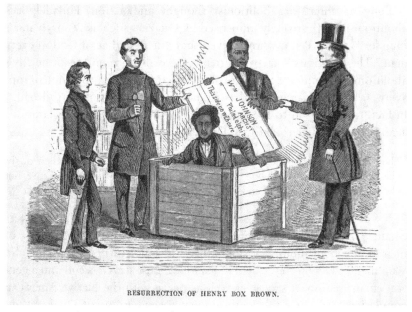

RESURRECTION OF HENRY BOX BROWN.

FIGURE 4.2 The Resurrection of Henry Box Brown, Engraving by John Osler, 1872; Public Domain.

Born in England, Kemble was not entirely familiar with the North/ South dynamics of slavery in the United States. She had lived a somewhat sheltered existence and had no experience with the actual institution of slavery and how it worked in America. She was not unlike many Englishwomen of a certain class who had relatives who quietly ran plantations in the Caribbean, but who themselves knew little of the institution of slavery and the activities of these relations in foreign lands.

Once married to Butler, as shown in Figure 4.3, Fanny became more curious and eventually consumed with the idea of visiting his plantations. Initially, he refused, but she would not relent. Eventually, he gave his consent, harboring the false notion that a season at his Georgia Sea Island plantations would bring his wife around to his pro-slavery views.

The visit finally took place in December 1838, but not before Fanny put her thoughts on paper about the injustice of slavery in letters to her long-time friend, Elizabeth Sedgwick. She was to assert categorically in those letters the humanity of the Black race and wondered about the fact that those who believed Blacks were inferior and incapable of learning were also the first to propose laws against them gaining an education.

If they really are brutish, witless, dull and devoid of capacity for progress, where lies the danger which is constantly insisted upon of offering them that of which

FIGURE 4.3 Pierce Mease Butler.
Hargrett Rare Book and Manuscript Library, University of Georgia.

they are incapable? But these themes are forbidden to slaves, not because they cannot, but because they can and would seize on them with avidity – receive them gladly, comprehend them quickly; and the masters' power over them would be annihilated at once and forever.[21]

She also asked herself why, for the white Southern planter, well known for having "a family more or less numerous of illegitimate colored children, there is no law in making a colored woman the mother of his children, but there is a law on his statute books forbidding him to make her his wife."[22]

Such were a few of the preconceived notions that Fanny Kemble had about slavery even before she set foot on Butler's plantations. Sedgwick encouraged her not to visit the plantations with already conceived prejudices, to which she replied:

Assuredly, I am going prejudiced against slavery, for I am an Englishwoman, in whom the absence of such a prejudice would be disgraceful. Nevertheless, I go prepared to find many mitigations in the practice to the general injustice and cruelty of the system – much kindness on the part of the masters, much content on that of the slaves.[23]

On December 21, 1838, Fanny Kemble and her husband Pierce Butler set off on their journey south with their two children, a White nanny named Margery, as well as Butler's aunt, who accompanied them as far as Charleston. This was to be a three-month visit. At this time, her first child named Frances (Fan) was three years old. Her second child, Sarah, was only a few months old.

The small party started from Philadelphia then traveled to Baltimore, through Virginia, and then further south. Fanny was fastidious about details and complained vociferously about the amenities in the railroad cars, the lack of cleanliness of their accommodations, and the varying modes of transport. In one "miserable inn" where they stayed in North Carolina, she wrote in her Journal:

We were shown up a filthy flight of wooden stairs, into a dilapidated room, the plastered walls of which were all smeared and discolored, the windows begrimed, and darkened with dirt.[24]

The countryside she described was by turns resplendent and dismal. Brandywine was radiant, but the swamps of North Carolina were gloomy. She found Wilmington beautiful and the architecture and city layout of Charleston reminded her of the older towns of England. She described the city as "genteel" and "picturesque." From Charleston, they traveled to "graceful" Savannah where she exclaimed about being treated to the luxury of a warm bath in their accommodations.[25]

As much as Fanny keenly recorded all these physical details, she was particularly interested in the people she met and observed along the way. In Portsmouth, Virginia, she encountered the first slaves she had ever seen and proclaimed that they were exactly as she had imagined them. Displaying her own prejudices, she described them in the following manner: "They were poorly clothed; looked horribly dirty, and had a lazy recklessness in their air and manner as they sauntered along, which naturally belongs to creatures without one of the responsibilities which are the honorable burden of rational humanity."[26]

Fanny got another glimpse of slaves in Suffolk, Virginia, where, while walking on the street, a slave was even offered to her young daughter as "a waiting maid." She promptly refused this offer. In another few days, on December 30, 1838, they had reached their destination – Darien, the town on the mainland closest to Butler Island. From there, they would take a schooner for the last leg of the trip to the island.

Such were the perceptions and misconceptions of Fanny Kemble as she approached Butler Island. She started the trip claiming that as an

Englishwoman, unlike her American husband, she was naturally prejudiced against slavery. Influenced by British and American abolitionists,
she spoke in bold strokes about the humanity of the slaves, yet even
so, she was ahistorical in her thinking about England and her English
identity. Why should she have been naturally opposed to slavery as an
Englishwoman? What evidence do we have in history that this was the
natural predisposition of the English?

To the contrary, in 1562, John Hawkins, known as Britain's first slave
trader, sailed from Plymouth with three ships to the West African coast
where he captured and kidnaped over 400 Africans. In the succeeding
years, he continued to kidnap over 1,200 Africans and trade them in the
West Indies. For these and other efforts, he was highly decorated by the
Queen of England. Thus began the British foray into the slave trade, with
other slavers not far behind.[27] Even in England itself, slavery was allowed
until 1772. Masters from the West Indies or other British colonies would
bring some of their slaves, usually trusted servants, on their trips home.
As such, there was eventually a small community of enslaved Africans
living in England. Some were able to secure their freedom, but most were
forced to continue serving their masters.

The Somerset case of 1772 made it subsequently illegal to enslave anyone on English territory yet it was not until 1807 that Black and White
abolitionists like William Wilberforce were able to secure a ban on the
slave trade altogether. Such a ban was not, however, a ban on slavery.
Slavery was a fact of life in the British Caribbean from the early 1500s
and continued to be practiced in the British colonies until the 1830s.
Between 1834–1838, slaves in the British colonies were emancipated but
not fully free.[28]

In the English-speaking Caribbean, slaves had to serve as "appren-
tices" to their masters for a period of a few years before they could
enjoy their freedom. This kept the labor force effectively immobile
and tied to their masters – a situation that was abhorrent to slaves in
the British West Indies. Furthermore, the conditions for slave emancipation were such that former masters would receive over 20 million pounds in compensation for their losses. Slaves would receive
nothing. The University College of London and Harvard University's
Hutchins Center for African and African American research have, as of
2013, digitized the records of those who received this compensation.[29]
This list includes ancestors of a number of England's leading families.
Historian Eric Williams's work makes clear that, at its core, the slave
trade and slavery contributed significantly to England's development.

At its height, over a third of England's profits came from its colonies. After its abolition, England's elite continued to profit at the expense of the Black population.[30] As such, the fates of Blacks and Whites were inextricably linked, just as they were in America, where the Butler slaves' lives were interwoven with their owners' livelihoods.

In the end, it was significant that the British abolition of slavery took place a full generation before the American abolition and was not preceded by a full-scale war. At the same time, the British, by the 1830s, had a long and checkered career in slave trading and plantation slavery. How could Fanny have been ignorant to these important details? That question cannot be definitively answered; all the gritty details of plantation slavery in the West Indies were not likely the subject of discussion in high-society gatherings. Such business might also have been censored in the company of women. And so, it appears that Fanny, not unlike her American husband, lived in her own world of denial. She may not have denied the humanity of the slaves, but she could not or would not see England's longstanding role in denying that very humanity. Ironically, Fanny too seemed to be a victim of a fragmented past. She saw England as the center of abolitionism, but did not put such efforts in their historical context. Finally, though she was more progressive than her husband in her desire for the slaves' freedom, she did not grasp the enormity of the link between Blacks and Whites. She did not see in complete context the phenomenon of their parallel lives and linked fates.

Notes

1 Fanny Kemble, *Journal of a Residence on a Georgia Plantation 1838–39*, (Athens, GA: University of Georgia Press, 1863) preface, p. 1.

2 Catherine Clinton, *Fanny Kemble's Civil Wars* (New York: Simon and Schuster, 2000) p. 27

3 Ibid., p.37.

4 Ibid., p. 48

5 Fisher, p. 186.

6 *Mr. Butler's Statement, originally prepared in aid of his professional council.* Butler, Pierce, plaintiff. 1807–1867. Kemble, Fanny, defendant. 1809–1893. (Philadelphia: J. C. Clark, printer, pref. 1850.) Also digitized by University of Michigan Library, 2005, quod.lib.umich.edu/m/moa/ABK2631.0001.001?view=toc, accessed August 31, 2016.

7 Clinton, p. 64.

8 Ibid., p. 56.

9 Ibid., p. 59–63.

10 Ibid., p. 69.

11 Ibid.

12 Ibid., p.75–76.

13 Ibid., p. 88.

14 Ibid., p. 89.

15 Ibid., p.108.

16 Ibid., pp. xiv–xv.

17 Ibid., p. 95.

18 Ibid.

19 Ibid., p. 98–99.

20 Willene Hendrick and George Hendrick, eds, *Fleeing for Freedom: Stories of the Underground Railroad as told by Levi Coffin and William Still* (Ivan R. Dee Publishers, 2004) p. 112.

21 Fanny Kemble, *Journal*, Preface, p. 2.

22 Ibid., Preface, p. 7.

23 Ibid., p. 7–8.

24 Ibid.

25 Ibid. p. 36, and Clinton (2000), p. 117–118.

26 Ibid., p. 17.

27 Harry Kelsey, *Sir John Hawkins: Queen Elizabeth's Slavetrader* (New Haven: Yale University Press, 2003). See also Anne Bailey, *African Voices of the Atlantic Slave trade: Beyond the Silence and The Shame* (Boston: Beacon Press, 2005).

28 Ibid.

29 "Legacies of British Slave Ownership," University College London, www.ucl.ac.uk/lbs/, accessed February 9, 2017.

30 See Woodville Marshall, "'We be wise to many more tings': Black's and Expectations of Emancipation," in Hilary Beckles, Verene Shepherd (Princeton, NJ: Markus Wiener Publishers, 1996); Legacies of British Slave Ownership project, www.ucl.ac.uk/lbs/project/, accessed September 2, 2016.

5

More Than "Hands": African Rhythms and Work on the Butler Plantations

"Dorcas prime woman – A1 woman, sa. Tall gal, sir; long arms, strong, healthy, and can do a heap of work in a day. She is one of de best rice hands on de whole plantation; worth $1,200 easy, Mas'r, an' fus'rate bargain at that."[1]

Mortimer "Doesticks" Thomson

The parallel lives and linked fates of the Butlers and their slaves centered around one thing: work. The epigraph above captures Jeffrey, sold the day before in the Butler auction, pleading in vain with his new owner to purchase his beloved Dorcas. The language he uses is not the language of a lover but the language at the heart of the institution of slavery. "She is one of de best rice *hands* on de whole plantation" (author emphasis). Slaves were not people with hopes, dreams, and desires, but hands – hands to plow, hands to plant, hands to weed, hands to harvest. Jeffrey's desperate plea speaks to the economic value and contribution of slaves of African descent. Among the many perceptions regarding African American slavery, one that is persistent is that the work of slaves was "just field work." Inherent in this view is a devaluation of the work that slaves performed and, by extension, of the slaves themselves. Jeffrey, Dorcas, and most of the other slaves listed in the 1859 auction catalogue were listed as "hands," but enslaved Africans were more than just hands.

Their work encoded and reflected memories of technology and know-how learned on the African continent from their forebears. Furthermore, not only were they more than hands, their work made an invaluable contribution to their masters' plantations, the American economy (both North and South), the New World, and the world at large. It was their work, as historian Eric Williams asserted in his groundbreaking book, *Capitalism and Slavery*, which made modernity possible.[2]

Because slave labor produced the large profits upon which Western economies were built, their fates were linked to their masters and others through their contributions to modernity. Yet their links to the past – their ancestors, through memory, never went away, even as the very technology of their forebears played a vital role in the modernization of the New World.

Links to the slaves' African past also fueled important mechanisms they adopted in the face of brutal and demoralizing labor, particularly in terms of music and resistance. Music was the ever-present backdrop to both work and resistance to it, and was not simply for entertainment purposes. Music has always played a prominent role in African cultures, so it is not surprising that it performed similar functions in African-descended cultures. Traditions and memories about their shared ancestry kept African technical skills and cultural practices alive in the slave communities of the Americas.

African Agricultural Traditions

At the blast of the conch shell, field hands like Jeffrey, Chattel no. 319 in the Butler auction, "prime cotton hand," and John, Chattel no. 99, "prime rice hand," went to work in the cotton fields and in the rice swamps. Cotton and rice were the plantation mainstays. Rice was grown in the muddy swamps of Butler Island, and cotton that was grown on the Hampton plantation on St. Simon's Island contributed to the brand Sea Island Cotton, or "Butler Cotton."

The planting of rice and cotton proved to be equally hard labor but there were some important differences. On a cotton plantation, "the negroes are generally healthy – all the work being of the dry kind." But on the rice plantations, as noted by a Captain Basil Hall on his visits to plantations:

The most unhealthy work in which the slaves were employed and in spite of every care, that they sank under it in great numbers. The causes of this mortality are the constant moisture and heat of the atmosphere, together with the alternate floodings and dryings of the fields, on which the negroes are perpetually at work, often ankle deep in mud, with their bare heads exposed to the fierce rays of the sun.[3]

Rice was central to Gullah-Geechee culture. Even today, it is said by many: "We are Gullah. We're rice eaters. If we don't have rice, we're miserable." Having enough rice was and is associated with a good life.[4] Slaves relished their monthly rations of rice even if it was difficult, back-breaking work to plant and to harvest it. They no doubt inherited this from their ancestors, for whom rice cultivation was a vital part of their identity. As it is still said on the Rice Coast of Africa: "Unless a meal includes rice, they claim not to have eaten."[5]

The rice season started in early March through April with the planting of the crop. Female slaves like Betsey, Chattel no. 100, listed as "rice hand unsound," and Dorcas, Chattel no. 278, listed as "rice, prime woman," would drop rice seeds into holes in the ground and would tamp down the seeds into the holes with their bare feet. In fact, it was often a pregnant or, at the very least, a young woman of child-bearing years, who would drop the rice seed at planting time. It was never someone older.

As Cornelia Bailey, Gullah Geechee folklorist, oral historian, and slave descendant, says:

You had to thresh all of that rice, and you had to put it in a mortar. You had to winnow it in the large baskets. You were still not allowed to eat any of it. You planted it and harvested and do all that back-breaking work. You could not enjoy it. So the women devised a way of tying the apron around them, and when they tied it up, they tied it in such a way where there was like a pocket here. So when they got the basket and they had took the rice out of the mortar and pestle, put it into the basket for winnowing, then they would shake it up and they'd go:

> Peas, peas.
> Peas and the rice done done, uh-huh.
> Peas, peas.
> Peas and the rice done done, uh-huh.

And when they go with the "uh-huh," some of it would always drop inside that apron pocket. So when they went home at night when work was over, they had enough rice to feed their families. And without being caught. So you have to be a little bit ingenious to feed your family. So the ladies were ingenious, of course. That's the only way you could do it.[6]

After they dropped the seed, the slaves would then hoe the fields from early June to August. They used a "fanner" basket to sort the rice grains and separate them from other plant matter. Finally, they pounded the rice by hand to take off its husk, often with large mortars and pestles, from late November to February. It took a special kind of skill in striking the rice in a way that prevented the grain from fragmenting. The enslaved population expertly used the mortar and pestle for milling the rice until the introduction of milling machinery at the end of the eighteenth century.

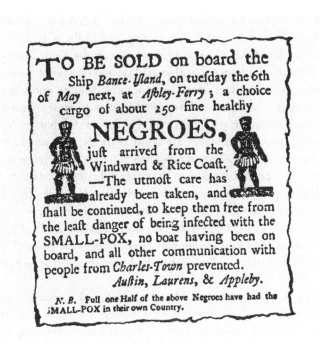

FIGURE 5.1 "To be Sold on board the Ship Bance Island … negroes just arrived from the Windward and Rice Coast".
Photograph and Prints Division, Schomburg Center for Research in Black Culture, The New York Public Library, Astor, Lenox and Tilden Foundations.

By the time Fanny Kemble had visited the plantation, there were three threshing mills, one of which was worked by steam.[7] But where did they learn to plant and harvest rice so efficiently?

These enslaved men and women acquired their agricultural skills from their mothers and fathers, who were from West Africa, specifically what is known as the Rice Coast: a 700-mile region that includes six nations: Senegal, Gambia, Guinea Bissau, Guinea, Sierra Leone, and Liberia. Sierra Leone in particular was one of the main sources of slaves for this region and the Carolinas in general. Slave traders and Low Country planters alike knew the value of Sierra Leone slaves and would often advertise or boast of such when reselling slaves as seen in the advertisement in Figure 5.1. According to Henry Laurens, a major slave importer in 1755 in the Carolinas and Georgia coast, for rice planting, "Gold Coast or Gambias are best, next to them the Windward Coast are prefer'd to Angolas."[8]

These aristocrats knew two things: 1) they didn't know how to plant rice and make it a successful commodity and 2) the African slaves did. They had for hundreds of years planted rice on the Rice Coast of Africa using various technologies that they had passed down for generations or improved upon over time. Even slave captains came to know this history and purchased rice from African communities to feed Africans during the Atlantic passage, to pacify them and to lessen the chances for revolt.[9] The thinking was that if slaves ate familiar foods, they would remain in fit condition to be sold. They would also be more likely to be compliant, if not hopeful, about their fate on the other side of the Atlantic. As historian Judith Carney shows in her pioneering book, *Black Rice,* from the Portuguese's earliest encounter with Africans on the coast, they and other Europeans came to depend on the surplus rice produced by African societies. Somehow, this knowledge was later suppressed. Instead, the myth was perpetuated that the Portuguese had introduced rice to Africa from Asia.[10]

Carney's work shows that Africans developed a separate species of rice – *glaberima* – which represented a distinct variation from the Asian *sativa*. In fact, rice planting was developed long before the European encounter in the 1400s. Islamic scholar Al-Bakri has documented the planting of rice along the Niger River in a record dating back to 1068.[11]

Enslaved Africans employed the same methods on the Georgia coast and in the Carolinas that their forebears had used in Africa to great effect. On the rice coast, they converted inland swamps to rice fields – a process that likewise required back-breaking labor. They developed a sophisticated process of controlled flooding to deal with weeds.[12] They also brought with them to the New World the mortar and pestle, which proved indispensable after the rice was harvested. Finally, the work they called "mud work" fed their masters and also fed themselves. When granted a small garden plot, they planted rice to supplement their meager monthly rations.[13] Their talents and know-how were then put to good use for their independent production.

Perhaps the main difference between rice production in West Africa and rice production on the Low Country plantations like the Butler estates was the division of labor. On the Rice Coast of Africa, women alone were responsible for both the milling and cooking of the rice crop. They also helped sell it in the market. Males were involved in irrigation, ditching, and banking, but women were still more often identified with the crop. It is for this reason that women were found to be just as valuable as men on the slave market – because of the traditional skills that they brought with them. Males continued to be involved in the heavy clearing, digging, ditching, and banking, as plantation records show, but at some point, however, they had to learn from their female counterparts how to process the crop. The demands of the market were such that countless arduous hours had to be spent milling the crop and preparing for market. That meant that men (and boys) would also have been required to use the mortar and pestle to pound the crop – something that traditionally only women would have done in West Africa.[14]

Contribution to Masters and Modernity

Africans put their skills and technology to good use on the plantations and on their independent plots, but whatever they were able to produce independent of the master was not to be compared to the huge profits that masters in the Low Country region enjoyed. They were the real beneficiaries of this technology that Africans transported across the Atlantic. In this way, the labor of enslaved Africans was directly linked to the profits of their masters. It was their work and creative use of their ancestral memories that was central to the agricultural history of not only this region but the Americas.[15]

From the 1720s to 1860, slaves made rice a most important commodity for Southern planters in particular and for the region and the country in general. On the eve of the Civil War, when secession efforts were hotly debated, Southern rice planters of the Low Country were among the richest men in America,[16] neither a small feat nor an accident. In the case of the Butler estates, it was the males in the Butler lineage who were the beneficiaries of this labor through their control of the estates from near or far. They relied on their representatives – overseers – to extract labor from their slaves and to ensure that their plantations were running smoothly.

As discussed in Chapter 3, the founder of the Butler estates, Major Pierce Butler, married Mary Middleton Butler in 1771, who was a part of a powerful and longstanding slave owning family. He quickly inserted himself into the management of their South Carolina estates even before the acquisition of his lands in Georgia. In fact, he did not purchase the 1,700 acres known as Hampton Point on St. Simon's Island until 1774. Up until that time, he was preoccupied with his and his wife's South Carolina interests. He later purchased the Butler Island tracts with money from the sale of his 29th Regiment Commission. He nurtured plans to transport a number of the Middleton-Bull slaves from South Carolina to new estates on St. Simon's Island (Hampton Point) and Butler Island. When his wife died in 1790, he seized the opportunity to transfer Middleton-Bull slaves in accordance with his new plans and also sold some of these slaves as well.[17]

"I purpose moving from your place about 15 workers and 2 or 3 from Carolina. Let Sambo point out a Driver for Hampton. In my next letter, I will send a List of Negroes that are to move."[18] In a 1793 list of 441 Hampton slaves, 295 were designated either PB, MB, or SG, with MB referring to the Middleton-Bull slaves that Butler transferred from South Carolina. It seemed not to concern Major Pierce Butler that many of these slaves were slated for his children. He had other plans for his children's inheritance.[19] "My sincere wish is to move 15 or 20 of my Negroes at Captain Saunders to my place Hampton Point on Great St. Simon's Island in order to prepare for planting about 130 acres of Cotton."[20] And so, many of the original Butler slaves had South Carolina roots and were related to other slaves left behind on the South Carolina estates.

For his part, Major Butler, as well as his eventual heirs, Pierce Mease Butler and John Butler, ran the estate as absentee owners. For example, during the period from 1810–1822, Major Butler visited his Southern estates only once.[21] As a result, the Butler males all depended on a variety of agents or overseers to run the plantation. For much of the period in question, the Kings – Roswell King and his son Roswell King Jr. – were the overseers. The senior Roswell King ran the Butler acquisitions for almost twenty years, starting in 1802. He was the son of a Confederate sea captain who moved to Darien County in 1789.[22] His son succeeded him and was in charge of the estate at the time of Fanny Kemble's one and only visit there. As overseers, they could make about $700 a year.[23]

Both Kings fancied themselves generous and indulgent. The junior King liked to talk about the even-handed way he managed the Butler estates. He claimed to have suppressed "brutality and licentiousness" on the plantation and boasted of controlling slaves with an "equitable distribution of rewards and punishments." Perhaps his most noteworthy claim was the following: "The reputed good condition of the Butler estate has been the work of time, and a diligent attention to the interest of the said estate and the comfort and happiness of the slaves on it." He even boasted of his initiative to have food (corn) prepared for the slaves so as to save time and to assure their proper nourishment. "Many masters think they give provision and clothing in abundance but lest they use means to have these properly prepared, half the benefit is lost. Another great advantage of grinding and cooking for them is, that the little Negroes are sure to get enough to eat."[24]

Of course, his concern for the "little Negroes'" welfare boiled down to his interest in their eventual ability to work hard and from an early age. "Young negroes," he says, "are put to work early, twelve to fourteen years old, four, five or six rated a hand. It keeps them out of mischief, and by giving light tasks, thirty to forty rows, they acquire habits of perseverance and industry."[25] The slaves no doubt did not find either King generous or indulgent, and their records also do not bear this out. In one account, the elder Roswell King talks about the importation of "new negroes" in the same discussion of oxen and ox machines:

> There is no accounts of the New Negroes. Mr. Mein informed me some weeks past they might be expected dayly. I have not seen Mrs. Cunningham but expect it will be difficult to purchase all her Negroes as I understand there is a *mortgage on them* and that she will have indulgence to try to clear them. If she sells them, these will come but very little to her share.

His reference here to their mortgaged bodies showed his total indifference to their utter dehumanization.[26]

Likewise, he claimed that the loss of so many babies had nothing to do with the harsh treatment of slaves but was rather the fault of the slaves themselves. "It appears difficult to save the lives of the young negroes … Not until the parents become more careful can it be effected. Towards themselves, they are thoughtless in the extreme."[27]

This claim was untrue: slaves made good use of the services of their midwives and root doctors whose Africanized herbal medicines at times provided some relief, if not minor miracles. These root doctors, like old Alexander, whom the slaves called "slim and berry black," existed between the world of faith and medicine and were highly respected individuals on the plantation. In the case of Alexander, his patients believed he could fly.[28]

Though Roswell King often blamed slaves for infant deaths, midwives like Midwife Rose, who Fanny Kemble met on her visit, did what they could to save many babies and mothers, drawing on African ancestral memories about health and healing.[29] Nothing, however, could take the place of sufficient rest before and after childbirth.

The overseers also depended on a number of slave "drivers" who in turn created the task or gang system by which slaves were organized, depending on the crop. Fanny Kemble commented on this system in her 1838 journal:

> These tasks, of course, profess to be graduated according to the sex, age, and strength of the labourer; but in many instances this is not the case, as I think you will agree when I tell you that on Mr. − − 's first visit to his estates he found that

the men and the women who laboured in the fields had the same task to perform. This was a noble admission of female equality, was it not? – and thus it had been on the estate for many years past.[30]

The drivers were a curious lot who lived somewhere in the netherworld between slave and master. Originally, a driver was a seasoned slave whose job it was to teach newly imported Africans how to use a hoe and the hand sickle.[31] Eventually, they came to be considered the plantation's most important slaves, who acted as "sole masters" when the overseer visited other plantations or was away during the height of malaria season. It was their job to assign tasks as instructed by the overseer and to supervise the execution of those tasks. This supervision took place under the weight and threat of the lash – a cowhide whip six feet in length with a small wooden handle.[32] Typically, the Butler estate had five or six drivers at any one time who were permitted to strike a fellow slave only six times (twelve for the head driver). Restraint was encouraged but was not always heeded.[33]

Drivers had considerable authority. "An order from a driver," Roswell King Jr. would say "is to be as implicitly obeyed as if it came from myself, nor do I counteract the execution (unless directly injurious) but direct his immediate attention to it. It would be endless for me to superintend the drivers and the field hands too, and would, of course, make them useless."[34] But in the end, this authority often proved to be hollow since a driver was still a slave and was subject to the whims and fancies of both overseer and owner. He could easily lose favor with both. Even in cases where he rendered good service, by no means was he and his family immune from sale, rape, or other acts of injury and injustice on the plantation. Most importantly, as evidenced by the number of slaves listed as drivers on the auction catalogue (at least seven), they were first and foremost slaves. They did not profit from their own labor; they labored to enrich their masters and could and would be sold for the same purpose. Their control of the slave population was ephemeral. In the end, their fate was no different from that of any other slave. Finally, their supposed influence could not be compared to the roughly $30,000 annual income earned by the Butlers during this period.[35] And so, slave labor contributed not only to the enrichment of their masters but to the Western world as the transatlantic economy expanded.

Contribution of Transatlantic Rice Culture

Rice was more than a commodity in the Low Country: it was a dominant part of both Black and White culture. For example, no celebration of New Year's day did not include a dish of rice and black-eyed peas (often with salt pork mixed in), called Hoppin' John in South Carolina and was supposed to bring good luck. Of the tradition, celebrants say that people "who eat poor New Year's Day eat rich the rest of the year."[36] Yet rice was everyday and every-season food, for, in the end, it was not only sustenance after a day's hard work in the field but also a bridge across the Atlantic between Africa and low-country Georgia and Carolinas.

Little did Butler slaves know that black-eyed peas and rice was practically the national dish for many Africans worldwide. Whether it was Suriname or Jamaica, Antigua or Brazil, black-eyed peas and rice in various mutations was sumptuously prepared with African herbal seasonings and always salt pork or beef. They could not have known that their counterparts had the same tradition; that they too had carried a pinch of Africa with them and added to that the new spices and flavors of what their masters were calling the New World. They could not have known that in Senegal the dish is called *chiebouniebe,* and that in Brazil it is called *arroz-de-Hauca.*[37]

It was as if some ancient ancestral memory refused to be forgotten and with every bite further left its mark. In both the preparation of the dish and in the technology used to plant the rice, the African past fused with the slaves' present, supporting Melville Herskovits' 1941 thesis in *The Myth of the Negro Past* that Africans did not arrive in the Americas as *tabula rasas,*[38] and challenging Black sociologist E. Franklin Frazier's claim that African Americans retained hardly any traces of their African past.[39]

Slaves may not have been able to bring many physical aspects of their cultures, but they brought their memories. These memories incorporated every aspect of their culture that could be reasonably replicated; in this case, agriculture and cuisine, which were important contributions to the New World and to modernity. Contributions like these prove that enslaved Africans were indeed more than just hands; their work more than just field work. Their labor enriched nations while simultaneously contributing to the development of New World cultures.

Cotton Planting

Cotton, too, served the Butlers well. Although it was not a crop native to Africa, the agricultural techniques that Africans practiced for thousands of years lent themselves to replication on the Butler estates and others in the South. Women, in particular, had a long tradition in cultivating crops on a subsistence level as well as for the purpose of trading.

For field workers like George, Chattel no. 1 in the first batch of slaves to be auctioned in 1859 and listed as a "prime cotton planter," and Noble, Chattel no. 256, cotton was a life of endless labor: the planting, plowing, and the picking of the crop. In mid-spring, the ground was prepared with hoes and plows drawn with mules. Roughly 100 pounds of seed per acre were planted in furrows plowed three to six feet apart. Solomon Northrup recalled in his narrative *Twelve Years a Slave*: "The women as frequently as the men perform this labor, feeding, currying, and taking care of their teams, and in all respects doing the field and stable work, precisely as do the ploughboys of the North."[40]

When the cotton was planted, soon after began the battle of the weeds.[41] An enormous amount of time and effort went into keeping the plant out of the grass. The last hoeing would take place by early July and cotton bolls would be ready for picking by August. This weeding continued straight up until late summer when the plant was harvested for a period of about four months. For the harvesting and picking of the cotton, usually every worker was needed, including those who worked in the plantation house. Profits for the planters were determined by how fast and how much the "hands" picked. Picking was an arduous task. Overseers across the South would lament that only those hands that had been trained from a young age could be "crack pickers." What is clear is that, as cotton became more and more profitable in the period from 1800–1860, there was a distinct growth in daily picking totals – in some places as much as 132 lbs a day, though 50–80 lbs appeared to be the average.[42]

The cotton was contained in four to five compartments in the boll, as seen in Figure 5.2, and an experienced picker could empty a boll quickly and efficiently into a bag around his shoulders. All the contents of each bag would be weighed and transferred to the gin house at day's end. Inclement weather could also slow down the process since rain not only made picking the cotton very difficult but posed a particular problem in terms of the drying out of the crop.[43]

Before the invention of the cotton gin by Eli Whitney in 1793, cotton had to be cleaned by hand, a grueling process. Inventive African slaves devised a rough comb to help them in their efforts, but the gin sped up the work and made this part of the process less labor-intensive, enabling a single worker to clean fifty pounds of cotton a day. This was a remarkable invention that earned cotton the title of King Cotton because of the tremendous profits that were now possible. The cotton gin allowed Major Butler and his grandsons, Pierce Mease and John, to make a healthy profit margin.

FIGURE 5.2 Cotton plant.
Courtesy of the Department of Agriculture, Public Domain.

The Butler slaves helped make the brand Sea Island Cotton famous. This was the long staple cotton used in the making of superior cloth that was in great demand in England among the upper class. Papers of the Butler Plantation estate affirm that the cotton was sold to factories in Savannah, as well as several markets in England, including Liverpool, London, and Manchester. It is ironic that among those same classes in England there was a cry for the abolition of slavery in this very period, only a short decade before the eventual British abolition in 1807. At the same time, they would accept nothing less than cloth made with cotton, cultivated by slaves from the Sea Islands and other slave states in America.[44]

Fanny Kemble moved in those abolitionist circles and by all accounts held strong anti-slavery views during and after her time in America, but as discussed earlier, still did not grasp the enormity of the problem. She said she could not understand slavery because she was an Englishwoman and so she knew nothing of such things, yet her very clothing belied this assertion. And so her battle against American slavery was not against America alone but was also against her original home, England, which was involved in almost every aspect of slavery from purchase to cotton production. Cotton production in factories in Manchester and other parts of England by the early nineteenth century was an important mainstay of the English economy. The by-product of slave labor, raw cotton, was refined and made into numerous items from shirts to tablecloths. These would in turn be sold on the open market around the world. In this way, slave by-products helped to fuel the Industrial Revolution in England and America, thus further linking Black and White lives together.[45]

Other Plantation Workers

In the end, whether it was rice or cotton, field labor was arduous work. However, working in and around the big house was not easy either. The auction catalogue revealed that slaves on the Butler estate worked as cooks, laundrywomen, dairywomen, housemaids, butlers, midwives, footmen, carpenters, masons, coopers, blacksmiths, and as other skilled craftsmen, all of whom had burdensome tasks.

When Fanny Kemble visited in 1839, she was attended to by several slaves including Jack, a young slave who often accompanied her when she rode horses or rowed in her boat, *The Dolphin*. She also was waited on by Mary, a housemaid, and two older boys were similar to footmen or butlers. She repeatedly exclaimed that the faces, feet, and hands of the boys were "encrusted in dirt."[46] One of them, Aleck, was a sixteen-year-old lad who begged her to teach him to read.[47] Her response revealed her abolitionist sentiments:

Unrighteous laws are made to be broken – perhaps – but then you see I am woman and Mr. Butler stands between me and the penalty ... But teaching slaves to read is a finable offense and I am a *femme couverte* (married woman) and my fines must be paid by my legal owner ... I certainly intend to teach Aleck to read. I certainly won't tell Mr. Butler anything about it.[48]

Aleck was the fortunate beneficiary of a rudimentary education at the hands of Fanny Kemble and, for reasons that are not entirely known, was not sold twenty years later on the auction block. He and the others who served her were also the recipients of a small wage that she paid to them.

There were special challenges for slave women who worked under the watchful eye of their masters because they were often raped or harassed. At the same time, as they confronted the unwanted attention of these masters, they also had to contend with the jealousy of their masters' wives, who often took out their anger on these defenseless slaves. The wives, while White, were not considered equal to men and so had little recourse in confronting their husbands. As historian Elizabeth Fox Genovese discusses in her work, it was much easier to blame female slaves for these indiscretions than their husbands.[49]

The Boatmen and their Musical Traditions

Before the auction, perhaps the slaves who enjoyed most a sense of "freedom" were the boatmen. Neither field workers nor house slaves, they were among the most important slaves on the plantation, carrying the plantation's cargo – human and material – they carried the rhythm of the plantation on their dugout boats, constructed by the estate's carpenters. They were highly valued because of their expertise on the water and the fact that they brought plantation produce to market. They were also expected to transport equipment back and forth, and for Butler Island, they were the only means of ferrying people from the mainland to the island.

On special days each year, they also played a leading role in regattas staged by the region's plantation owners, much to the delight of slaves and masters, Black and White. Their racing boats, made of cypress logs hulled out in the form of shells, were 25–50 feet in length, with 12-foot oars.[50] As they rowed, the boatmen sang in unison with the rhythm of the rowlocks. Like a persistent drumbeat, the rowlocks would undergird their a capella voices above the waves of the Altamaha River. Many of them sang in high tenor – a tenor that Kemble compared to an opera.[51]

These were, however, distinctly African rhythms – African rhythms that lightened the heavy load not only for the boatmen, but for all the slaves that labored on the plantations. These rhythms were from the Congo, Nigeria, Gambia, Sierra Leone, and Angola.

Boatmen were known for singing in good humor and high spirits, so much so that the casual visitor tended to believe the Butler's estimation that his slaves were a happy lot. A song like "Zion" was a playful twist of the Bible story of the foolish and the wise bridesmaids:

> Five were wise an' five were foolish
> When the bridegroom come
> Five were wise an' five were foolish
> When the bridegroom come[52]

The slave Liverpool Hazzard was a Butler boatman. He was also one of the last surviving slaves in Darien County after the war and famously rowed a sick Pierce Mease Butler to the mainland in Darien in the year 1867.[53] Liverpool, who had not been sold in the 1859 Auction, was one of the last slaves to participate in the rowing regattas. As an old man living in Darien, he recalled in the early 1900s:

Old Marster was good to his oarsmen. For three months before the race he wouldn't let us do any work. He'd lock us up if we did and we'd just eat and practice and make our muscles strong. He'd sit in the stern of the boat and would keep urging us on – calling us by name when would slack up. At ou best, we could do the mile in 6 ¼ minutes. Old Marster loved the races and used to bet $500 on us every time and when we would win there was sure some celebratin' on the plantation.[54]

Fanny Kemble enjoyed the boatmen's music and lyrics, even when they were at her expense. During her visit to the plantation, they gaily sang of her "wire waist," in reference to her slim figure. They sang too of the haughtiness of her three-year-old daughter. "Little Missis Sally," they would sing, "That's a ruling lady."[55] It seemed as if in song and good humor, they could get away with saying almost anything. And they did. The meaning of some songs, like boatman Cesar's, was sometimes hard for Fanny to understand, yet Cesar and the slaves understood it well: "The trumpets blow, the bugles sound – oh stand your ground," they would sing as if striking a defiant pose.[56]

This African rhythm of plantation work was especially evident in the music played and sung by the boatmen and many other slaves. Some songs had more than an African rhythm; they were American versions of songs sung by their ancestors. Mrs. Amelia Dawley, a Gullah-Geechee resident of Harris Neck, McIntosh County, Georgia, taught the following song to her daughter Mary Moran, who, with the help of scholars, found the small village of Senehun Ngola where their family originated. There, thousands of miles across the Atlantic, they still sing the same song in the Mende language as a funeral song:

> Ah wakuh muh monuh kambay yah lee luh lay tambay
> Ah wakuh muh monuh kambay yah lee luh lay kah
> Ha suh wileego seehai yuh gbangah lilly
> Ha suh wileego dwelin duh kwen
> Ha suh willeego seehi yuh kwendaiyah[57]

> Everyone come together, let us work hard
> The grave is not yet finished, let his heart be perfectly at peace
> Everyone come together, let us work hard
> The grave is not yet finished, let his heart be perfectly at peace

> Sudden death commands everyone's attention,
> like a firing gun
> Sudden death commands everyone's attention
> Oh elders, oh heads of family
> Sudden death commands everyone's attention
> Like a distant drumbeat.

African rhythms thus played a major part in the world of plantation work, beginning with the driver's blowing of the conch shell an hour before daylight and ending with the blowing of the same at sundown.

Butler slaves knew the meaning of that call. Though it may have seemed that they had barely slept, it was time to labor in the fields, in the big house, in the rice mill and wherever else they were needed. Just as soon as the call went forth, it would not be unusual for a song to be heard. It was a song of hope and a song of encouragement for the day that would otherwise be dark with hardship.

> Breddren, don' git weary,
> Breddren, don' git weary,
> Breddren, don' git weary,
> Fo'd work is most done.[58]

> (Brothers, don't get weary, Bbrothers, don't get weary,
>   brothers, don't get weary, for the work is almost done.)

Butler slaves knew many such songs. These were songs that their forefathers had sung which helped them keep time and wile away the time during the long night that was slavery. When almost all hope was lost in this side of the world, they looked to the next:

> 'E got 'e ca'go raidy. Raidy. Raidy.
> 'E got 'e ca'go raidy.
> Fo'to wait on de Lawd.[59]

> (He got his cargo ready. Ready. Ready. He got his
>   cargo ready. Just for to wait on the Lord.)

The African rhythms and the Gullah language, itself a mixture of English and African words, made for a powerful mix of pathos and hope. They were work songs, but they were often religious in nature too. These rhythms undergirded them from sunup to sundown and would touch every key in the emotional spectrum – from desperate sorrow to raucous humor accompanied with the stamping of feet and the waving of hands. These are the same songs of which W. E. B. Dubois would later declare: "I know these songs are the articulate message of the slave to the world."[60]

And that they were, but they were also the beats that held their hearts and minds and souls together and kept them from the brink of despair. These beats kept together the threads of family and community. Without music as background and foreground of their experience, who knows how many would have survived the cruel hand of slavery? Who knows how many would have survived the back-breaking labor that was required on a daily basis?

Music and Resistance

When this sad rhythm of life got to be too much, some slaves attempted to run away. Whether they knew it or not, they were continuing a long African tradition of seeking freedom. From the first days of their capture in the interior of Africa and on its Slave Coast, Africans never stopped longing for freedom. Even when grouped together in such a way that it was difficult to communicate given the mix of languages, some still found a way to upset the plans of their captors. Some sabotaged slave ships, killed ship captains and crew, and set the vessels on fire; others wrested themselves free of chains and jumped overboard and swam ashore. When they arrived in the New World, still others were no less restless in their pursuit of freedom.

Resistance was widespread and multifaceted, armed and unarmed. In America, there were famous slave revolts by Denmark Vesey and Nat Turner, but there was also nonviolent resistance by slaves who engaged in everything from work slowdowns to crop sabotages. Still others like Frederick Douglass or Kemble's footman, Aleck, in their determination to read and write, used pen and paper to defy a system that would confine them to ignorance.[61]

On the Butler estates, notwithstanding Butler and his overseers' proclamations of the good life they afforded the slaves, some slaves tried to run away multiple times. Sarah, Stephen's wife on Hampton Point estate, once ran away and was severely flogged when found. She ran away again to the woods but was found and this time appeared to have become deranged (probably from hunger and isolation) since when they found her, she was naked. She was driven back to the plantation and was never quite the same again.[62]

The story of Louisa most impressed Fanny, as witnessed in the following exchange. Perhaps not so surprisingly she was one of those mothers who had lost many babies. One day after she was lashed by Bram the driver for not completing her work, fearing another punishment, she ran away to the swamp. She stayed there for days until she was forced to return due to hunger. They then tied her up by her wrists with her feet barely touching the ground for what would prove to be the worst lashing of all.

According to Kemble:

"Tie you up, Louisa!" Said I, "what is that?"

"Oh," said Fanny, "Louisa, but the rattlesnakes – the dreadful rattlesnakes in the swamps, were you not afraid of those horrible creatures?"

"Oh missus, "said the poor child, "me no think of dem; me forget all bout dem for de fretting."

"Why did you come home at last?"

"Oh, missus, me starve with hunger, me most dead with hunger before me come back."[63]

The slaves that were sent to Philadelphia to help in the Butler household appeared not to fare much better. These slaves also showed a keen awareness of the changing times and looked for opportunities to flee or be freed by abolitionists. In 1804, Major Butler decided to send his household slave Ben back to the Georgia plantations after an eleven-year tenure in Philadelphia. Ben promptly went to the Society of the Quakers, one of whose members came knocking at Butler's door with a writ of *Habeas Corpus* for Ben. In the end, the whole matter was taken up in court, with Major Butler protesting that his slaves were not subject to Pennsylvania's law that a slave residing in the state was free after six months. He continued to assert, as he always did, his good treatment of his slaves. To which the representative of the Quakers replied: "Thou benevolent! Why thou are not even just. Thee has sent back into bondage two men who were legally entitled to freedom by law. If thou had a proper sense of Justice thou wouldst bring them back and let them take the liberty that rightfully belongs to them."[64]

Ben did eventually gain his freedom – not from the benevolent Major Butler, but from the Pennsylvania court system.

At the end of the day, as the curtain came down on their African opera, the conch bell was blown again, and slaves could finally rest from their long hours of work. Their work was more meaningful than even they would realize. It was, after all, the fruits of their labor – raw materials turned into manufactured goods in the capitals of North America and Europe – that would usher in modernity. Using their "hands" and minds, they had made an important contribution that neither they nor those around them would recognize for centuries to come.

This lack of acknowledgment notwithstanding, they did have some small comforts. They maintained some connection to their African past through the technological know-how of their forefathers and the music that fueled their work. They also continued the African tradition of retaining their faith in the notion of freedom, and sometimes actively seeking it through acts of resistance big and small. Religion, as we will see in the next chapter, gave them the strength to believe in something larger than slavery.

These themes are perhaps best expressed in the Negro spiritual, "Wade in the Water," whose lyrics are below. On one level, this song appears to have only a spiritual significance, with its references to Old and New Testament Biblical principles. Upon closer examination, like many other Negro spirituals, it was a coded message to runaway slaves on the trail of the Underground Railroad. "Wade in the water," they were instructed, so that the bloodhounds that were sent by slave masters would be unable to pick up their scent. If they waded in the water and moved swiftly, they would not be detected. Every note and every lyric was an act of resistance.

There is perhaps no better example of the African survivals of music and resistance –not to mention faith – the subject of our next chapter.

Wade in the Water
Wade in the Water
Wade in the water children
Wade in the water
God's gonna trouble the water.

Now if you should get there before I do
(I know) God's gonna trouble the water
Tell all my friends that I'm comin' too
(I know) God's gonna trouble the water
Sometimes I'm up lord and sometimes I'm down
(You know my) God's gonna trouble the water
Sometimes I'm level to the ground
God's gonna trouble the water
(I Know) God's gonna trouble the water

FIGURE 5.3 Darien Gullah Geechee Shouters today reviving African rhythms of yesterday.
Courtesy of Griffin Lotson.

Notes

1 Thomson, p. 16.
2 See Eric Williams, *Capitalism and Slavery* (Chapel Hill: University of North Carolina Press, 1944), and Edward Baptist, *The Half has Not been Told: Slavery and the Making of American Capitalism* (New York: Basic Books, 2014).
3 Bell, p. 127.
4 John H. Tibbetts, "African Roots Carolina Gold," *Coastal Heritage*, South Carolina Sea Grant Consortium, Summer 2006, Vol. 2. No. 1, p. 4–5.
5 Judith Carney, *Black Rice* (Cambridge, MA: Harvard University Press, 2001) p. 31.
6 Interview with Cornelia Bailey, folklorist, *Africans in America* PBS series, www.pbs.org/wgbh/aia/part4/4i2970.html, accessed October 28, 2016.
7 Tibbetts, p. 5, and Judith Carney, "Rice Milling, Gender and Slave Labour in Colonial South Carolina," *Past & Present*, no. 153 (1996): p. 111–117, www.jstor.org/stable/651137. Daniel Littlefield, *Rice and Slaves* (Baton Rouge: Louisiana State University Press, 1981) p. 105, Fanny Kemble's *Journal*, p. 9–10.
8 Bell, p. 90.
9 Tibbetts, p. 5.
10 Carney 2001, p. 5–6.

11 Carney 2001, p. 35.

12 Ibid., p. 86 and 93.

13 Tibbetts, p. 5.

14 Butler Plantation Papers, Reel 3 Collection 1447, Box 2, folders 1–26, letter of September 17, 1803 by Overseer Roswell King, and Carney 1996, p. 126–132.

15 Carney 2001, and Edda Fields, *Deep Roots: Rice Farmers in West Africa and in the African Diaspora* (Bloomington: Indiana University Press, 2008).

16 Eric Foner, *Forever Free: The Story of Emancipation and Reconstruction* (New York: Penguin Random House, 2005), and Carney 1996.

17 Bell, p. 55.

18 In a September 1791 letter to Roger Parker Saunders in Bell, p. 57.

19 Bell, p. 58.

20 Ibid.

21 Dusinberre, p. 215.

22 Dusinberre, p. 216.

23 Ibid.

24 Roswell King, "On the Management of the Butler Estate and the Cultivation of Sugar Cane," *Southern Agriculturalist I* (1828): 527.

25 Ibid.

26 Letter of September 17, 1803, Butler Plantation papers pamphlet.

27 Dusinberre, p. 239.

28 Bell and Yvonee P. Chireau, *Black Magic: Religion and the African American Conjuring Tradition* (Berkeley:University of California Press, 2003).

29 Dusinberre, p. 240.

30 Fanny Kemble's Journal, p. 17.

31 Bell, p. 144.

32 Ibid.

33 Bell, p. 146.

34 Roswell King.

35 Interview with William Dusinberre on the Weeping Time, *Africans in America, Part 4*, PBS, www.pbs.org/wgbh/aia/part4/4i2971.html, accessed October 28, 2016.

36 Tibbetts, p. 6.

37 Karen Hess, *The Carolina Rice Kitchen: The African Connection* (University of South Carolina Press, 1998) p. 101–102. See also the work of anthropologist Sheila S. Walker, ed., *African Roots American Cultures* (Lanham, MD: Rowman and Littlefield, 2001).

38 Carney, Introduction.

39 Frazier 1939.

40 Jean West, "King Cotton: The Fiber of Slavery," *Slavery in America*, p. 7–8, cuwhist.files.wordpress.com/2012/07/king-cotton-the-fiber-of-slavery.pdf, accessed October 29, 2016, and Solomon Northrup, *Twelve Years a Slave, A Narrative of Solomon Northrup*,(Auburn: Derby and Miller, 1853). See also Catherine Clinton, *Tara Revisted* (NY: Abbeville Press, 1995) p. 31.

41 Pietra Rivoli, *The Travels of a T shirt in a Global economy: An Economist examines the markets, power and politics of world trade* (New Jersey: John Wiley and Sons) p. 11–13.

42 West, p. 7–9, and Edward E. Baptist, *The Half Has Never Been Told: Slavery and the Making of American Capitalism* (New York: Basic Books, 2014) p. 125–128; p. 112–113.

43 Rivoli, p. 11–13.

44 Bell, p. 111, *"A Statement of the Cotton Crop for the Year 1802, what Shipped, what packed on hand & what supposed to be on hand unpacked…"* Reel 3, Collection 1447, Box 2, folders 1–26.

45 See Eric Williams, *Capitalism and Slavery,* and "Revealing Histories, Remembering Slavery," Revealing Histories, www.revealinghistories.org.uk/home.html, accessed October 28, 2016.

46 Bell, p. 271

47 Kemble, p. 271.

48 Ibid., p. 272.

49 Elizabeth Fox Genovese, *Within the Plantation Household: Black and White Women in the Old South* (Chapel Hill: University of North Carolina Press, 1988).

50 Buddy Sullivan, *Memories of McIntosh: A Brief History of McIntosh Island, Darien and Sapelo* (Darien News, 1990) p. 16.

51 Kemble, p. 260.

52 Bell, p. 148.

53 Bell, p. 408. He also sang boat songs for Lydia Parrish in the 1930s.

54 Sullivan, p. 18.

55 Kemble, p. 142.

56 Ibid., p. 260.

57 "Amelia's Song: A Song led them home," Harris Neck Land Trust, www.harrisnecklandtrust1.xbuild.com/amelias-song/4529751671, accessed October 28, 2016. Scholars Joseph Opala and Cynthia Schmidt were instrumental in this effort. A film called *The Language You Cry In* was made of Amelia's song and its connection to the village in Sierra Leone.

58 Elieen Southern and Josephine Wright, *African American Traditions in Song, Sermon, Tale and Dance, 1600's-1920* (Westport, CT: Greenwood Pub. Group, 1990).

59 Shane White and Graham White, *The Sounds of Slavery: Discovering African American History Through Songs, Sermons and Speech* (Boston: Beacon Press, 2005) p. 65.

60 Wilbur Cross, *Gullah Culture in America* (Winston–Salem: John F. Blair Publisher, 2012) p. 205 and Chapter 3.

61 Bailey, p. 96–98.

62 Kemble, p. 229–231.

63 Ibid., p. 215–216.

64 Bell, p. 141.

6

Faith on the Butler Estates

"The night before, they (Dembo and Frances) had found a minister among those attending the sale and begged him to join them in Holy matrimony."[1]
Mortimer "Doesticks" Thomson

This moment captured by the newspaperman Doesticks, posing as a buyer at the Auction of 1859, belies one of the most striking ironies of the period of slavery. Dembo and Frances considered themselves fortunate to have found a minister among the buyers to marry them in order to prevent their separation on the auction block. Given the rampant disregard for family bonds beyond nuclear units, this appears to have been a ray of hope, but what was a Christian minister doing at a slave auction? Was he just another buyer, or prospector, or was he simply a bystander? Or, like his counterparts on slave ships, was he there to bless the proceedings?

This moment is further evidence of the parallel yet linked fates of both slave and master, Black and White. Both master and slave ostensibly shared the same religion – Christianity. To that end, not only were their fates linked on earth, but presumably in the afterlife. Their vastly different interpretations of the same religion, however, meant that they had largely parallel spiritual lives.

On the Butler plantations in the period before the sale, Fanny Kemble (and to some extent the slave preachers of the plantation) served as a bridge between master and slave in matters of the spirit. Pierce Mease Butler, by contrast, showed little interest in such matters for much of his life. It was not until the end of his life, in his provision of a slave burial ground, that he appeared to gain a greater respect for the spiritual lives of his former slaves.

Shadrach's Funeral

A great example of masters' and slaves' parallel yet linked fates is the story of the funeral of Shadrach, a young Butler slave, which Fanny Kemble recalled in her diary.

It was a chilly winter evening in 1839 during Fanny Kemble's stay at the Butler estate. Just after twilight, all the slaves on Butler Island met at the house of Cooper London, the slave who made and repaired barrels on the plantation but was also the plantation preacher. All eyes were fixed on Mr. and Mrs. Butler. Aside from the stars and the moon, only the light from the pinewood torches of the slaves illuminated the scene.[2]

Shadrach was said to have been "a very valuable slave." He had succumbed to a peripneumonia – a disease that felled many a slave during the winter months. He, like many adult slaves, had a compromised immune system due to repeated bouts of malaria. In January 1839, he sank rapidly and died within days.[3]

The slaves laid his coffin on trestles in front of the house and Cooper London and another Black slave stood before it officiating the service.[4] London first led the group in a wailing hymn that they sang in perfect unison. Then, as he called for prayer, humbly knelt in the sand. All the slaves and Fanny Kemble bent their knees in the presence of God and the dead, except Mr. Butler, who would not kneel. As London gave the closing invocation, he called for blessings on Mr. and Mrs. Butler and their children, and, at these words, Fanny burst into tears.

After prayer, the coffin was brought to the burial ground and another round of prayers ensued from the funeral service of the Prayer book and, once again, they knelt as Cooper London said, peering over the grave: "I am the resurrection and the life." All the slaves and Fanny Kemble bent their knees, except Butler, who again would not kneel.

London then gave a short address in plain speech and without flourish on Lazarus and how Jesus raised him from the dead. At his sermon's end, the coffin was lowered into the grave. But the grave was filled with water because of the swampy land. At the sight of the water-filled grave, then and only then did the small congregation depart from their somber service with exclaims and cries.

Kemble, who was still crying quietly to herself, turned with her husband to head back to the main house. Butler was stoic and silent, but the slaves, amidst their grief, were moved by Kemble's. "God bless you, missis, don't cry," they repeatedly said. "Lor, missis, don't you cry so!" Finally they said, "Farewell, good night, massa and missis."[5]

Enslaved by Religion but Freed by Faith

Notwithstanding his wife's sympathetic cries, Butler was largely indifferent to the spiritual lives of his slaves. Generations of slaveholders before him in the South held vastly different interpretations of the Christian religion. For many of the slaves, the Christian Bible was incompatible with slavery, yet slave owners used the same Bible to provide the ultimate rationalization for the system of slavery. They cherry-picked the text and selectively interpreted it for their own purposes. Christianity was made to conform to economic and social realities, not the other way around. But Black slaves read that same Bible, many of whom risked brutal punishment, perhaps even death, for learning how to read. Others committed much of it to memory such that they came to rely on their interpretations that centered on freedom and hope.

For many slaves, they saw in their faith freedom and hope of a better life in the next. Kemble made this discovery when she overheard a conversation between her three-year-old daughter Sally and Mary the chambermaid:

"Mary, some persons are free, and some are not (to which the woman made no reply.)

"I am a free person ... I say, I am a *free* person, Mary – do you know that?"

"Yes missis."

"Some persons are free and some are not – do you know that Mary?"

"Yes Missis, *here,*" was her reply; "I know it is so here, in this world."

Here my child's white nurse, my dear Margery, who had hitherto been silent, interfered saying:

"Oh then you think it will not always be so?"

"Me hope not, missis."[6]

She was a slave in the here and now, but one day she would be free. Holding onto hope, some even saw themselves as free, even though they were still in bondage. Whether they worshiped Christ of the Bible or Allah of the Koran or the gods of Africa, there were many slaves who enjoyed a certain freedom that was only afforded by their faith. Long before their shackles fell to the ground at the signing of the Emancipation Proclamation, many of them were free. They did not need a bitterly fought war to determine their fate.

They were freed by faith.

Fanny Kemble: Bridging the Divide
Between Master and Slave

Fanny seemed to spend much time assessing the spiritual lives of the slave population on the Butler plantations and noted that "there was an immensely strong devotional feeling among these poor people ... yet light is light even the poor portion that may stream through a keyhole."[7] She appeared to understand and to reject the parallel way in which Christianity was practiced on Southern plantations. A century before Martin Luther King Jr. would say that the most segregated day in the South was a Sunday, Fanny made the same observation and was a bridge between these two vastly different worlds.

On the one hand, she knew that slave owners had their ideas of how much light they would let through. "Slaveholding clergymen and certain piously inclined planters undertake to enlighten these poor creatures with a safe understanding," Kemble would say, "however, of what truth is to be given to them and what is not; how much they may learn to become better slaves and how much they may not learn, lest they cease to be slaves at all."[8] There was something "dangerous" about the scriptures and the slave owners knew it right well.

In fact, there was a quietly fought contest between the slaves and their masters about how much religion was enough. The slaves appeared always to want more – more time to have their services, more prayer books, more Bibles and more opportunities to get baptized. It was a tug of war with each side pushing against the other, a stark example of their parallel yet linked lives.

The Butler Island slaves were only allowed to worship at the church on the mainland in Darien once a month, but they wanted more. Similarly, the slaves on the St. Simon's plantation also had little access to the White church there called Christ Church, a beautiful structure flanked by magnificent live oaks as seen in Figure 6.1. Once inside, however, the slaves were obliged to sit at the back of the church and heard the usual sermons that told them to be content with their lot. They wanted more but were often refused, as was the slave Morris, whom Fanny describes as handsome with fine features. During her stay, he had requested permission to be baptized but Butler would not grant it.[9]

Like his employer, Roswell King had no tolerance at all for religion for Blacks and, as it turns out, for Whites as well. In this, he was consistent. He was not keen on religious instruction for slave or free, White and Black, and had no problem letting everyone know so.[10] His chief concern

FIGURE 6.1 Christ Church, St. Simon's Island.
Courtesy of Georgia Historical Society.

was the management of the estates, and he felt strongly that slaves getting together in groups, especially with slaves from other plantations in a church setting, was a dangerous thing. So he did everything he could to stand in their way.

If slave owners were not exactly preoccupied with present or future judgment, Fanny Kemble certainly was. During her visit, she thought a lot about emancipation and supported the notion of a gradual emancipation.[11] Like the slaves, she could not wait for that moment to come.

"Beat, beat the crumbling banks and sliding shores, wild waves of the Atlantic and the Altamaha! Sweep down and carry hence this evil earth and these homes of tyranny and roll above the soil of slavery and wash my soul and the souls of those I love clean from the blood of our kind."[12] This was literally her prayer and it was a theme that was repeated again in her journal when, like a real-life Lady Macbeth, she asked herself out loud: "where and how is one to begin the cleansing of this horrid pestilential immodest (foulness) of an existence?"[13]

Fanny Kemble also felt strongly about what she saw as the eventual judgment on those who held others in bondage. Until the day she died, she was convinced that there would be some eternal judgment meted out to those who had used the Christian faith as a weapon against the poor and the oppressed. That same light, she would say, would eventually sweep them all away.[14] There was a great deal of hypocrisy in white Christian circles in the county of Darien, the home of the Butler plantations. The church backed the slave owners on every point and in some cases the clergy owned slaves. Even in those cases where slaves were allowed to attend certain churches, as in the case of the Baptist Church in Darien, there were strict rules of segregation. Communion was administered to Whites first, then afterwards administered to Blacks.[15]

In her heart and mind, Fanny seemed to understand the linked fates of master and slave. Her heart pined for the freedom of those around her as if somehow in their freedom, she would find her own. After all, she was the wife of a slave owner of very large Southern plantations. Her comforts and her leisure and that of her children were directly connected to their enslaved status. The two were inextricably linked. This she could not escape. But neither could she escape her intense desire to be just to those held in bondage. As she waited for their emancipation, she found some absolution in devoting herself to good works – rehabilitating the infirmary and holding prayer services for the slaves in the house she shared with Butler.

During her time on St. Simon's Island, she held several prayer services for the slaves in her living room. She would read the scriptures out loud, sometimes overwhelmed with emotion and losing her composure. They received them solemnly, and in the end would express gratitude without overwhelming her with the usual petitions and complaints.[16]

Aside from Fanny's interventions during her stay, the plantation appeared to be well served by various slave preachers, the most notable of which was Cooper London, who had officiated Shadrach's funeral. One of the most remarkable things about Cooper London, besides the fact that he was so well respected on the plantations, was the fact that he could read and write. This Fanny found out when London asked her for Bibles for the slaves.

I had a long talk with that interesting and excellent man, Cooper London, who made an earnest petition that I would send him from the North a lot of Bibles and Prayer Books; certainly the science of reading must be much more common among the Negroes than I supposed, or London must look to a marvelously increased spread of the same hereafter. There is, however, considerable reticence upon this point, or else the poor slaves must consider the mere possession of the holy books as good for salvation and as effectual for spiritual assistance to those who cannot as to those who can comprehend them.

For all of this, London would not tell Kemble how he had learned to read. Even to the end, he evasively offered:

"Well, missis, me learn; well, missis, me try"; and finally: "Well, missis, me 'spose Heaven help me"; to which I could only reply that I knew Heaven was helpful, but very hardly to the tune of teaching folks their letters. I got no satisfaction."

Kemble did not get any satisfaction on this point and given the stiff penalties against teaching slaves to read and write, it is no wonder.[17]

Just as their ancestors had multiple spiritual authorities (outside of an official priest), so did the slaves on the Butler estates in Low-Country Georgia. Men as well as women were able to occupy these positions. Sinda, the prophetess, was an excellent example. She was not a preacher and there is no evidence that she could read and write like Cooper London. But she was highly revered on the plantation, and her words carried much weight; her prophesies even more.

So one day when Sinda gave forth the prophesy that the end of the world was nigh, and thus the Great Emancipation could be expected soon, the slaves listened. They also stopped working altogether in anticipation for the great day. No amount of cajoling them back to the field worked, not even the lash or threat of the lash. They summarily had abandoned the rice swamps and the cotton fields and there was nothing that anyone could do. Roswell King was duly frustrated.[18] All King could do was to threaten a great and terrible punishment if, on the appointed day, no such occurrence took place.[19]

And thus it was that when the dreaded day came, nothing dreadful happened save that Sinda, the prophetess, was whipped with full force for having for a short, sweet time led the slaves into believing that their freedom was around the corner. Even Fanny was saddened not to see her prophesy fulfilled, as she mused:

Freedom without entering it by the grim gate of death, brought down to them at once by the second coming of Christ, whose first advent has left them yet so far from it, Farewell; it makes me giddy to think of having been a slave while that delusion lasted and after it vanished.[20]

Christianity, Islam and Other Dieties

The slaves had a "turn for religion" according to Kemble. This, however, was not a new phenomenon. That religion in the main tended to be Christianity, to which they were introduced on New World plantations and through the eighteenth-century "Great Awakening," which included multiracial revival meetings. Still, it is important to note that the African continent was introduced to Christianity from as early as the fourth century AD. The great kingdom of Aksum, a major trading empire in Ethiopia from the fourth through ninth century, was a Christian kingdom whose kings worshipped Christ and put the image of the Cross on their currency. Christian churches in East Africa – the Coptic Church – stood and stand to this day as strong evidence of their early adherence to the Christian faith.

While most slaves tended to be Christian converts, others held fast to African ancestral gods and to Islam. Historian Michael Gomez and others have expounded well on the latter.[21] The sacred has always held a special importance in African life. Notions of the sacred are not relegated to specific days or rites; instead, they are infused in daily life and actions.[22] As such, indigenous African religions were alive and well at the time of their encounter with Europeans via the Atlantic slave trade. Africans brought with them to the "New World" their profound understandings of the sacred. Their perception of God or gods was as complex as it was pervasive.

Whether they were local deities or those shared with neighboring communities, they retained a strong sense of who they were with respect to the sacred with particular attention to the afterlife and respect for their ancestors. What early travelers and anthropologists in Africa mistakenly referred to as ancestor worship was, in fact, simply veneration of the wisdom of those who had gone before and preparation for the role that those living would one day occupy. At the same time that they served local deities that would vary from region to region and community to community, they were also introduced to Islam through Muslim traders from as early as the seventh century. In fact, the accounts of Muslim travelers like the famous Ibn Battuta and others continue to be great sources of written knowledge about Africa's history in the period prior to the European encounter. Muslim traders who traversed the Sahara with their goods found West and Central Africa ripe ground for conversions to Islam, though often with a twist: Africans often embraced Islam but also held onto to their indigenous beliefs, creating a syncretic mix that is still evident in some quarters today.[23] Furthermore, a significant number of slaves that were taken from these regions were Muslims, though, for a long time, this was not widely understood or acknowledged in the literature.

What did that mean for the Butler slaves who retained much of their African heritage and memory? A multifaceted religious picture was very

present on the plantation, although Christianity appeared to be the dominant religion. The duress of the slave system did little to alter their "turn
for religion." Even when the prophesies such as Sinda's did not come
true, the slaves did not falter in their beliefs. Some continued to hold onto
the Christian promise; others whose ancestors had brought to America's
shores the God they called Allah held on too. And still others held onto
the gods and the faith lore of Africa, sometimes combining the former
with the latter. They held onto hope.

Not surprisingly, if some slave owners in the region were hardly interested in the spiritual growth of their slaves as far as the Christian religion,
they were even less interested in anything that was reminiscent of Africa.
They wanted nothing to do with this kind of worship. Some found it
frightening, others considered it superstition, and still others suspected
it was witchcraft. In all cases, it was threatening to slave owners, to say
the least.

That said, there were and are signs of these Africanized beliefs all over
Low-Country Georgia and in Savannah in particular. Haint blue, the
color that "ain't blue and ain't green," was the color of choice for the
doors and windows of slave houses which, according to lore, warded off
the evil spirits. The haint blue color represented water, over which it was
said the spirits could not pass.[24] These doors and windows pointed to the
mysterious side of the region where spirits, ghosts, and "haints" (ghosts)
are considered by some to be part of the landscape.

In the 1930s, folklorist and St. Simon's resident Lydia Parrish asked
former slaves in the region about other religious practices. One said:

Now, ole man Dembo he use tuh beat duh drum tuh duh fewnul, but Mr. Couper
he stop dat. He say he dohn wahn drums beatin roun duh dead. But I watch em
hab a fewnul. I gits behine duh bush an hide an watch an see wut dey does. Dey
go in a long pruhcession tuh duh buryin groun an dey beat duh drums long duh
way an dey submit duh body tuh duh groun. Den dey dance roun in a ring an dey
motion wid duh hans. Dey sing duh body tuh duh grabe an den dey let it down
an den dey succle roun in duh dance.

Dey ain hab no chuch in doze days an wen dey wannuh pray, dey git behine duh
house aw hide someweah an make a great prayuh. Dey ain suppose tuh call on
duh Lawd; dey hadduh call on duh massuh an ef dey ain do dat, dey git nine
an tutty.

(Translation: Old man Dembo used to beat his drum to the funeral but Mr.
Couper (one of Butler's slaveowner neighbors) put a stop to that. He said he
doesn't want any drums beating around the dead. But I watch them have a
funeral. I got behind the bush and hide and watch and see what they do. They
go in a long procession to the burial ground and they beat the drums along the

day and they submit the body to the ground. Then they dance around in a ring and they motion with their hands. They sing the body to the grave and they let it down and they circle around it in a dance. They didn't have no church in those days and when they want to pray, they get behind the house and hide somewhere and make a great prayer. They are not supposed to call on the Lord. They had to call on Massa because if they did not do that they would get nine and thirty (lashes).[25]

Butler's Evolution

Wariness notwithstanding, slave owners appeared to have a grudging respect for the spiritual authorities on their plantations because, on the list of 440 slaves that were to be sold at the auction on March 2 and 3, there does not appear to be one such figure. Even valued drivers like Bram were listed as "prime cotton, dri'r, high character, age 47," and sold for $1,410. Cudjo was also one of three drivers sold listed as "prime rice, driver, age 49," and sold for $710, yet there is no record of a preacher being sold. In fact, it is almost a certainty that there was not one amongst them since when Dembo and Frances made their little plan to get married, they had to ask one of the white preachers in attendance of the auction to marry them, as opposed to one of their number. In the contest between slaves and slave owners for more religion not less, those with spiritual authority were nonetheless valued.

When the Civil War was over and the period of Reconstruction had begun, there was less controversy and debate around the issue of religion. During this postwar period, Pierce Butler and his youngest daughter and staunch ally, Frances Butler Leigh, went back to the estates to help restore them to their former glory. They found much hardship and difficulty, yet on this question of faith, there was less struggle. For the South, the war was over. The battle was lost and now there was much to be done. The South and Southern estates lay in shambles. Restoration and reconstruction were the order of the day and there was no time, nor did former slave owners have any authority, to keep the slaves from worshipping as they pleased.

When the Civil War was over, according to Leigh, "our own clergyman at Darien told me he had been working among the negroes all his life to the best of his powers, but felt now that not one seed sown among them had borne any good fruit."[26] The slaves may have lost interest in the Darien church in the early years after the war, but this did not mean that their interest in matters of faith had diminished at all. As C. Eric Lincoln and Lawrence Mamiya show in their seminal book on the historical

Black church, it is this period after the Civil War when African American churches experienced the most growth. These independent Black churches were involved in every aspect of the lives of ex-slaves, but, above all, were sites of great religious fervor.[27]

The Enduring Ring Shout

Leigh, like her mother Fanny Kemble decades before, was to witness the extent of the religious devotion and fervor of the ex-slaves on her birthday, when she was treated to the famous "ring shout." This ring shout can be witnessed even today as the cultural group the Georgia Gullah-Geechee Shouters (headed by Reverend Griffin Lotson, community activist and Gullah advocate, himself related to former Butler slaves in the area as seen in Figure 5.3) entertain audiences all over the country with their version of what was called the sacred circle:

I spent my birthday at the South, and my maid telling the people that it was my birthday, they came up in the evening to "shout for me." A negro must dance and sing, and as their religion, which is very strict in such matters, forbids secular dancing, they take it out in religious exercise, call it "shouting," and explained to me that the difference between the two was, that in their religious dancing they did not "lift the heel." All day they were bringing me little presents of honey, eggs, flowers, &c., and in the evening about fifty of them, of all sizes and ages and of both sexes, headed by old Uncle John, the preacher, collected in front of the house to "shout." First they lit two huge fires of blazing pine logs, around which they began to move with a slow shuffling step, singing a hymn beginning "I wants to climb up Jacob's ladder." Getting warmed up by degrees, they went faster and faster, shouting louder and louder, until they looked like a parcel of mad fiends. The children, finding themselves kicked over in the general *mêlée*, formed a circle on their own account, and went round like small Catherine wheels.[28]

By this time, the main preacher on the plantation was Old John Bull, about whom stories abound. Marriage was still important and had taken on even more importance now that they were free, and it was John Bull who was called into service for every nuptial. Leigh talked about how much he encouraged the girls to be "moral and chaste" and how she provided all the veils, the cakes, the wreaths, and whatever else they could to dress up what was always a simple ceremony:

The parson, old John, received them at the reading-desk of the little church, and after much arranging of the candles, his book, and his big-rimmed specs, would proceed and read the marriage service of the Episcopal Church, part of which he knew by heart, part of which he guessed at, and the rest of which he spelt out with much difficulty and many absurd mistakes. Not satisfied with the usual text appointed for the minister to read, he usually went through all the directions too, explaining them as he went along thus: "Here the man shall take the woman by the right hand," at which he would pause, look up over his spectacles and say, "Take her, child, by de right hand and hold her," and would then proceed. On one occasion, after he had read the sentence, "Whereof this ring is given and received as a token and pledge," he said with much emphasis, "Yes, children, it is a *plague*, but you must have patience."

As Leigh listened in horror, the service continued:

When it was all over he (Old John, the preacher) would say to the bridegroom with great solemnity and a wave of his hand, "Salute de bride," upon which the happy man would give her a kiss that could be heard all over the room. The worst of John's readings and explanations was that they differed every time, so we never could be prepared for what was coming, which made it all the more difficult not to laugh.[29]

Eventually, Leigh tried to get Old John licensed because of a new law that prohibited an unlicensed preacher from performing the marriage rite. She sent him up to Savannah, but they found him too untutored to pass muster for the license. Unfortunately for both Leigh and John, it put a damper on all her weddings and forced him to retire.[30]

Preachers for the former slaves, as for their former masters, were important because they were the ones who conducted major rites of passage and everything in between, especially at life's end:

I left the South for the North late in July, after a severe attack of fever brought on by my own imprudence. Just before I left an old negro died, named Carolina, one hundred years old. He had been my great grand-father's body servant, and my father was much attached to him, and sat up with him the night before he died, giving him extract of beef-tea every hour. My sister had sent us down two little jars as an experiment, and although it did not save poor old Carolina's life, I am sure it did mine, as it was the only nourishment I could get in the shape of animal food after my fever. When Carolina was buried in the beautiful and picturesque bit of land set apart for the negro burying-ground on the island, *my father had a tombstone with the following inscription on it erected over him.* (Author's emphasis.)

CAROLINA,

DIED JUNE 26, 1866,

AGED 100 YEARS.

A long life, marked by devotion to his Heavenly Father and fidelity to his earthly masters.[31]

And so, by this time, Butler, who decades before refused to kneel in respect at Shadrach's funeral and who sold half of the estate's slaves at the great auction of 1859, came to respect the faith traditions of his former charges. In giving a burial stone to old Carolina and eventually a burial ground not only on the estate but on the mainland, he made peace with the expression of the faith of his former slaves.

When Butler was only days away from death himself, his old and faithful slave, boatman Liverpool Hazzard – who was not sold at the great sale of 1859, but whose friends and fellow slaves were sold to keep Butler in fine style – facilitated his last days on earth by transporting the gravely ill Butler to the mainland by boat.

Years later, Hazzard was buried in the burial ground that Butler had bought and designated for the slaves and their descendants. Liverpool's grave can still be found on that burial ground. The tombstone reads:

Liverpool Hazzard
Born 1851 died 1938; age 87;
Last of the Butler Island Darien Ga. Butler slaves
"He faithfully served his God and his Master."[32]

Notes

1   Thomson, p. 18.
2   Bell, p. 286 and Kemble, p. 147.
3   Dusinberre, p. 74, 227, and 263.
4   Dusinberre, p. 227.
5   Kemble, p. 147–150.
6   Ibid., p. 60.
7   Ibid., p. 106 and 260.
8   Ibid., p. 107.
9   Ibid., p.121.
10 Ibid., p. 344.
11 Dusinberre, p. 221.
12 Kemble, p. 233.
13 Ibid., p. 271.
14 Ibid., p. 107.
15 Ibid., p.106.
16 Ibid., p. 262.
17 Ibid., p.194.
18 Ibid., p. 118–119.
19 Fanny's Diary does not specify the day that Sinda gave forth the prophesy; we only know that the story was told to her during her trip in 1838–1839.
20 Kemble, p. 119.
21 See Michael Gomez, *Black Crescent: The Experience and Legacy of African Muslims in the Americas* (New York: Cambridge University Press, 2005), and *Exchanging Our Country Marks: The Transformation of African Identities*

in the Colonial and Antebellum South (Chapel Hill: University of North Carolina Press, 1998) for more.

22 See Bailey, *African Voices of the Atlantic Slave Trade*, chapter 6.

23 See also Basil Davidson, *African Civilization Revisited* (Africa World Press, 1991).

24 "The Culture of Gullah," Exhibit of Cindy Ensminger, Museum of the City, www.museumofthecity.org/project/the-culture-of-gullah/.

25 Mary Granger, *Drums and Shadows: Survival Studies Among Georgia Coastal Negroes* (University of Georgia Press, 1940) p. 171–172.

26 Leigh, p. 150.

27 "The Church in the Southern Black Community," Documenting the American South, docsouth.unc.edu/church/intro.html, and C. Eric Lincoln and Lawrence H. Mamiya, *The Black Church in the African American Experience* (Durham: Duke University Press, 1990).

28 Leigh, p. 59–60.

29 Ibid., p. 161–163.

30 Ibid., p. 163–164.

31 Ibid., p. 71–72.

32 Burial Grounds Record, Record 2, Burial Grounds, Darien, Ga. See also efforts to preserve the burial ground today, jacksonville.com/news/georgia/2011-04-07/story/butler-cemetery-key-mcintosh-slave-era-past-0, accessed October 26, 2016.

7

A Family Divided, a Nation Divided

In the intervals of active labor, the discussion of the re-opening of the slave trade commenced, and the opinion seemed to generally prevail that its reestablishment is a consummation devoutly to be wished, and one red faced Major or General or Corporal clenched his remarks with the emphatic assertion that "We'll have all the niggers in Africa over here in three years – we won't leave enough for seed."[1]

Mortimer "Doesticks" Thomson

The Butler slave community may have experienced a certain freedom through their faith, but, on the eve of the Civil War, their physical freedom was anything but assured. This recorded conversation at the auction points to the deep divisions that preceded the Civil War. The fact that as late as 1859 – two years before the onset of the Civil War – there was talk of *reopening* the Atlantic slave trade that shows how far apart both North and South were on the question of slavery.[2] The nation was truly divided if the debate was not just about the right to preserve slavery in Southern territories or the right to extend slavery further west, but also the right to reopen the trade. After all, that battle had been fought and won by Black and White abolitionists on both sides of the Atlantic over a period of decades culminating in the British Abolition of the slave trade in 1807.

Long before the auction or the war, however, the division between Pierce Butler and his wife, Frances Kemble, proved just as wide and in many ways foreshadowed the sharp division that was to characterize the Civil War era. That said, the experience of the war and its aftermath showed that North and South, Black and White could not escape the fact that their fates were linked. As the war raged, family life on both sides was the real casualty of war, best exemplified when brothers on both sides of the family could be found fighting for different causes. At the same time, though Blacks suffered great losses too, the war afforded them a great opportunity to fight for and gain their freedom.

Division in the Butler Family

By the time the Butlers returned to Philadelphia in May, 1839, their marriage was in shambles. They had spent a total of five months on the Southern plantations and had fought and squabbled continually over the treatment of the slaves and the very institution of slavery itself. It had only been five months in a five-year marriage, but it may have seemed much longer to both parties. Their conflicts seemed insurmountable. To Fanny, he was a miserable tyrant. To Butler, she was an unstable hypo-crite.[3] Fanny delivered an ultimatum. If he continued in this slavery busi-ness, she would leave.

What followed over the next few years was a series of temporary sep-arations and reunions. Throughout this unstable period, there were con-stant rumors of Butler's adulterous affairs. Kemble's reaction to Butler's exploits was often to flee. In fact, in 1845, leaving her children behind, she left the household and sailed to Europe, where she stayed for about a year. By 1848, communications had broken down to the point that Butler was now seeking an official divorce. She accused him of adultery and abject cruelty. He accused her of desertion and abandonment of their home and sought sole custody of the children. What ensued was a cus-tody battle that was so notorious it was the talk of Philadelphia society as the various ins and outs of the case were actively covered by newspapers.

At the time, fathers had presumptive rights in Philadelphia, and so Fanny had little chance of getting custody of her children. As if she expected such a result, she said of her first Philadelphia court appear-ance: "Upon this afternoon to Philadelphia, I feel as if I were going to (my) execution."[4]

While their divorce battle raged, Butler was reportedly involved in a relationship with a certain Miss Coleman.[5] These claims of infidelity seemed to have largely gone unheard. At the heart of the matter seemed to be his view that women were not equal to men and should submit to them in all matters.

In the end, Butler need not have worried about the outcome of the divorce. Under American law at the time, a wife and minor children had few rights and a woman certainly had no legal standing outside of her husband. Butler could even claim all her earnings. The divorce was granted on September 22, 1849 and Butler was given sole custody of their two children, Frances (Fan) and Sarah, except for the two summer months when Fanny could see them in her newly acquired home in Lenox, Massachusetts. She was also required to give up her rights to his estate.

In spite of this agreement, for much of the time until the children were twenty-one years old, Fanny did not see her daughters very much. Not long after the divorce was settled, Butler refused to meet his financial obligations towards Fanny. During these early years, he would also arbitrarily refuse to let the children stay with her for the agreed-upon two months of the year. This was to be a source of great heartbreak for Frances Anne Kemble – not only the breakdown of her marriage but her estrangement from her children.[6]

Pierce Butler had won this battle, but it was a pyrrhic victory, because his family was truly in tatters. Throughout, Fanny had struggled to keep her family together in much the same way that she had witnessed the slave families on the Butler plantations trying to do the same. But her cause, their cause – the abolition of slavery – was the stumbling block and the source of the breakdown of the Butler family. In time, the children, too, would take sides. The younger daughter, Frances, took the side of her father, and Sally took the side of her mother in the abolition debate.

Family Life: a Casualty of Slavery

The Butler family was torn apart by the institution of slavery, even as they actively worked to dissolve the ties that bound them to their Southern plantations. Ownership of these plantations afforded them substantial wealth and social standing, but they did not escape the legacy of dislocation and dissolution of family life from which they so greatly profited. This was the ultimate irony of the Butler family and their state of affairs. How could they have known that the dissolution of their own family bonds was to foreshadow the further dissolution of family bonds of the slaves of their own estate ten short years later in 1859, in the Weeping Time auction? How could they have known that the dissolution of their own family bonds was to foreshadow the dissolution of the American family – with North and South pitted against each other over the institution of slavery and states' rights? How could they have known that the threads of connection that had unraveled in their family life were to unravel likewise across the nation?

The Butler divorce had cast a foreboding shadow over the future. Without their knowing it, their domestic affairs demonstrated that family life was the real casualty of the institution of slavery. And, in the end, it was but a warning shot of the devastation that was to come as North and South went to war.

Division in the Nation

Scarcely a decade later, there were real shots fired at the Federal outpost in Charleston, South Carolina. In 1861, Southern Confederate forces fired on Fort Sumter, thus beginning the American Civil War. President Abraham Lincoln responded by quickly commissioning the Union army for war.

From the beginning of this turmoil, four million slaves, including many from the Butler estates, took their fates into their hands rather than await the outcome of the war. One month after the firing on Fort Sumter, slaves were on the move. They left their plantations in great numbers, first seeking shelter at the Fort under the auspices of the Union army. The Federal government called them "contrabands of war," but they saw themselves as freedom fighters. Soon after hostilities broke out, they were conscripted, first informally, and then more officially, in the war effort. By August of 1861, the year leading up to war, there were over 900 slaves, including women and children, residing at the fort. All over the rest of the South, slaves were not waiting for the outcome of the war.[7]

This fact was no more evident than on St. Simon's Island in particular and the Sea Islands in general. St. Simon's Island – the site of one of Butler's major plantations – was a pocket of freedom. First a trickle, then a flood. Many of these so-called contrabands of war were sent to St. Simon's, since Federal ships had been posted there as early as October 1861 to maintain a naval blockade.[8] This blockade was set up with the intent to stop commerce in the area and to enable the Federal government to patrol the coastline. As a result, there was great fear amongst the planters, who now felt the effects of the war being waged in their backyard.[9]

The war itself could have started at least a year before official hostilities began in the firing of the first shots at Fort Sumter.[10] When the lower South left the Union and declared the newly formed Confederacy a country, from the perspective of some, this was already an act of war. The Confederate States Constitution was the supreme law of the Confederate States of America, as adopted on March 11, 1861, and in effect through the conclusion of the American Civil War. The Confederacy included eleven states: Alabama, Arkansas, Florida, Georgia, Louisiana, Mississippi, North Carolina, South Carolina, Tennessee, Texas, and Virginia. Structured as a country, delegates appointed Jefferson Davis the Confederacy's one and only president for a six-year term and established the Confederate Congress. Central to their constitution was the protection of slavery in all their states.

The Confederate soldiers saw this war as the second war for American Independence. Time and again in their letters and their diaries, they speak of resistance to being subjugated by Northern forces. A homesick soldier in the 24th Mississippi infantry told his fiancée, "I am here because a numerous and powerful enemy has invaded our country and threatened our subjugation."[11] Most missed the irony of fighting so hard for freedom – the freedom to enslave others.

One Georgia soldier wrote to a friend three months before dying at Spotsylvania: "the Deep still quiet peace of the grave is more desirable than Vassalage or Slavery."[12] Such it was that a number of Confederate soldiers used the terms "slave" and "slavery" as both something they were fighting to preserve as well as a condition they wanted to avoid. The letter of a Georgia officer to his wife during the Atlanta campaign of 1864 suggests as much: "In two months more we will perhaps be an independent nation or a nation of slaves." If we lose, "not only will the negroes be free but ... we will all be on a common level."[13]

The Confederacy was a country with its own rules and regulations. It had its own trading partners and ambassadors, and, most of all, adherents who felt they were fighting for their new motherland. The Union soldiers from the North also saw themselves as fighting for their country, but, in their case, for the preservation of the Union. In a wider context, they saw themselves as fighting for liberty, democracy, and republican ideals.

The South may have started the war, but it could be said that war was brewing between the North and the South for many years prior. Though both sides were economically dependent on the other, there were great tensions pertaining to the question of the extension of slavery into new territories such as Kansas and Nebraska. The difference in each region's economies also contributed to the conflict. The South, with its four million slaves, was largely agrarian, whereas the North was a center for highly industrialized factories. Ironically, these same factories depended on the raw materials harvested by slaves, such as cotton and tobacco, for their operation. Both regions also differed in character. The Southern Gentleman, for example, saw himself as associated with the older notions of European nobility. He was the lord of his manor, and those four million slaves were expected to be loyal vassals who served him at will.[14]

In defending slavery, Southerners were not simply defending the institution itself, but their very identity. White Southerners tended to aspire to be like European nobility, in particular English nobility, and this colored their view of slavery. The slave was at the bottom rung of society and even whites who did not own slaves were persuaded by "the near fiction" that they could one day become a part of the planter aristocracy. To defend slavery, then, was to defend the pecking order and to defend one's place at the top of it.[15]

In fairness, aside from the issues surrounding the institution of slavery, many of the Confederate soldiers fought out of a sense of duty and honor to the values described above. Their Northern counterparts also fought out of a sense of duty – duty to the preservation of the Union. Some have suggested that only a sense of duty and honor, as well as an undying commitment to their comrades, could have caused them to defend their home and hearth with the ultimate sacrifice: their lives.[16]

Before the war, the Southern defense of lifestyle, character, and values took place in a war of words. "Through bloodless conquests of the pen," they hoped to "surpass in grandeur and extent the triumphs of war."[17] Southerners saw themselves as responding to the attacks of William Lloyd Garrison's newspaper *The Liberator* that was established in the 1830s. They were also responding to attacks on the ground from Nat Turner in the Virginia slave revolt in 1831 and later John Brown in 1859. The editor of *The Southern Review*, John Underwood, declared defiantly: Northern assailants should be met and "never suffered to enter the citadel till they walk over our prostrate bodies."[18]

This war of words underscored a war between two ideologies. Many Southerners like John Calhoun did not believe that all men had a right to liberty and rejected Jefferson's claims of inalienable rights.[19] They could not accept the notion that Black people could be accepted as free persons into the national fabric of American life. Such a fundamental conflict ultimately was not resolved in words but in war, with the South striking the first blow but finding themselves eventually outmanned and out resourced by Northern forces.

Black Agency and Colored Troops

In response to the onset of war, planters, including Butler, moved as many slaves as possible to the mainland for protection. Butler's slaves were specifically moved to Waycross, Georgia, while the planters fortified the islands with Columbiad guns and 1,500 Georgia troops.[20] There, as elsewhere in the South, these slaves helped in the rebel Confederate war efforts. This assistance was in the form of cooking, cleaning, and other duties off the battlefield.

But soon, slaves were to distinguish themselves on the battlefield as well. Just as scores of slaves fled to the British during the Revolutionary War, more than 180,000 slaves joined forces with the Union army to fight for their freedom. Ex-Butler slaves Noble Walker (Chattel no. 256) and Thomas Baker, son of Ned and Scena Bleach (Chattel nos 127 and 128), sold on the auction block in 1859, fought on the battlefield.

As can be seen from his military record, Thomas Baker, born in St. Simon's, Georgia, enlisted in 1863. He served in Charleston, South Carolina until December 31, 1865, when he was last paid for his services. He is listed as a waiter, which is likely a reference to the kinds of duties he performed for the Union army.[21]

Also of note was a brave group of free Black soldiers, a regiment from South Carolina, who had volunteered to join the Union war effort. In the summer of 1862, they raided and burned many dwellings on St. Simon's under the command of a White officer who said:

I started from St. Simon's with sixty two colored fighting men. As soon as we took a slave from his claimant we placed a musket in his hands, and he began to fight for the freedom of others.[22]

In June 1863, Union Colonel Robert Gould Shaw, commander of the all-Black 54th Massachusetts regiment, visited Butler's Hampton Estate on St. Simon's and declared that there were hardly more than ten slaves on the estate, including an old slave named John who still remembered Fanny Kemble fondly. That same Colonel Shaw was responsible for the burning of Darien County in June, 1863, and was later to charge against Fort Wagner in South Carolina. He died in that raid alongside his Black soldiers.[23]

Others who served their country valiantly included Edward King from Darien, who crossed over and joined one of the first combat units in the Union army. His wife was Susie King Taylor, a literate slave from Savannah, who wrote her memoir of the Civil War years, *Susie King Taylor, Reminiscences of My Life in Camp*. Born into slavery, she became a "contraband slave" who fled Liberty County in Georgia for Union lines and joined countless Black women serving in the war effort as nurses and laundresses without pay. She was a staunch supporter of Black and White

Union soldiers of the First South Carolina Volunteers who later became the 33rd US Colored Troops.[24] She became well known for having taught newly freed slaves to read on St. Simon's Island, and later she opened her little schoolhouse at her home on South Broad Street in Savannah.[25] Throughout, she never forgot the extraordinary trials of the war and the costs and sacrifices made by Black and White alike:

My dear friends! Do we understand the meaning of war? Do we know or think of that war of '61? No, we do not, only those brave soldiers, and those who had occasion to be in it, can realize what it was. I can and shall never forget that terrible war until my eyes close in death. The scenes are just as fresh in my mind to-day as in '61. I see now each scene,– the roll call, the drum tap, "lights out," the call at night when there was danger from the enemy, the double force of pickets, the cold and the rain. How anxious I would be, not knowing what would happen before morning! Many times I would dress, not sure but all would be captured.[26]

Another slave in the region, March Haynes, was engaged not only in military-style raids from the Sea Islands but also collected intelligence for the Union army.[27] He was a part of a larger phenomenon across the South in which Black slaves served formally and informally as intelligence agents in the war effort. Unbeknownst to their Confederate masters, who plotted strategies in their midst, they were just as busily collecting information and passing it onto the Union officers. Their "Black Dispatches" – the term used for the intelligence collected by Blacks during the war – were invaluable to the Union war effort. Slaves like Mary Elizabeth Bowser served as an effective spy. She actually lived for a time in Jefferson Davis' home, the Confederate White House, eavesdropped on important conversations between Davis and his generals, and took note of key documents left around the house.[28]

At the same time, many plantations, including Butler's, were abandoned by the slaves; an extremely upsetting phenomenon for masters.[29] First and foremost, this marked a loss of property in the person of their slaves. It also meant that their land and other goods were left unsecured, which left the estates open to looting and vandalism. From the perspective of the Union army officers, many did not want to be seen as vandals. They too were cognizant of the property rights of these planters but, were at the same time obliged to obey Federal orders regarding the protection of the slaves who were called "contrabands of war."

The following notice put up in Beaufort and signed by a Union navy officer showed Northerners' sensitivity to this issue: "Every effort has been made by us to prevent the negroes from plundering their masters' homes. Had the owners remained and taken care of the property and negroes, it would not have occurred. I only trust that we will not be accused of vandalism."[30]

Northerners knew that they were vulnerable to this kind of criticism and could even be accused of plundering these abandoned homes themselves if they were not careful. Still, the slaves continued to leave their plantations, first a trickle and then a flood. By all accounts, the slaves descended on the Union army in droves. In the Low Country region, they were either taken into service of the army or, more often than not, sent to St. Simon's Island. In this way, long before the Emancipation Proclamation of 1863, St. Simon's Island, the site of Butler's Hampton Estate, became a colony of slaves who had sought and won their freedom by the deceptively simple act of abandoning their estates.

Susie King declared that the settlements on St. Simon's Island were "just like little villages, and we would go from one to the other on business to call or only for a walk."[31] They were the "free islands," colonies of ex-slaves who had the boldness to even "trade" and sell provisions to the bands of soldiers on the mainland.[32] At one point, Susie King's outfit, the South Carolina Volunteers, gathered eighty bushels of rice that they used as provisions.[33]

As during slavery, they continued to plant, but with one huge difference: now it was for themselves. They continued to harvest but now for the betterment of their new and growing community. They did not need a hallowed document or groundbreaking law to make their freedom a reality. They had taken hold of this unique opportunity afforded by the war and had taken matters into their hands.

For a time, they were masters of their own fate.

The Brothers' War

All the while their masters were heavily engaged in what is often called The Brothers' War:

It will be a glorious day for our country when all the children within its borders shall learn that the four years of fratricidal war between the North and South was waged by neither with criminal or unworthy intent, but by both to protect what they conceived to be threatened rights and imperiled liberty: that the issues which divided the sections were born when the Republic was born, and were forever buried in an ocean of fraternal blood.

Lieutenant General John B. Gordon, CSA

The Civil War is often called the Brothers' War because in some memorable cases it pitted brother against brother. The Crittenden family of Kentucky was in just such a precarious position. Senator John C. Crittenden had two sons: one served successfully as a Union General and the other less successfully as a Colonel in the Confederate army. Where one saw victory on the battlefield, the other saw defeat and was eventually relieved of his post.[34]

The threads of the American nation had unraveled. Over a quarter of the South's White males of military age were killed, leaving behind 200,000 widows and 400,000 fatherless children.[35] The conventional estimate is that 618,222 men lost their lives in the Civil War. Recent recalculations of nineteenth-century Census data and other sources suggest that the toll, however, may be as high as 750,000. But for the slaves in their midst, the war had an altogether different meaning: it was an opportunity to gain their freedom.[36]

They had suffered abject misery for hundreds of years, and they were helpless to prevent their families from being torn apart on the auction block and elsewhere. They could do nothing to prevent sisters and brothers from being sold away from one another; husbands and wives and mothers and fathers and their children going their separate ways. At times, they were successful – as in the cases of Frances and Dembo, and Doctor George and Margaret, who were spared being separated on the auction block in 1859 – but these examples were more the exception than the rule. The dramatic separation of Jeffrey and Dorcas was more common. The legacy of slavery was dislocation and breach of that universal institution – family. Family life was the real casualty of slavery and, as it turns out, not only for the slaves themselves. They may have been largely powerless to determine their fate and the fates of their loved ones, but even those who towered over them did not escape this legacy of dislocation.

Fanny and her husband Pierce were a vivid example of how slavery's legacy cast a wide shadow. Not only were they torn apart by their separate and opposing views about the liberty of slaves, but their children, in taking sides with one parent over the other, were also torn asunder because of these opposing views.

This unraveling was even more evident with the break-up of the United States, which precipitated the United States Civil War; the only American war fought on its soil. In this sense, the Weeping Time of 1859 and all the other weeping times before that foreshadowed the tragic effects of war in America. If family life was the real casualty of slavery, then the American family suffered a huge blow in the form of the Civil War. Three hundred and sixty thousand Union soldiers and 260,000 Confederates died on American soil. This was a huge number given the fact that there were only thirty-five million people in the country at the time. This number also did not include the thousands of injured.[37]

Georgia itself suffered many deaths, leaving sad and broken families in the midst of a battle-scarred South. Most of its large cities, as in much of the South, lay in ruins, and the surrounding countryside was equally ravaged. The image of Atlanta burning in 1864 is well known, but the area where the Butler slaves lived and worked, Darien County, also experienced similar devastation one year earlier, when it was burned to the ground in June, 1863 by the 54th Massachusetts infantry: an act that foreshadowed General William Tecumseh Sherman's march through Georgia.[38]

Indeed, many thought of Georgia, along with Virginia, as the cornerstone of the Deep South. It was said that, if Georgia fell, the battle would be over. Much was riding on Georgia.[39] Southern generals like Robert E. Lee were responsible for several brilliant military maneuvers, but, by 1863, the war was beginning to turn in the North's favor.

By 1862, Lincoln was committed to drafting a preliminary version of the Emancipation Proclamation. This was to prove an important turning point in the war. The Battle of Gettysburg, beginning in July, 1863, gave the North a decisive edge, with the battle ending with Lee's army retreating into Virginia. Up to that point, there had been losses on both sides, but the tide was turning in favor of the North. Kentucky, when invaded by Northern forces, had changed sides in favor of the Union and other Southern states were also leaning in that direction.

Beginning in May, 1864, Sherman marched toward Richmond. His path included the fall of Atlanta in September, and, by April, 1865, Union Generals Philip Sheridan and Ulysses S. Grant attacked Confederate General Robert E. Lee's army in the last major battle of the war. On April 9, 1865, Lee surrendered to Grant at the Appomattox Court House in southwestern Virginia and the war was effectively over.

Not surprisingly, the Butler family – Pierce, Fanny Kemble, and their daughters – had differing reactions to the end of the war. Pierce Jr. was disconsolate and was particularly concerned about his property in the Sea Islands which by this time had been in his family for several generations. From the firing on Fort Sumter, his daughters had been worried that he would involve himself in the war effort to his detriment. And though it appeared that his was mostly a war of words and quiet sympathies with

the Confederate cause (versus actual enlistment or other active engage-
ment in the war effort), Northern officials still suspected him of the latter. He was arrested in Philadelphia on August 18, 1861 and taken to
New York, where he was imprisoned for a short time. This was possible
because President Lincoln had suspended *habeas corpus* – the right of a
prisoner to know the charge upon which he is imprisoned (US Const. Art.
1 Sec. 9). This effectively allowed Northern local authorities and others
to imprison suspected Confederate sympathizers in their midst.[40] It was
only through the intense lobbying of Butler's friends and family that he
was declared innocent and released a month later by order of the State
Department on September 21, 1861.[41]

For her part, when the war broke out, Fanny Kemble was away in
Europe with her daughter Fan. They each had different reactions to the
news. Fanny was to write: "I with joy and she with sorrow."[42] Frances,
now a grown woman, had long since expressed her sympathies for
the Southern cause. Like her father, she was also a strong pro-slavery
advocate.

And so, there were parallel views of this war not just between North
and South, but Black and White, with a similar devastating impact on the
family. Yet, although many Blacks lost their lives, it was still a tremendous opportunity for freedom, which they had seized for themselves by
leaving the plantations en masse.

Two Groundbreaking Documents:
the Emancipation Proclamation and Sherman's Field Order No. 15

Perhaps it was the recognition of Lincoln and some of his generals of what
was actually taking place on the ground that led to two groundbreaking
documents: The Emancipation Proclamation of 1863 and later Sherman's
Field Order no 15. Susie King, who had served the Union army so well on
St. Simon's Island, recalled the exhilaration of Emancipation Day:

On the first of January, 1863, we held services for the purpose of listening to
the reading of President Lincoln's proclamation by Dr. W. H. Brisbane, and
the presentation of two beautiful strands of colors ... It was a glorious day
for us all, and we enjoyed every minute of it, and as a fitting close and crown-
ing event of this occasion we had a grand barbecue. A number of oxen were
roasted whole, and we had a fine feast ... The soldiers had a good time. They
sang and shouted "Hurrah!" all through the camp, and seemed overflowing
with fun and frolic until taps were sounded, when many, no doubt, dreamt of
this memorable day.[43]

Frederick Douglass, an ex-slave and tireless fighter for slave freedom, greeted the Proclamation with jubilance and said in an editorial
at the time: "We are ready for this service in this we trust the last struggle with the monster slavery."[44] Indeed, Douglass and so many others
fought for this brave and momentous act of justice not only during
the war, but for years before and in a variety of ways. For example,
Douglass's profound speech, "The Meaning of the 4th of July to the
slave," delivered on July 5, 1852 at the Corinthian Hall in Rochester,
called for freedom all over the land in a most eloquent way: "The
4th of July is *yours*, not mine," he said, "You may rejoice, but I must
mourn." (Emphasis in original.)

In his journals, including *The North Star* and *The Frederick Douglass
Paper*, he was one of the principal advocates for an end to slavery long
before the war. Early on, Douglass pressed Lincoln to consider liberation
of the slaves as a goal and called on him to utilize Black slaves as soldiers
in the war effort.[45]

Lincoln would eventually call Douglass a friend, but the president had
not always been convinced of the immediate need for Emancipation. As
the war progressed, however, he soon saw that it was as necessary as it
was morally correct. His views about Blacks had always been compli-
cated. Though it was clear that he never believed in slavery as an institution, with the help of advocates like Douglass he came gradually to the
position of full outright Emancipation being one of the important goals
of the war effort.[46]

Not everyone, however, greeted the passage of the Emancipation Act
with as much enthusiasm as Douglass and the slaves. As a Georgia Lt.
wrote his wife regarding the possibility of Atlanta and Richmond falling:

We are irrevocably lost and not only will the negroes be free but ... we will all be
on a common level ... The negro who waits on you will then be as you are and as
insolent as she is ignorant.[47]

A number of Union soldiers were equally dismayed at the passing of
the Act and showed their displeasure by deserting the army. Desertion
or resignation were the only options for some who claimed that the
Proclamation had changed the purpose of the war and they had not,
in fact, enlisted, in their words, to fight a "nigger war," but rather had
fought to preserve the Union.[48]

Even those individuals who saw the war as some sort of Christian
crusade of the nineteenth century, such as Capt. Oliver Wendell
Holmes Jr. of the 20th Massachusetts regiment did not explicitly

describe the war effort as a war for the liberation of the slaves. Rather, they saw it as a cause for democracy worldwide. Accordingly, he wrote to his wife:

Sick as I am of this war and bloodshed, as much oh how much I want to be home with my dear wife and children…every day I have a more religious feeling, that this war is a crusade for the good of mankind … I cannot bear to think of what my children would be if we were to permit this Hellbegotten conspiracy to destroy this country.[49]

To understand how significant a document this was from an American perspective as well as a global perspective, one has to appreciate the fact that, since the fifteenth century, slavery had been sanctioned on almost all official levels in Europe and in many of its colonies. By the early seventeenth century, the US saw the arrival of the first Africans in 1619 and the institution only grew from there. Black slavery was sanctioned on every level and, even though it was largely a reality in the South and had dwindled in the North, Northern factories depended on the by-products of slave labor.[50]

Furthermore, the Northern shipping industry was heavily involved in slave trading itself. Northern investors commissioned ships from New York, Rhode Island and Boston in the nineteenth century when the institution was near its demise but also witnessing a rise in demand. The fact that so many global economic forces depended on this institution directly or indirectly made the Emancipation Proclamation a revolutionary act of great proportions.

The Emancipation Proclamation
January 1, 1863
A Transcription
By the President of the United States of America:

A Proclamation.

Whereas, on the twenty-second day of September, in the year of our Lord one thousand eight hundred and sixty-two, a proclamation was issued by the President of the United States, containing, among other things, the following, to wit:

"That on the first day of January, in the year of our Lord one thousand eight hundred and sixty-three, all persons held as slaves within any State or designated part of a State, the people whereof shall then be in rebellion against the United States, shall be then, *thenceforward, and forever free*; and the Executive Government of the United States, including the military and naval authority thereof, will recognize and maintain the freedom of such persons, and will do no act or acts to repress such persons, or any of them, in any efforts they may make for their actual freedom. (Author's emphasis.)

... And I further declare and make known, that such persons of suitable condition, *will be received into the armed service of the United States* to garrison forts, positions, stations, and other places, and to man vessels of all sorts in said service. (Author's emphasis.)

And upon this act, sincerely believed to be an act of justice, warranted by the Constitution, upon military necessity, I invoke the considerate judgment of mankind, and the gracious favor of Almighty God.

In witness whereof, I have hereunto set my hand and caused the seal of the United States to be affixed.

Done at the City of Washington, this first day of January, in the year of our Lord one thousand eight hundred and sixty-three, and of the Independence of the United States of America the eighty-seventh.

By the President: ABRAHAM LINCOLN
WILLIAM H. SEWARD, Secretary of State.[51]

No less groundbreaking was the lesser-known Sherman's Field Order No. 15, which was in direct response to what was happening on the Butler estates and the other estates in the Low Country Southern region. Given that the slaves had not only abandoned their estates but also set up little colonies of their own, particularly on St. Simon's Island, Lincoln's generals were forced to deal with the matter at hand and attempt to make official what had already taken place in reality.

The order came about in part because of a meeting between General Sherman and Lincoln's Secretary of War Edwin Stanton, along with several important Black and White Christian ministers from the region. This historic meeting took place exactly four days before the Field Order was issued. Several of the Black ministers were self-made men who bought their freedom and established church communities. These were not ordinary men. They defied the odds in every way and now were seated at the table with men of enormous influence and power. Garrison Frazier, age sixty-seven, of North Carolina was a prime example. Only eight years prior, he was said to have bought himself and his wife for $1,000 in silver and gold. He was a retired minster in the Baptist church, where he had served for thirty-five years. Such a man as this was the spokesperson for the group.

And what did this group ask of General Sherman and Secretary Stanton? This was their request: "The way we can best take care of ourselves is to have land, and to turn it and till it *by our own labor* ... we want to be placed on land until we are able to buy it and make it our own"[52] (author emphasis).

The ministers must have made quite an impression because a mere four days later, General Sherman issued his famous Field Order No. 15 granting ex-slaves in the region such land, popularly referred as "Forty acres and a mule."[53]

The first two articles of William T. Sherman's order given at the Headquarters Military Division of the Mississippi, in Savannah, Georgia, January 16, 1865 were as follows:

1. The islands from Charleston south, the abandoned rice-field along the rivers for thirty miles back from the sea, and the country bordering the St. John's River, Florida, are reserved and set apart for the settlement of the negroes now made free by the acts of war and the proclamation of the President of the United States.

2. At Beaufort, Hilton Head, Savannah, Fernandina, St. Augustine, and Jacksonville, the blacks may remain in their chosen or accustomed vocations; but on the islands, and in the settlements hereafter to be established, no white person whatever, unless military officers and soldiers detailed for duty, will be permitted to reside; and the sole and exclusive management of affairs will be left to the freed people themselves, subject only to the United States military authority, and the acts of Congress. By the laws of war, and orders of the President of the United States, the negro is free, and must be dealt with as such ... but the young and able-bodied negroes must be encouraged to enlist as soldiers in the service of the United States, to contribute their share toward maintaining their own freedom, and securing their rights as citizens of the United States.[54]

Here there was a distinction made between the Sea Islands and the mainland. The Sea Islands were truly the free islands according to this order with whites, save for the military personnel of the United States army and navy, having no rights to reside on their own former properties, much less possess their former charges.

Who could have thought that, scarcely four years prior, these self-same slaves would now not only be free but also the owners of the very properties upon which they toiled for years and years without pay? No one could have imagined that such a phenomenon could take place in so short a time span.

According to the order, Sherman instructed General Saxton to execute a radical act of land redistribution: 40,000 slaves were to be settled on 400,000 acres of land, which came at first to be known as Sherman's reservation. They were also to be loaned mules for the purposes of farming.[55]

This was to be simultaneously compensation for years of unpaid labor and a punishment to the Confederate South for their rebellion.

Sadly, no one could have anticipated that this order could have been so short-lived. Shortly after Lincoln's assassination in 1865, President Andrew Johnson promptly rescinded the order and returned the said lands back to their original owners. It had been a bold experiment, now it was over. Whatever became of these slaves that tasted not only freedom but property ownership in so short a span of time is not immediately known, but we do know that most of the slaves in the region as in the South in general remained on their former estates as sharecroppers.

The Butlers were by now long divorced, and the slave families were separated on the auction block of 1859, but these divisions had fore-shadowed the ultimate division between North and South. The consequence of war was devastation for everyone on all sides including the state of Georgia. When Georgia looked back on its war years, it had switched from cotton to food production to accommodate its soldiers, and its extensive railroad lines were mostly in ruins by 1864. Sherman's March to the Sea had destroyed at least sixty miles of land leaving parts of the state in shambles. The only thing to do was to attempt to rebuild the damaged foundations and to restore broken ties.[56]

Out of the scourge of war, four million slaves declared themselves free by moving toward Union lines and fighting for their freedom. This declaration would finally be made official by the signing of Emancipation Proclamation in 1863. They too had lives to rebuild and ties to be restored and would attempt to do so in the years to come.

Notes

1   Thomson, p. 3.
2   See Sylviane Diouf, *Dreams of Africa in Alabama* (New York: Oxford University Press, 2009), and Eric Foner, *Forever Free* for more information.
3   Clinton 2000, p. 128.
4   Ibid., p. 148.
5   Ibid., p. 149.
6   Ibid., p. 155–156.
7   Harold Holzer, Edna Greene Medford, Frank J. Williams, *The Emancipation Proclamation: Three Views* (Baton Rouge: Louisiana State University Press, 2006) p. 16.
8   Clinton 2000, p. 181.
9   Bell, p. 252.
10 Clinton, p. 167–168.

11   James M. McPherson, *For Cause and Comrades: Why Men Fought in the Civil War* (New York: Oxford University Press, 1997) p. 29.

12   "Volunteers in Blue and Gray," Encyclopedia Brittanica Blog, blogs.britannica.com/2011/07/volunteers-blue-gray-fought/, accessed October 24, 2016.

13   Ibid.

14   John Hope Franklin, *The Militant South 1800–1861* (Cambridge: Harvard University Press, 1956) p. 63–64. See also James M. McPherson, *Ordeal By Fire: The Civil War and Reconstruction* (New York: Alfred Knopf, 1982) on the Cavalier image of the Southern gentleman, p. 48–49.

15   Franklin, p. 66.

16   James M. McPherson, *For Cause and Comrades: Why Men Fought in the Civil War* (New York: Oxford University Press, 1997) p. 5–6.

17   Franklin, p. 81.

18   Ibid.

19   Ibid., p. 82.

20   Clinton, p. 181.

21   The United States Colored Troops, National Archives; see also The Civil War Pension Application Files, National Archives for information on Noble Walker.

22   Bell, p. 361–368.

23   Kemble, p. 184.

24   Susie King Taylor, *Reminiscences of My life in Camp: An African American Woman's Civil War Memoir* (New York: Arno Press, New York Times, 1968) p. 50.

25   Ibid., p. 54.

26   Ibid., p. 50.

27   F. N. Boney, *Rebel Georgia* (Macon, GA: Mercer University Press, 1997) p. 56–57.

28   See P. K. Rose, *Black Dispatches: Black American Contribution to Union Intelligence During the Civil War* (Washington, DC: Center for the Study of Intelligence, Central Intelligence Agency, 1999).

29   Bell, p. 353.

30   Ibid., p. 354.

31   King, p. 12.

32   Bell, p. 361–362.

33   Ibid., p. 362.

34   McPherson, *Ordeal by Fire*, p. 153. This was the case even in Lincoln's family; four of Mrs. Lincoln's brothers and three brothers-in-law served in the Confederate army.

35   McPherson, *Battle Cry of Freedom*, p. 854.

36   See new war casualty figures by David Hacker, "Disunion: Recounting the Dead," *The New York Times*,opinionator.blogs.nytimes.com/2011/09/20/recounting-the-dead/#more-105317, accessed October 24, 2016. For one of the most noteworthy and groundbreaking books on the human toll of the war, see Drew Gilpin Faust, *This Republic of Suffering: Death and Dying and the American Civil War* (New York: Knopf, 2008).

37   McPherson, *Battle Cry of Freedom*, p. 854.

38 Boney, p. 35; event documented in the movie *Glory*.

39 Boney, p. 4.

40 McPherson, *Ordeal by Fire*, p. 152 and p. 294–296.

41 Clinton, p. 173.

42 Ibid., p. 188.

43 King, p. 18.

44 Holtzer et al., p. 14.

45 David Blight, *Beyond the Battlefield: Race, Memory and the American Civil War* (Amherst: University of Massachusetts Press, 2002).

46 Holzer, p. 16.

47 McPherson, *For Cause and Comrades: Why Men fought in the Civil War*, p. 109.

48 Ibid., p. 122–123.

49 Ibid., p. 43.

50 Holzer, p. 16.

51 Emancipation Proclamation transcript, National Archives, www.archives .gov/exhibits/featured_documents/emancipation_proclamation/transcript .html, accessed October 24, 2016.

52 Freedmen and Southern Society Project, "Newspaper Account of a Meeting between Black Religious Leaders and Union Military Authorities," http:www.freedmen.umd.edu/savmtg.htm, accessed October 24, 2016; clipping from *New-York Daily Tribune* [February 13, 1865], "Negroes of Savannah," Consolidated Correspondence File, series 225, Central Records, Quartermaster General, Record Group 92, National Archives.

53 McPherson, *Ordeal by Fire*, p. 506–508.

54 Reprinted in William Tecumseh Sherman, *Memoirs of General William T. Sherman*, vol. 2 (New York, 1875), p. 730–732; author's emphasis.

55 McPherson, *Ordeal by Fire*, p. 506–508. See also Richard Zuczek, *Encyclopedia of the Reconstruction Era* (Westport, CT: Greenwood Press, 2006).

56 Charles E. Jones, *Georgia in the War, 1861–65* (Augusta, GA: C.E. Jones, 1909).

PART III

HEALING THE BREACH

8

Reconstruction and Reconnecting Threads

None of the Butler slaves have ever been sold before, but have been on these two plantations since they were born. Here they have lived their humble lives, and loved their simple loves; here were they born and here have many of them had children born unto them; here had their parents lived before them, and now are resting in quiet graves on old plantations that these unhappy ones *are to see no more forever*; here they left not only the well-known scenes dear to them from very baby-hood by *a thousand fond memories*; and homes as much loved by them, perhaps, as brighter homes by men of brighter faces; but all the clinging ties that bound them to living hearts were torn asunder, for but one-half of each of these two happy little communities was sent to the shambles, to be *scattered to the four winds*, and the other half was left behind. And who can tell how closely intertwined are the affections of a little band of four hundred persons, living isolated from all the world beside, from birth to middle age? Do they not naturally become one great family, each man a brother unto each?[1] (author emphasis)

Mortimer "Doesticks" Thomson

In describing the devastating impact of the 1859 auction, Doesticks felt sure that these auctioned slaves, "scattered to the four winds," would never again see the old plantations where they were born and had toiled. He imagined they would never again be able to rekindle "a thousand fond memories" of hearth and home albeit in very trying circumstances. Though the conflict between North and South was rising by the day, war was not yet an option. Emancipation certainly was not a tangible point of discussion. In 1859, neither Doesticks nor the slaves themselves could have anticipated war, emancipation, and thus the possibility of reuniting with their families and returning to their plantation homes.

Theirs had been a story of a series of weeping times – the weeping time of backbreaking plantation labor, the weeping time of families split up on the auction block, and ultimately the weeping time of families, both Black and White, who suffered great losses during the war. But this was also a story of restoration and redemption.

American slavery was one very long night. For the slaves, there were few bursts of light such as the creation of a unique musical tradition and the fervent expression of religious faith. But when freedom came, this one very long night had finally come to an end. But what did it mean to be free? What would they do next?

As we will see, freed slaves reconnected with families torn asunder, they pursued and created for themselves new work arrangements with former masters or others, and amidst the turmoil of Reconstruction with its gains and its losses, they would continue to struggle for their civil rights – the right to vote and the right to war pensions.

Families First

But first and foremost came family. They desired to reconnect with their families; to restore the breach. During Reconstruction they systematically attempted to reconstruct their family bonds just as the nation was in the process of solidifying the union. Ironically, as we shall see in the next chapter, 150 years later, African American families are determined to piece together and make sense of their fragmented past.

Family was first, and this could be seen in what individuals did soon after the Emancipation Declaration came into effect in January, 1863. Blacks all over the lower South headed towards the Upper South or headed West in search of their loved ones. They took with them scraps of cloth, strands of hair – small mementos that they had kept in remembrance of those they had lost. They combed African American churches for clues as to the whereabouts of loved ones, and they put advertisements in African American newspapers to let the world know whom they were looking for. The following ads in the August 12, 1865 copy of the black newspaper, *The Colored Tennessean*, were typical:

SAMUEL DOVE of Utica, NY – Looking for ARENO, his mother, his sisters MARIA, NEZIAH and PEGGY and his brother, EDMOND DOVE. Their former owner was GEORGE DOVE of Rockingham County, Shenandoah Valley, Virginia. His mother and sisters were sold in Richmond, Virginia, and he, and his brother were taken to Nashville.

HENRY HILL of Nashville, TN – Looking for my wife, LUCY BLAIR, of Jonesboro (Washington County) Tennessee. Five years ago she was last living with WILLIAM BLAIR. I was raised by JOHN BLAIR.

LEVY DONE of Nashville, TN – Looking for KISSY DONE of Corinthe, Mississippi, my mother. Last saw her in 1862. Also looking for JOSEPH DONE, my brother.

MARTHA McDERMIT of Nashville, TN – Looking for ELIAS LOWERY McDERMrr, my brother, who used to belong to THOMAS LYON of Knoxville, Tennessee. ELIAS was sold to a MR. SHERMAN about 1855. He worked on a steamboat between Memphis and New Orleans.[2]

In rare cases, these ads were successful, but most had to take to the road to find their far-flung relatives. Those that could not afford horse and buggy rides (which was the case for most slaves) walked for miles on foot in search of their loved ones.[3] Some, including various Butler plantation slaves, returned to the old plantation and reconnected with family members who were left behind. For many slaves after the war, home was where their family was. A former slave who returned to Savannah explained: "This was my home. My children and friends and my husband were all here."[4] Home was family and so there was no contradiction in returning to the place of their birth. For others, it was also an affirmation of faith.[5] Slaves had prayed for a Union victory and for emancipation. Going home to the place where it all began was a way to show and assert their gratefulness to God in answering their prayers. The events of the last few years affirmed their belief that there was equality under God and so the idea of going "home" was sometimes an act of celebration if not vindication. Finally, some of those who searched and did not find their relatives returned to their plantations and made it once again their home. They stayed and attempted to accommodate to unique working relationships with their former masters. In the end, they were searching for the familiar – for the ties that bound them to people and to place. They were not as concerned with what they would eat or how they would live. They thought largely about reconnecting those bonds and restoring the breach.

Slavery had brought about what seemed like an impassable breach. Most families split up on the auction block could neither keep in contact nor did they even know the final destinations of their loved ones. If they were fortunate, as seen in some of the ex-slave narratives from Georgia, their family members were sold to a nearby plantation. That would leave open the possibility of occasional visits. A good example comes from the narrative of ex-slave Amanda McDaniel. Her mother, Matilda Hale, was originally sold away from her first husband with two small children to a plantation in Georgia. She later married again, to a man named Gilbert Whitlew, and had two more children, one of whom was Amanda. Amanda herself had never been on the auction block or witnessed an auction but her very existence was sadly informed by an auction event. In her account of the times she called "King Slavery," she remembers that her father lived on a nearby plantation and was allowed to visit often.[6]

Otherwise, slaves put up to auction would have to depend on overhearing the state and location of the new buyer: information they would keep close to their heart until the right opportunity afforded itself. This was feasible more for those who were sold shortly before Emancipation, like the Butler slaves sold in 1859. But what about those slaves that had been sold on other plantations generations before? How likely was it that they could be found in the place where they were originally sold when the average slave was sold at least six times in his lifetime? How likely was it that even the most determined freedman or freedwoman would be able to find a mother, a brother, a husband, or a wife sold even twenty years before Emancipation, much less longer? Even for the Butler slaves, this must have been a great challenge, since the nature of the auction experience meant that all ties would be broken. Once the bill of sale was drawn up, there was to be no communication between interested parties.

The current owner signed away his rights to the new owner for an agreed-upon sum. This document was a legal document that ensured the property rights of the new owner and the legality of the transfer. Copies were usually sent to the Court office, as court office records all across the South and elsewhere are evidence of these simple yet devastating transactions. What was paperwork for the owners and the legal system was the destruction of slave families and relationships. For masters, this was about property transfer, just as cattle or land would change hands, but it was a case of deep sorrow for those whose lives were disrupted.

Those families that managed to stay together on the auction block, like Frances and Dembo, who surreptitiously married the day before the 1859 auction, were the fortunate ones. They had a chance to stay together and were sold to an Alabama plantation. But what about the ill-fated relationship of Jeffrey and Dorcas? As far as we know, they were never reunited. Perhaps they would have tried to find one another, but it was likely in vain. They would have had no access to official records, and the federal government was barely concerned about the reconnection of Black families once the war was over.

Reconstruction was not about reconstructing Black family life; it was about rebuilding a war-torn country and about reorganizing its new political life and fate. The freedmen were a concern, but they were not the most important postwar concern. On January 31, 1865, President Lincoln proposed the 13th Amendment, banning slavery in the United States, except as a punishment for a crime. In conjunction with the Emancipation Proclamation of 1863, the amendment was a signal achievement, so much so that Charles Douglass who was seated in the gallery wrote the following to his father, Frederick Douglass: "I wish you could have been here the day that the constitutional amendment was passed forever abolishing slavery in the United States."[7] It would not be until after Lincoln's assassination that the bill was ratified on December 18, 1865. Soon after, President Andrew Johnson overturned Sherman's Field Order No. 15, demonstrating once again that the welfare of the slaves was not everyone's priority. The South was plundered, and Whites too suffered great losses at war. Cities like Atlanta had been burned to the ground during Sherman's March to the Sea, and so the order of the day was the rebuilding of cities and towns, not families. To be sure, White Southern families were also attempting to restore some stability to their family life, but this was often in the context of rebuilding their former plantations or transforming them to meet the needs and exigencies of a new age.

Freedmen's New Work Arrangements

In Frances Butler Leigh's diary, *Ten Years on A Georgia Plantation*, she vividly recalls her return with her father to the South after the war. Her first entries speak of the apparent willingness of their former slaves to receive and work for their former masters. Her husband, James Wentworth Leigh, who was later to build the church, St. Cyprian's on the mainland in Darien, was also under the impression that the freedmen had a high regard for his father in law, Pierce Mease Butler, "(They) loved him so dearly and to whom he was very much attached."[8]

Many of the slaves returned, including seven who were sold to plantations in the Upper South in 1859, including Bram, a driver. Bram took the surname of Butler and professed undying loyalty to Pierce Butler to a Freedman's Agent who was quite astonished by his words. It was his actions, not his words or the words of the other slaves that spoke to what was important to them: reconnection with family and the place they called home; establishment of new work arrangements with their former masters and advocating for their civil rights including the right to vote and the right to pensions.

'Why, Bram, how can you care so much for your master – he sold you a few years ago?' 'Yes, sir,' replied the old man, 'he sold me and I was very unhappy, but he came to me and said, "Bram, I am in great trouble; I have no money and I have to sell some of the people, but I know where you are all going to, and will buy you back again as soon as I can." 'And, sir, he told me, Juba, my old wife, must go with me, for though she was not strong, and the gentleman who bought me would not buy her, master said he could not let man and wife be separated; and so, sir, I said, "Master, if you will keep me I will work for you as long as I live, but if you in trouble and it help you to sell me, sell me, master, I am willing."' And now that we free, I come back to my old home and my old master, and stay here till I die."[9]

For their part, the Butlers were at first excited about the possibility that their former slaves were willing to work for them. They took their words on face value and believed the professed loyalty of slaves like Bram. They soon were to come face to face with a new more startling reality, as Leigh described: "their idea of work, unaided by the stern law of necessity," she said, "is very vague, some of them working half a day and some even less."

The slaves, buffered by their new free status, had their own ideas about what kind of arrangements they wanted to work out with their former owners. Without any experience in these types of negotiations, they were nonetheless skillfully trying to carve out for themselves a work routine that suited *their* purposes, not those of their former masters. For this, they earned the moniker of "hopelessly lazy," when in truth, they were simply reorganizing their lives to suit their own tastes for the very first time.

It seemed that they had decided that half a day's work was sufficient not to starve, and so it was half a day's work that they performed, much to the consternation of Leigh and her father:

Half a day's work will keep them from starving, but won't raise a crop. Our contract with them is for half the crop: that is one half to be divided among them according to each man's rate of work, we letting them have in the meantime necessary food, clothing, and money for their present wants (as they have not a penny) which is to be deducted from whatever is due to them at the end of the year.[10]

At the same time, Leigh had to admit that during the war these very slaves, when they were working for themselves, appeared not to be so "hopelessly lazy" after all. They had planted corn and cotton to a considerable extent. When they thought they were the new owners of St. Simon's Island (because of the short-lived Sherman's Field Order no. 15), Butler's slaves and others had performed an economic miracle.[11] A similar phenomenon had also taken place in Confederate President Jefferson

Davis' own backyard, the Davis Bend plantation in Mississippi. His brother, who owned the plantation, was forced to flee in 1862, but his slaves left behind during the war had planted cotton and made profits to the tune of $160,000.[12]

Leigh's testimony is one important testimony of their dejection regarding the reversal of this order, which, though it had granted only "promissory titles" dependent of the outcome of the war, was nothing short of revolutionary.

They were perfectly respectful, but quiet and evidently disappointed to find they were not the masters of the soil and that their new friends the Yankees had deceived them. Many of them had planted a considerable quantity of corn and cotton, and this my father told they might have, but that they must put in twenty acres for him.[13]

Again, it was very hard to tell what these slaves really thought, since their words and their actions were often far apart. Eventually, the Butlers had to acknowledge that their former charges were serving themselves much more than they were serving them.

Bram, for instance, appears to be the perfect example of what W. E. B. Dubois called "double consciousness." His professed loyalty may have been just that – professed. As community activist James Simms, the tireless African American advocate for the rice country freedmen in Savannah in the early twentieth century, was wont to say: "The white race had never understood or known us perfectly because we have always dissimulated. This was the natural result of tyranny – of the tyranny of slavery."[14] Others have described this dissimulation as a masquerade that masks the intensity of the pain beneath. Sometimes that masquerade takes the form of apparent obsequiousness; sometimes it has more destructive manifestations. As writer Louis Simms said in James Alan McPherson's piece on his father, "Going Up to Atlanta:" "Those black folk who did not have other escape mechanisms had to masquerade, or face the sure prospect of being blown to pieces physically and psychologically." Throughout, it was a way to survive the depths of disappointment and loss.[15]

And so, to their former masters, Bram and the other freedmen showed one face that often hid another reality. Their loyalty in the end may have been thin at best, and, at other times, eminently practical. Two amusing incidents among many recorded by Leigh spoke volumes in this regard:

My cook made all the flour and sugar I gave him (my own allowance of which was very small) into sweet cakes, most of which he ate himself, and when I scolded him, he cried ...

My white maid, watching my sable housemaid one morning through the door, saw her dip my toothbrush in the tub in which I had just bathed, and with my small hand-glass in the other hand, in which she was attentively regarding the operation, proceed to scrub her teeth with the brush. It is needless to say I presented her with that one, and locked my new one up as soon as I had finished using it.[16]

These transgressions, though small, would have been unheard of or greatly punished during the time of slavery. The influence of the whip, the stocks or most devastatingly the auction block were great deterrents. With no such deterrent in sight, these former charges were trying out their freedom wings and exploring new relationships with their former masters that once would not have been possible. Furthermore, when one older slave professed to Mrs. Leigh after being informed of her freedom: "No missus, we belong to you, we be yours as long as we lib (live)," she may very well have been displaying pragmatism in the face of her limited options. How realistic would it be for her as an old former slave to find work and start a new life elsewhere? Where would she go? Who would take care of her? After all, Butler and his daughter had put in place a policy in which infants of up to three years and very old slaves would be taken care of. She could at least rely on that much, which was perhaps more than she would be able to expect had she moved away.[17] If her remarks belied a masquerade, these might have been the reasons behind it.

Indeed, the Butlers had so much trouble with the freedmen that they, like other Southern owners in those early years after the war, became increasingly frustrated and sometimes turned to other workers of Asian and Irish descent for a source of labor. "Some don't want to work on Saturdays, others won't sign at all," was Leigh's report regarding the process of getting the freedmen to sign a work contract. This frustration led them to consider the use of Chinese laborers. Butler Leigh and family eventually hired at least seventy Chinese laborers for the propagation of their property on General's Island – an act followed by many of her white neighbors in the area.[18] So-called "coolie indentured labor," very much the norm in much of the Caribbean and Latin America in the post-slavery period, was also a factor in the American South.

Leigh's hiring of the "coolie labor" from China was nonetheless controversial on many levels. As early as 1862 a bill had been signed that prohibited the transport of "coolies" by American ships, with jail and fines to be levied to transgressors.[19] Companies like the Central Pacific

Railroad company hired Chinese laborers on five-year contracts to build the transcontinental railroad in Western states. At the same time, labor leaders and others debated and expressed concern about the influx of Chinese laborers and did what they could to halt it, including the Chinese Exclusion Act of 1882, which forbade Chinese immigration.[20]

For Southerners like the Butlers, however, there was little to debate. Many saw Chinese laborers as the antidote to Black emancipation. Butler and his daughter went so far as to lease General's Island, land they owned jointly with John Butler's estate, to an "enterprising planter" who further imported thirty Chinese workmen.[21] As historian Moon Ho-Jung points out in his book, *Coolies and Cane: Race, Labor, and Sugar in the Age of Emancipation*, coolie labor was not just a factor in the Caribbean and Latin America. It also had "profound and lasting effects on the historical formations of race and nation in the nineteenth century" in the American South.[22] But that was not all. Southern planters, including the rice-planting Butlers, also brought in Irishmen to dig the rice ditches, since the newly freed blacks refused "to go to the ditch."[23] The ditch had represented the hardest part of rice planting, and now, in their freedom, they exercised their right not to dig ditches, notwithstanding the fact that it was a necessary part of the planting process.

Reaching for the Future: Voting and Pension Advocacy

If they were frustrated with Black labor relationships, Leigh, Butler, and other Southerners were outright aghast about the idea of Blacks voting. The Butlers and their neighbors did everything in their power to disrupt the process. They felt personally aggrieved and saw this new policy as the supreme method employed by the North to control the South.

Meanwhile, Blacks saw this as the heart and soul of their freedom. Not only were they free to reconnect with their loved ones and negotiate new kinds of work arrangements, but they were now free to vote. All over the South, Blacks were lining up at the polls and exercising their rights. Braving numerous efforts at intimidation, they continued to assert a core benefit of their freedom. They faced unjust literacy tests and the like, but they still kept going to the polls. They were harassed and provoked, but they still kept going. Whites like Butler Leigh attributed their ardor to the Yankees sending people to stir them up, but the truth was that they did not need any stirring up. They had watched life unfold from the sidelines long enough.

Now that they were free, they were determined to vote. And vote they did. For ten short yet significant years, they voted up to the day that their enfranchisement was reversed in the Compromise of 1877. They voted for an unprecedented number of Black politicians and whites who sympathized with their cause. They needed little encouragement to take hold of this – the brass ring of freedom – the right to determine their fate through representation in all levels of government. Sixteen Blacks sat in Congress from 1867–1877, including Robert Smalls, and Hiram Revels of Mississippi, who was the first African American Senator in 1870. All in all, approximately 600 blacks served as legislators on the local level as a part of "Radical Reconstruction," which was led by Thaddeus Stevens. Radical Reconstructionists, in opposition to President Johnson, led the effort to grant newly freed Blacks citizenship through the 14th Amendment in 1868 and the right to vote by means of the 15th Amendment in 1870. They, along with Black activists and preachers, pushed for equal rights for Blacks during this period and achieved significant gains.

One notable beneficiary of Radical Reconstruction was Robert Smalls, who bravely steered the Confederate naval vessel, *The Planter*, from Charleston into the hands of the Union forces in May 1862. He was still a slave, and Abraham Lincoln had not yet given official permission for slaves to join the war effort by means of the Emancipation Proclamation. For his efforts, Smalls won a reward of $1,500 and an officer's commission in the Union Army. With these funds, he purchased land in Beaufort, Georgia and was thus well-positioned to be elected to Congress five times in the 1870s and 1880s.[24]

His efforts were forgotten – when President Wilson removed the remaining Black appointees from office. Smalls's contribution to African American and Southern history has faded in historical memory to the extent that even some of his purported family members do not know the full extent of his deeds. James Alan McPherson, in his aforementioned piece, "Going up to Altanta," in which he tries to piece together this family tree, shares that he learned only late in his life that Robert Smalls was an ancestor. This was the very same Robert Smalls whose bravery earned him unparalleled recognition for a slave at that time; the same man who was a part of the grand experiment of Radical Reconstruction in which Black self-determination was a reality if only for a short time. McPherson could only say to his Aunt Eva in reaction to this revelation: "I asked her why I had never been told these things. Eva said she did not know."[25] For ten important years in the aftermath of slavery, newly freed slaves experienced self-determination at the polls. Notwithstanding the fact they often had to vote under the protection of Federal troops, they continued to struggle for this basic right. During this time, the Freedman's Bureau was also established, and it provided food, medical aid, schools, and assistance with working out of new labor arrangements.[26] The Bureau also helped to register Black voters.

It was a heady time: a time of great promise and hope. They were trying new ideas like new garments. They were reaching for the past only insofar as they tried to reconnect with loved ones. The rest was about grasping for a new future. For their part, white Southerners were most concerned about regaining their wealth and, more importantly, their position in the nation. In accordance with the Reconstruction Act of 1867, the South had been divided into five military districts, with a US army general in charge of each. This division was a major bone of contention. Southerners felt dejected and spoke about being "enslaved" by the Yankees. New conditions that were placed on them, such as taking the oath of loyalty to the Union, were considered onerous and overbearing. Furthermore, in their backyards, they were taking orders from Northern military commanders, and this infuriated them the most. Georgia was in the second district along with Alabama and Florida. The Butlers, like many other Southerners, chafed at the presence of the military and considered the efforts of Northern representatives in the South to protect the freedmen's newfound rights obtrusive and unnecessary.

They were not alone in their opposition. The Compromise of 1877 meant that Northern troops were removed from Southern territories, and Black leaders were removed from office. Poll taxes and literacy tests were instituted to deter Black voters. The Ku Klux Klan, now already a decade old, was emboldened and the practice of lynching helped to enforce Jim Crow laws and customs.[27] Reconstruction had succeeded in the short-term in ushering in new rights for Black citizens, but failed in the long-term in guaranteeing those rights. Historian Allen Guelzo, in his narrative of the Civil War and Reconstruction, *Fateful Lightning*, points to the many political reasons for Reconstruction's failure, but also suggests that the dwindling support for Reconstruction's original goals coincided with the death of some of its most ardent leaders. Thaddeus Stevens, for example, died in August 1868. He died true to the cause, but in some ways, the cause, at least on the Federal level, died with him. Guelzo poignantly points out that it was the final wish of this American hero to be buried in a segregated cemetery for African American paupers in order that "I might illustrate in death the principles which I advocated through a long life, Equality of man before his Creator."[28]

Still, the ex-slave population was not deterred. Their fight would continue in pursuit of pensions and other benefits they felt were due to them.

Ex-Slave Pension Advocacy

On their return to the plantations, Frances Butler Leigh and her father agreed to take care of the very old "till they die."[29] That was their provision for those who could no longer work as well as for infants till the age of three. Though we can assume that this was not a monetary transaction, it did mean that old Butler slaves would receive some degree of protection in these perilous years. They would not have to work in the fields or leave to find work when age had gotten the better of them. They could remain close to their families who, as in the time of slavery, would provide support and sustenance. Now that slavery was over but their material conditions had hardly changed, the slave community would continue to nurture and take care of the old and the young alike.[30] It may also be that the Butlers' gesture was in direct response to their recognition of how the old people on the plantation protected the livestock, including sheep and cows, during the war years. They even sold chickens to a Yankee captain and collected five dollars for this transaction.[31] Whatever the reason, the old people on the plantation must have been duly relieved to know that there was some measure of security for them in their old age.

We do not know, however, how often this happened on other plantations in the South. What we do know is that the majority of slaves that were freed by means of the Emancipation Proclamation and the 13th Amendment were not guaranteed pensions of any sort, but nonetheless, they sought them.

Callie House, resurrected by historian Mary Frances Berry, was one of the most notable proponents of pensions for ex-slaves. House was born a slave in Tennessee and was a seamstress and washerwoman for most of her adult life. She expanded the original efforts of Walter R. Vaughan, a white Democrat, who had responded to the call of freed slaves for pensions with the founding of the organization, the National Ex-Slave Mutual Relief, Bounty and Pension Association. In the early 1900s it is estimated that there were 600,000 members – all of whom were petitioning the Federal government through the organization to receive pension benefits for 246 years of uncompensated labor.

House, in conjunction with Isaiah Dickerson, a school teacher and a minister, traveled the country to organize chapters. Members would pay about 10 cents per month to aid in advocacy efforts. The dual mission was to attain federal pension legislation for ex-slaves and mutual aid for poor members, including maids, cooks, and washerwomen. House herself was bold enough to make the case as to why such compensation was due. As she declared in 1899: "If the Government had the right to free us, she had a right to make some provision for us and since she did not make it soon after Emancipation she ought to make it now."[32] This was one of the first mass movements of its kind in the African American community, and it was met with fierce resistance. Court records and government documents show how the Pension Bureau as well as the Postmaster General attempted to thwart their efforts and to destroy the movement and its leaders. In 1916, House was charged with mail fraud and sentenced to one year in Missouri State prison, in spite of the fact there was no evidence of fraud and none of the members had claimed they were defrauded. Her sentence effectively ended the momentum of the movement. Though House's mass movement did not secure pensions for ex-slaves like herself and countless others across the country, it was an important achievement in that it was further proof that people of African descent could and would advocate for their rights at the turn of the twentieth century. The call for reparations would continue throughout the century and inspire other calls not only in America but also in the Caribbean.

At the time of writing (2017), buoyed by the important historical work on slavery in the Caribbean by Caribbean authors, including Professors Hilary Beckles and Verene Shepherd, fourteen Caribbean nations are calling for reparations for slavery from Great Britain, France, Sweden, Norway, the Netherlands, and other European nations. According to a recent article,

CARICOM's 10-point plan will pursue a full formal apology for slavery, repatriation to Africa, a development plan for the native Caribbean peoples and funding for cultural institutions. It also seeks to address chronic diseases and psychological rehabilitation for trauma inflicted by slavery, technology transfer to make up for technological and scientific backwardness resulting from the slave era, and support for payment of domestic debt and cancellation of international debt.[33]

Callie House's ex-slave organization, perhaps the first organized effort to request reparations, may not have succeeded in the strictest sense of the word, but it laid the foundation for such efforts then and now.

Civil War Pensions

In 1862, the US Pension Bureau was given the mandate by Congress to administer pensions to Whites and Blacks who were disabled as a result of service to the Union cause, as well as survivors of war dead. Approximately 200,000 African American men served in the war effort, and many women worked also in ancillary capacities such as nurses and spies. Thousands of them applied for these pensions, although only 80,000 soldiers and sailors received them, according to the records.[34] These pension applications also happen to be a valuable source of information on slave life, since pension bureaucrats demanded detailed biographical information as well as affidavits of former masters.

Pension bureaucrats demanded this information with little understanding that the institution of slavery largely did not afford slaves such luxuries as birth certificates and marriage records. Furthermore, according to historians Elizabeth Regosin and Donald Shaffer's study of these files, more than half of the African American claimants were asked to submit to "special examinations." Special examinations were requested when pension bureaucrats were skeptical of the documentary evidence that ex-slaves provided. At the same time, they asked only a quarter of the White claimants to submit to such examinations – a fact that Regosin and Shaffer suggest indicates bias.[35] They seemed unaware or lacking in any sympathy for what Frederick Douglass claimed was one of the most devastating impacts of slavery: the denial of identity. As he said in his 1855 narrative, *My Bondage and My Freedom*:

I never met a slave who could tell me how old he was. Few slave mothers know anything of the months of the year, nor the days of the month. They keep no family records with marriages, births and deaths. They measure the ages of their children by spring time, winter time, harvest time, planting time, and the like; but these soon become undistinguishable and forgotten. Like other slaves, I cannot tell how old I am. This destitution was among my earliest troubles. I learned when I grew up that my master – and this was the case with masters generally- allowed no questions to be put to him, by which a slave might learn his age. Such questions are deemed evidence of his impatience, and even of impudent curiosity.[36]

Given this reality, the fact that thousands of ex-slave veterans made applications for pensions speaks volumes. It is a testament to their determination to advocate for their rights. They had shown their mettle in the war effort. They would not sit on the sidelines while others fought for their freedom. They would fight, and they would win this war. And when the war was over, they would continue to fight for their rights, and this they did in part by advocating for their hard-earned pensions. Family members of the war dead were no less tenacious. One such claimant was the widow of Noble Walker, Mrs. Millie Walker. Noble, a slave on the Butler plantation, had participated in the war effort and his wife sought compensation for his service. Though claimants were often frustrated with the repeated requests for documentation that was hard to find or unavailable, they often persisted in their demand for pensions. The result was that over 80,000 received pensions, often against all odds.

Reconstruction represented a small window that opened wide for a decade and ushered in new and unprecedented opportunities for the Black American population. That decade of opportunity came to a close in 1877, and the end of Reconstruction looked more like the twenty-five previous decades of the denial of such opportunity. Blacks were left landless and in a constant tug of war with their previous owners and planters. And so, for many, even today, Reconstruction represents a period of loss; lost opportunities to bridge the divide between Black and White and lost reparations and other compensations for 246 years of unrequited labor. Still today, Black communities across America associate the phrase "40 acres and a mule" with that loss and for many it represents a debt unpaid.

Yet amidst these very real losses, the Black population coming out of slavery was determined to reconnect with families torn asunder. They were determined to carve out for themselves more favorable work conditions than they had experienced in the past, and most of all, they kept their eyes on the prize of obtaining the full benefits of their newfound citizenship. They voted, they sought pensions, and fought for other civil rights. If the government would not or could not do it, they would reconnect the threads of their humanity on their own.

Notes

1 Thomson, p. 5.
2 Bobby L. Lovett, *The African-American History of Nashville, Tennessee, 1780–1930* (Fayetteville, AR: University of Arkansas Press, 1999) p. 59, quoted in Antoinette G. van Zelm, *Hope Within a Wilderness of Suffering: The Transition from Slavery to Freedom During the Civil War and Reconstruction in Tennessee,* Tenessee Civil War Heritage Area.
3 See "Sylvia Dubois (Now 116 Years Old) A Biografy of the Slav who Whipt Her Mistres and Gand Her Fredom," in Bailey, ch. 4.
4 Jacqueline Johnson, *Saving Savannah: The City and the Civil War* (New York: Alfred A. Knopf, 2008) p. 214.

5 Ibid.
6 Narrative of Amanda McDaniel, *Born into Slavery: Slave Narratives from the Federal Writers' Project 1936–38*, Georgia Narratives, Library of Congress, Washington, DC.
7 Allen C. Guelzo, *Fateful Lightning: A New History of the Civil War and Reconstruction* (New York: Oxford University Press, 2012) p. 472.
8 Bell, p. 414.
9 Leigh, p. 34–35. See Bram's recovered family tree in Appendices.
10 Ibid., p. 25.
11 Ibid., p. 27–28.
12 Catherine Clinton, *Tara Revisited: Women, War and Plantation legend* (New York: Abbeville Press, 1995) p. 117.
13 Leigh, p. 32–33.
14 Jones, p. 22.
15 James Alan McPherson, "Going Up to Atlanta," www.almostisland.com, p. 24–25, accessed October 26, 2016.
16 Leigh, p. 38.
17 Bell, p. 396.
18 Leigh, p. 146.
19 1862 Anti-Coolie Law, "An Act to prohibit the 'coolie trade' by American citizens in American vessels," library.uwb.edu/guides/usimmigration/1862_anti_coolie_law.html, accessed October 26, 2016.
20 Lakshmi Gandi, "A History of Indentured Labor gives 'Coolie' its sting," www.npr.org/blogs/codeswitch/2013/11/25/247166284/a-history-of-indentured-labor-gives-coolie-its-sting, accessed October 26, 2016; see also Gaiutra Bahadur in *Coolie Woman, The Odyssey of Indenture* (Chicago: University of Chicago Press, 2014).
21 Bell, p. 418.
22 Moon-Ho Jung, *Coolies and Cane: Race, Labor and Sugar in the age of Emancipation* (Baltimore: Johns Hopkins University Press, 2006) p. 5.
23 Bell, p. 411.
24 Foner, *Forever Free*, p. 41.
25 James Alan McPherson, p. 12.
26 Guelzo, p. 497.
27 Guelzo, p. 511. See also C. Vann Woodward, *Reunion, and Reaction: The Compromise of 1877 and the End of Reconstruction*, (New York; Oxford: Oxford University Press, 1991).
28 Guelzo, p. 504.
29 Leigh, p. 24, and Bell, p. 396
30 See Deborah Gray White, *Arn't I a Woman: Female Slaves in the Plantation South* (New York: Norton, 1985).
31 Bell, p. 396.
32 Mary Frances Berry, *My Face is Black, Is true: Callie House and the struggle for ex slave Reparations* (New York: Alfred A. Knopf, 2005) p. 50–60.

33 Aileen Torres-Bennett, "Caribbean nations agree to seek slavery reparations from Europe," Reuters, http://www.reuters.com/article/2014/03/11/us-caribbean-slavery-idUSBREA2A1ZR20140311, accessed October 26, 2016; see also Beckles and Shepherd, *Liberties Lost.*

34 Elizabeth Ann Regosin and Donald Robert Shaffer, *Voices of Emancipation: Understanding Slavery, the Civil War and Reconstruction through the U.S. Pension Files* (New York: New York University Press, 2008) p. 2–3.

35 Ibid., p. 3.

36 Ibid., p. 10.

9

Out of the Silence: Descendants Restore Family Names

Chattel no. 37, Quacco (Cooper), age 47, cooper and rice field hand
Chattel no. 38, Jean, age 34, prime woman
Chattel no. 39, Delia, age 14, prime girl
Chattel no. 41, Chaney, age 3 months, infant girl[1]

Out of the ashes of the auction experience there is beauty in that our story is fundamentally about redemption and restoration of not only African American families torn asunder on the auction block some 150 years ago, but also the restoration of historical memory. The latter is particularly evident in the brave and noble efforts of modern-day descendants' attempts to stitch together the pieces of their fragmented pasts.

As we saw in the last chapter, freed slaves after the war were preoccupied with reconnecting families and reconnecting threads of the past. Part of this process was the selection of names. On March 2–3, 1859, the 436 men, women, and children on the auction block were little more than numbers to those who bought them, despite the fact that they were not chattel at all, but human beings with names and histories. Against all odds, the slaves of the 1859 auction and their descendants found relative success in retrieving and maintaining family bonds through a variety of measures, such as preserving family names, serving in the Civil War, engaging in new and diversified work opportunities, entering bonds of marriage, and pursuing the goal of literacy.

Descendants Discover Their
Family Lineages

Three descendants of the Butler estates and the 1859 auction Annette Holmes, Mabel T. Hewlin, and Tiffany Shea Young have conducted their own exhausting yet rewarding research. Their findings, including the findings of this study, constitute fifteen percent or ten families consisting of fifty-nine men, women, and children from the original 436 on the auction catalog that have been found in the historical record. It is an ongoing process of recovery, but one that reminds us that out of displacement and loss, there can be redemption. The descendants' recovery process extends not just to the 1859 auction itself, but back to the Butler estates and even further back to Africa, where the very clues that descendants and researchers alike have depended on – names – were central to West and Central African societies.

Annette Holmes' Story

Chattel no. 99, John, age 31, prime rice hand
Chattel no. 100, Betsey, age 29, rice hand, unsound
Chattel no. 101, Kate, age 6
Chattel no. 102, Violet, age 3 months[2]

For Annette Holmes, it all started with a name. A resident of Oakland, California, Holmes has worked for the University of California system for over thirty years, starting in the mailroom to become the Assistant to the President of the University of California and, at the time of writing, is a researcher in the Office of Institutional Research and a financial consultant.[3]

As a young person, she was always curious about her family history but her "grandparents did not talk about where they were from." This silence only made Holmes more curious about her family's past. About eighteen years ago, she started exploring the family's history. She spoke with every elder she could find and developed a family tree of several generations. Then, in 2003, she was watching a documentary that alluded to the Butler plantation of the Georgia Sea Islands. Knowing her mother's maiden name was Butler, she decided to investigate. It was a longshot because, as far as she knew up until that time, her family originally came from Louisiana.

Holmes continued doing some research on her own and joined several genealogy websites serving American families, including some that cater to African American families. What she found helped to confirm what little oral history she was able to glean from the family. She knew the names of her ancestors going back several generations and, with those names, she was able to trace her family to Chattel nos 99–102: John, Betsey, Kate, and Violet at the Savannah auction.

Though a key primary source did not say more than how they were listed in the catalog and how much they were sold for, she searched through archival records at UC Berkeley and on Ancestry.com and learned that they were sold to Mr. Archibald Baird of the Baird plantation of Natchitoches Parish, Louisiana. She further confirmed this information when she found them listed on the 1860 Slave Schedule and the 1870 Census.

This is the reason family members would say that they were from Louisiana; as if the memory of that auction and the loss of their former life in Georgia was too painful to recall, they suppressed it for many years. Only when Holmes had this evidence in hand and shared it with her Uncle Charles did he admit that they were originally from Georgia. Doing further research, she made another interesting discovery. Some of the family (Captain and Dorcas) originally came from South Carolina in 1793 as a part of the Bull-Middleton lot of slaves that Major Pierce Butler brought with him for settlement in Georgia. So she now found that she not only had roots in Georgia but also in South Carolina. Like many Black communities all over the world, her family covered up their trauma with a blanket of silence. Ms. Holmes says: "You could have knocked me over with a feather. I could not believe that this was my family being sold like animals. Although you know that there were slaves in the family, it doesn't quite hit home until you see their names, ages, chattel numbers and the price for which they were sold."[4]

On this slave schedule was another surprising and important detail: John Butler (Chattel no. 99 on the auction list) could read and write. This was phenomenal for a slave since it was against the law for them to receive any formal education.[5] Even after the war, the 1870 Census for this area shows that very few ex-slaves could read and write.[6]

Annette Holmes was overwhelmed by all this information. While at first glance it might seem unusual for a family not to disclose its origins, it turns out this is not an unusual occurrence for families who have experienced a traumatic event. Armed with this knowledge, Holmes then went through all the subsequent land and census records and kept finding references to the original family as it expanded. For example, we find the family on the 1900 Census in Red River Parish in Louisiana with two

FIGURE 9.1 James Butler, 1865–1931, son of John and Betsey of Weeping Time auction.
Courtesy of Annette Holmes.

more children – Abraham and James. James, as seen in Figure 9.1, grew up and eventually married Hannah Stewart from the plantation adjacent to the Baird's and they had eleven children. The last of the eleven was Henrietta Butler – Ms. Annette Holmes' grandmother. Henrietta Butler married O. V. Cox and had nine children, including Ms. Holmes' mother, Betty Jean Cox.

After the Butlers gained their freedom as a result of the Emancipation Act of 1863 and the subsequent end of the Civil War, they decided to remain in Louisiana. We do not know much about what happened to their other family members who remained on the Butler plantation. We know that her family also included the preacher Cooper London, who helped officiate the funeral of Shadrach, as we saw in Chapter 6, and countless others. He was the brother to one of Ms. Holmes' family ancestors named Kate, who was born in 1800. London and his family were not sold at the 1859 auction, and after the war they took the surname Blake. They were not one of the six separate family groups that took the name of Butler.[7] The rest of the family that was sold must have consciously decided to stay in Louisiana, where John and Betsy Butler eventually bought land in Nachitoches County and attempted to rebuild their lives.

This was not an easy task. The rest of their time in Louisiana and later in Houston was peppered with stories illustrative of the challenges faced by Black families in the decades following the Civil War. Jim and Hannah discovered two oil wells (named Butler #1 and #2) on their property in Louisiana, but were soon driven off the land once this discovery became public. Another story of note concerned the eldest sister of O. V. Cox (Ms. Holmes' grandfather), who was said to have beaten up the sheriff in Louisiana. According to Cox, the sheriff was so embarrassed that he did not report them, but the incident left them with a reputation as "hellraisers."

Then there was Henrietta Cox, Ms. Holmes' grandmother, who represents one of the fascinating threads of the contemporary history of the Butler/Cox family. Like many women in the family before her, she was known for being a fierce protector of her children. At the same time, they were known in the community for being kind but strong. As Holmes says, "they were bad actors ... the type of people who weren't afraid. They did not get off the sidewalk when whites were coming." Henrietta was also known to fight physically with those threatening the welfare of her children. In fact, it is for this reason that they were eventually encouraged to move to Texas in 1938, their last stop before moving to California, where much of the family still lives.

Unfortunately, on September 15, 1940, while still in Texas, their oldest child, eighteen-year-old Leo James Cox, was killed with an ice pick when he got into a fight with a White man nicknamed Lumsey. Hauntingly, Holmes' Aunt Nell and Aunt Marie were on the bus headed to town when they saw Lumsey on the same bus sharpening his ice pick. They heard him say that he was "going to get him a nigger, tonight." They had no idea that it would be their brother who would be killed. "In 1944," according to Holmes, Grandpa Cox moved to California first to find work and "set up shop" for the rest of the family to come. His plan was to send for two family members at a time, starting with the eldest daughters, Marie and Nell. As luck would have it, Grandpa won the "Chinese lottery" and was able to move his entire family to California all at once. Betty Cox was four years old at the time. She remembers that Hayward Walker (who would later marry Aunt Nell) carried her to the car to make the trip to the train station."[8]

More than half-a-century later, Ms. Holmes occupies a significant position in the University of California system and her daughter is a graduate of UCLA. Both are descendants of slaves sold on the auction block in Savannah on March 2–3, 1859. These and other family stories are illustrative of the strength and resilience of some African American families after slavery. What is particularly interesting about these families is the length to which they took to stay together and to make a home for themselves in spite of the odds. At the same time, while attempting to find the best way to survive and surmount very difficult circumstances, they suppressed a lot of their personal history. The search for these family members was like unraveling secret threads of the past.

Mabel Audingston Thompson Hewlin's Story

Chattel no. 43, Bram (driver), age 47, prime cotton, dr'r, high character, $1,410

Chattel no. 44, Joan, age 42, woman, $1,410

Chattel no. 45, Morris, age 15, cotton hand, prime boy, $1,410

Chattel no. 46, Lucy, age 6

Chattel no. 47, Zephora

Chattel no. 48, Mary, age 4

Chattel no. 49. Pierce, age 3 months[9]

Like Annette Holmes, Mabel Audingston Thompson Hewlin (Mabel T. Hewlin), a retired nurse in California, started with a name – Jennie – the name of her great grandmother, also known as Jane. Similar to most slaves, she also had a nickname: Mudda (Mother). Jane was a slave on the Butler plantation and was a teenager when freedom came. While she was not sold at the Auction of 1859, she remembered well the horrible tales about it, including the violent rainy weather. She told these stories to Mabel's mother, who she reared in her home and who was the vessel through which some of this history was passed.[10]

When Mabel's mother shared these stories with her, she was in her thirties. She found them fascinating but did not pursue them any further until she read a brief description about the Weeping Time in a book. All of a sudden, these stories came rushing back, and she recognized that this incident may have had something to do with her family. She traced Jane/Jennie back to her parents, Chatham Dennis and Peggy, who are not only found on the postwar 1870 Census but are also to be found on the list of slaves that remained on the Butler estates after the sale. Chatham and Peggy were part of that group that belonged to Pierce Butler's brother John and his wife Gabriella. These men, women, and children would not be sold and so largely would remain in the county until and sometime after Emancipation. On that list, Chatham is listed as thirty-eight years old and appraised at $1,000, and Peggy is listed as twenty-nine years old and appraised at $800. Their daughter Jennie/Jane is later found on the 1870 Census list as being married to George Hall at the age of eighteen years.

On her mother's side, Mabel is connected to Chatham Dennis and Peggy, who were not sold, but lived and worked on the Butler plantation and recalled the painful story of the Weeping Time. But on her father's side, Mabel is related to slaves that were sold. Her father, Christopher Butler, was the son of Israel Butler, who was born in freedom. Israel, in turn, was the son of Morris, who was fifteen when sold with his parents, Bram and Joan Butler, at the auction in 1859. On both sides, Mabel is connected in some way to this traumatic event. Her story vividly shows how families were split apart.

Mabel often found herself one of the few family members interested in this history. Throughout her travels, she continued to visit Darien, her birthplace, to meet and talk with members of her family. One relative, Singleton Butler, a cousin of her father, shared some of this family history with her only over a long period. "He knew we were relatives. He looked after my stepdad and my brother and ended up having some job as keeper on Butler Island but still he didn't talk a lot about it," Mabel says. "He would talk about children and how they didn't listen to their elders or about ministers today and how they were out for your money. He'd say there were not like the old days where you could go to Reverend Young – those were real ministers, he would say... but now for some reason, he never spoke of slavery or what his grandmother had told him."[11]

It was after Mabel and her family left Darien as a part of the second wave of the Great Migration North that she began to fully recognize the rich history of Darien and Butler Island. It was only years later that she developed an interest in unraveling some of these threads. As with Annette Holmes, only after she had found out certain details on her own in the records did family members like the elder Singleton Butler confirm what she now knew to be true. She was a descendant of the slaves who were sold at the great auction of 1859.

Her reaction?

It made me feel that I didn't just get here. I have come through a line of very strong people. I think of all the things that they had to go through for their survival, and here we are and we made it. It gives me such respect. When I read Frances Butler Leigh's book and things she said about blacks being docile and needing to be taken care of like little pets, what would she say now if she could see black people today? It made me feel a strong sense of connection to that time. And made me realize the contribution made to this country.[12]

And this journey all started with a name.

Tiffany Shea Young's Story

Tiffany Shea Young also didn't have much to go on because her family did not tell a lot of stories about times past. But she too started with a name – the name of her grandfather James King, who was born in 1917. He was married to Mrs. Shirley King, who was over twenty years his junior and born in 1939.

"I was raised on these stories," she says as she recounts how she unearthed the trail that led her to Butler Island. "My grandfather always told me how life was different for him. He didn't know he was from Butler Island; they were sharecroppers. He knew though that he was from Africa. Some of his friends went missing, and they figured they were lynched."[13]

With this scant information and a few more names, Ms. Young traced her family tree back to Roswell King Jr., one of the overseers for the Butler plantation, who we met in Chapter 5. The family was owned by the junior King but lived all the while on Butler Island according to family oral history. She was able to go as far back as Bristoe and Leah King, who were found on the 1870 Census with two children including Bristoe Jr. (born 1845) and living on Broughton Island, a stone's throw from Butler Island in Darien County. He is listed as a fisherman, and he married Minerva and had sons Morris, Moses, Michael, and daughter Hannah. By this time, they had moved to Montgomery County in Georgia. Bristoe Jr. also owned his own farm of sixty acres, four of which are still in the family today. In fact, Ms. Young's grandfather not only bequeathed the stories to his granddaughter but also left her this homestead that is steeped in history.

"I am so glad he chose me. Others may have sold it off because it is deep rural Georgia." Young wants to build a museum in the family's honor to mark what they went through and how they came through it. "All I can do is pay homage and maybe create some kind of museum, give them some respect and be thankful." The KKK burned a cross on that land, and the family endured many hardships there, but the fact that it is still there is a testimony to the strength and resilience of this family.

Ms. Young was not content with the records she found in the archives. She had to see for herself where her forebears were from, so she traveled to Darien County and to Butler Island. She was struck by how little she knew and how little her family had spoken about "dem dark days." "You are all holding this back," she would say to them out loud, but then in reflective moments add,

It's embarrassing to tell you what they endured. You have to beg and coerce them … and then it is confusing. It's got to be confusing for people like my grandfather's sister, Ms. Homelee King (who is still alive), to have had a Black President in Barack Obama. She has seen it all … They were beat and spat on. She would tell stories how the Klan would come to their land and threaten her brothers and burn a cross and tell them it was time to get out. But get out and go where? This on the same land they gave me.[14]

For Ms. Young, this explained the silence that she experienced much of her life when she inquired about the family history. Only her grandfather, Mr. James King, who died in 2014, cared to share freely with her, most likely because she grew up with him, and he somehow knew she would be a good steward of this history.

Like many descendants connected to the Butler estates, Young is hopeful because she understands the great significance of knowing her history. She knows she is a different person because of it and is now actively promoting Gullah-Geechee culture and its preservation. In recent years, she has started a tour company in the area to share this history with others. She has also joined Rev. Griffin Lotson and others at the Georgia state capitol to talk with the governor about the preservation of Gullah-Geechee culture.

Griffin Lotson is a longtime and formidable community activist from Darien, Georgia, who has traced his Gullah-Geechee family history back seven generations. He has also been active in preservation efforts for many years, and sits on the Gullah-Geechee Cultural Heritage Corridor Commission that was established by Congress in 2006. The Corridor goes beyond Butler Island and Darien and extends north from Wilmington, North Carolina and south to Jacksonville, Florida. The Commission can already count many important achievements, including lending support to local festivals and helping to identify and preserve historical sites of interest.[15]

Their efforts will ensure that Gullah-Geechee culture and language, which once was looked down upon even by those who spoke and practiced it, will now have its place in history. No longer will her children and their children be able to say, as she has said: "I was born in Georgia and go all the time to museums and you see nothing. Where are the graves of the slaves? You have built on top of them." Now she and others see themselves as getting back to their roots and advocating for the healing and reconstruction of their families and their history. And it all started with a name.

Other Families Recovered

There are several other families associated with the Butler estates whose names also tell a significant story that circles back to those fateful days in 1859 on the auction block. The names of these individuals helped restore the breach between and amongst families: Bram and Joan Butler, George and Margaret Goulding, the Walker Family (Sally, Noble, and James), Primus and Daphne Wilson, the Ferguson family, Ned and Scena Bleach, Matty and Brister McIntosh, and George and Sue Broughton – the first family sold in the 1859 auction. Together, in addition to the families of Annette Holmes and Mabel T. Hewlin, they represent ten families and fifty-nine men, women, and children who were sold on the auction block in 1859 in Savannah, Georgia.

There are many recurring threads in each of their stories. First, there is the continuity of names. Because of the practice of fathers naming their first-born sons after themselves and their second-born after their fathers, we find many common patterns. In one family, an unusual name Singleton keeps coming back each generation. Wiseman, of the Ferguson family, also reappears from census to census. Although this practice is not uncommon across the globe, it is particularly significant given the patchwork nature of African American history. There are also parallels between elements of these stories and important periods in African American history.

Most important is what we learn about how the Butler slaves and their descendants lived. These families clearly did all they could to stay alive and to stay intact as families. Sold on the auction block to lands far away, it was no small feat for them to stay together; yet together they remained. We see time and time again how elder fathers and mothers remained a part of the household until death and even extended family members are listed in the same household in census records. If family life was the great casualty of the period of slavery, then we see attempts at restoration after emancipation. We see attempts to reposition and to restore the family to a stronger foundation. A good example is Chattel no. 45, Morris Butler in Mabel T. Hewlin's family, who on the 1880 Census is married to Pheobe; their eldest son is Israel Butler. As late as the 1910 Census, Morris is still listed as living with his Israel and assorted grandchildren. Later we see Israel, at sixty, continuing the same practice and living with his children and grandchildren, including Singleton Butler, who was thirteen at the time.[16]

> Chattel no. 256, Noble, twenty-two, cotton prime man, $1,236
> Chattel no. 260, James, age nine, $1,236[17]

In the Walker family, two brothers, Chattel nos 256 (Noble Walker) and 260 (James Walker), who were ages twenty-two and nine, respectively, and sold for $1,236 on the auction block, did not return to Butler Island but ended up in Macon in Bibb County, Georgia and lived only two doors away from one another with their wives and families for many years. Similarly, as late as 1910, the whole Ferguson family lived together in spite of the great hardships they endured.[18]

Families like the Fergusons and the Walkers, who suffered the trauma of separation and also displacement from Butler Island, understood the importance of family and staying together and seemed to make every effort to do so. By the same token, marriage seemed to be of continuing importance to the ex-slaves and their early descendants. Certainly, it was important during slavery in part because it was often denied them, but after slavery, they seemed to take even more advantage of the institution of marriage. In our fifteen percent sample, almost all of the individuals sold stay married and, if a partner died, they remarried. Their children tended to follow the same pattern, and created large families. Ex-Butler slaves sometimes officiated at marriages as well, such as Noble Walker (Chattel no. 256), who must have been a lay minister of sorts since he is listed in the records as marrying the following couples in Bibb County: Madison Thomas and Luvena Harps on July 18, 1871, and Nelson Thomas and Susan Randall on April 10, 1872.[19]

> Chattel no. 422, Hannah
> Chattel no. 127, Ned, age 56, cotton hand, $485
> Chattel no. 128, Sena, age 50, cotton-cook, $485
> Chattel no. 422, Hannah, age 23, cotton, prime woman[20]

From the record, we see that marriage was important. Interestingly, we see evidence of some interracial marriages in the records, such as in the Bleach family, where Hannah Bleach (Chattel no. 422), the twenty-three-year-old daughter of Ned and Scena Bleach (Chattel nos 127 and 128), is married to a White physician named Samuel W. Wilson.[21] He was listed on the 1870 Census as originating from Pennsylvania with a personal estate of $1,000. Hannah had no children at the time of the auction, which is surprising since many young women on the plantation had children from as early an age as sixteen. This relationship is significant not only because of its interracial nature but because these two made their relationship official via marriage. Certainly were relations between the races usually forced – but even when of free will, marriage was rare.[22]

Sold at auction at twenty-three years of age, Hannah was married to a white Northerner of some personal wealth a scant eleven years later. Again, it speaks to the priority placed on marriage for the ex-slaves and their early descendants. To be sure, in our fifteen percent sample, we do have some female heads of households like Mattie (Chattel no. 209) and her son Brister (Chattel no. 211) of the McIntosh family, but these are not the norm.

Marriage was important but so was the variety of work opportunities these families pursued. All the Butler slaves had talents. Most were field hands whose foreparents had taught them the intricate art of planting and harvesting rice and cotton. Some had gained experience on the South Carolina rice plantations and before that in West Africa, where rice was an important commodity for hundreds of years. Still others were skilled blacksmiths, carpenters, and coopers. When freedom came, many still remained as farmers working the land as they had for years. Many became sharecroppers on the same land on which they had been slaves. In the beginning, those who returned to Butler Island and the neighboring plantations carved out new work agreements with their former masters and tried to see how they could make this land work for them. Our fifteen percent sample shows this trend but also reveals how Butler ex-slaves gradually diversified in terms of their work. This diversification had a lot to do with the growth of literacy. We know that some slaves, like Cooper London in Annette Holmes' family, during his enslavement learned to read and write, although we don't know how he accomplished this feat.

Chattel no. 1, George, age 27, prime cotton planter
Chattel no. 2, Sue, age 26, prime rice planter
Chattel no. 3, George Jr., age 4, boy child
Chattel no. 4, Harry, age 2, boy child[23]

In even the early census and Freedman's Bank records, furthermore, we find evidence that others too learned to read and write after slavery. In the case of the Broughton family (Chattel nos 1–4), the first family sold at the auction in 1859, there is a steady growth in the literacy of the family, illustrated by George's youngest son, Harry, who was sold at auction at the age of two for $620 and by 1910 is listed in that year's census as having seven children – all of them literate. Harry died in 1925 at age seventy and is listed as being a minister in his later years – a profession often associated with some degree of education. In the Ferguson family, of which Chattel no. 227, Wiseman Ferguson, plays a prominent part, we have two of his sons listed as being "in school" as early as the 1880 Census.[24] Two of his other sons, Edward and Wiseman Jr., are later listed as railroad laborers by the 1900 Census and another relative, William Baldwin, also living in the same household at the time, is listed as a railroad engineer.[25] Others are by 1910 listed as railroad tie-cutters or stokers; again occupying positions of great importance in the Black community at that time.[26] We see a continued connection to the land as well as the growth of literacy that opened up new opportunities and new doors literally across the nation via the railroad.

We can only imagine how hard-won all those gains were. W. E. B. Dubois talks about the zeal that many a freedman had for learning and education and how they craved new opportunities on and off the land.[27] But notwithstanding the commitment of several Black and White missionaries in the period after slavery and even the Freedman's Bureau created on March 3, 1865, many of these opportunities were sorely lacking. Many slaves simply had to fight to get an education and to open doors to more prestigious employment. They were free, but they were hardly the most important priority for a nation that was trying to recover from a bloody and tumultuous war; a war in which several of these ex-Butler plantation slaves fought on the side of the Union troops.

> Chattel no. 256, Noble, age twenty-two, cotton prime man
> Chattel no. 423, Thomas, age twenty-one, cotton hand[28]

There is a strong thread of war service in our fifteen percent sample (from the Civil War to World War II) but nowhere is it more poignant than in the military records of Thomas Baker (Chattel no. 423), son of Ned and Scena Bleach, who were sold at auction in 1859. Baker enlisted in the 21st Regiment, Company D, US Colored Troops. On April 25, 1866, he mustered out from Charleston, South Carolina. He was also one of the brothers of Hannah (Chattel no. 422), whose interracial marriage is discussed above.[29]

But he was not alone. Noble Walker (Chattel no. 256), who at age twenty-two was listed in the auction catalogue as "cotton, prime man" and was sold for $1,236, also fought for the freedom of his family and others held in bondage at the time. He served in the Unit Co. I. 137th US Colored Infantry 2, a regiment organized on April 8, 1865, and mustered troops on June 11, 1865 at Macon, Bibb County, Georgia. The unit mustered out on January 15, 1866. His wife and later widow, Millie Walker, applied for a Civil War pension in 1893 on behalf of their family. Although we are only able to trace this family till the 1880s, Walker's service to his country and his fellow ex-slaves is remarkable.[30]

Noble Walker and Thomas Baker are but two examples of the enduring contribution made by ex-slaves for their country. Pierce Butler's slaves, auctioned off in 1859 to pay his debts, went on to play a pivotal role in the redefining of the American nation. They served their country with honor and helped to gain freedom for themselves and their fellow slaves. Service in war and emancipation gave them the chance to redeem what was lost during "The Weeping Time." Their service in the US Colored Troops enabled them to restore the breach.

Unlike thousands of others, both of these men managed to survive the war and lived out their remaining years with their children and grandchildren, but this was not the case for all the freedmen. Littered within the record is evidence of some gruesome deaths and, in some cases, death of unusual or unknown circumstances. These stories speak to the precariousness of life for the freedmen, a number of whom died at an early age. For example, Primus Wilson (who with wife Daphne was sold with children Dido and the infant born on Valentines's Day to Tom Scriven of South Carolina), remarks on his Freedman's Bank record that most of his closest relatives, including his brothers, Louis and Frank, and his sisters, Judy, Abba, Dido, Rachel, and Sarah, who had been split up by the auction, were "all dead." And this is 1869, only ten years after the fateful auction. It appears, from the Freedman's records, that this was by no means an isolated case.

Many who lived through the auction and survived the Civil War made fruitful contributions to their families and their communities, but others appeared to have suffered greatly at the end of their lives – cancer of the stomach, knife wounds to the chest, tuberculosis. We can only imagine that, with inadequate housing and health care, among other needs, freedmen were particularly vulnerable to numerous perils and misfortunes.[31]

Throughout, the determination to remain together is the recurring thread through the lives and experiences of these families. They seemed determined to reestablish themselves as families in spite of their history of dislocation and displacement. Sometimes, they were helped by fate, as we saw in Chapter 1 with Frances and Dembo – the couple that married just in time to be sold together to an Alabama plantation. Although their trail runs cold after the auction, we hope that they had a better life being together rather than being apart.

> Chattel no. 138, Doctor George, age 39, fair carpenter
> Chattel no. 139, Margaret, age 38
> Chattel no. 140, Maria, age 11
> Chattel no. 141, Lena, age 6
> Chattel no. 142, Mary Ann, age 3
> Chattel no. 143, Infant, boy born February 16[32]

Fate may have also been at the side of the Goulding family, Chattel nos. 138–143, headed by Doctor George and his wife Margaret. They were listed in the auction catalog and expected to be sold and separated like the others, but, by a strange twist of fate, Pierce Butler was persuaded to give them a reprieve. Margaret gave birth only four days before she and the rest of the slaves were scheduled to be carted off to Savannah in railroad cars fit for animals, and so, for this, she and the family were allowed to stay on the plantation. Why they were spared and others like Daphne, who had also been pregnant and gave birth around the same time were not, no one knows. All we know is that Doctor George and Margaret were able to stay on the plantation and maintain continuous residence in the area before and after the Civil War.[33]

That they were able to stay together was no ordinary accomplishment for the era. They remained married, and by 1900 daughter Mary was also married to a Joe Mandees, with Henry Goulding listed as one of her sons, along with his stepbrother Frank. Henry Goulding is later found alternately loading vessels and doing carpentry by 1910 and married Hagar McFarlane, and his mother Mary Mandees is living on her own by 1920. She is described as a widow who worked as a laundress and owned her home free of mortgage: very noteworthy accomplishments for the times. Mysteriously, her son, Henry Goulding, died tragically at the age of forty-one in August 1924 from, according to his death certificate, knife wounds to the chest: "murdered by unknown parties." His grave is an unmarked tombstone in Butler's Cemetery in Darien and no other descendants beyond him can be found for this family. It is ironic that, despite the fact his family was spared full and total separation on the auction block, it was still subject to the vagaries of life as freedmen. They were not immune. Their stories were full of tragedies, some on the auction block, others reserved for a future date. Escaping separation from house and household did not mean the end of weeping.

For all of these struggles, the stories after the war and the search for family are still filled with hope because living descendants are finding meaning in their past and its pains, triumphs, sadness, and joy. In the threads of the patchwork quilt called African American history they have found their stories and, in so doing, have found themselves.

Out of the silence, they have found their voices in the search that begins and sometimes ends with family names. But in between the lines, they have seen the contributions of their families who worked hard, who strove for literacy and the right to vote, and who fought for their freedom. But perhaps their greatest accomplishment was their determination to restore the breach caused by slavery and the auction and to reestablish their family life; to put back together what was denied them in the past. For that feat, they would win no awards or receive any honors, but their living descendants are the greatest testimony to their tireless efforts. In that, there is victory and joy.

The process of recovery by descendants does not end with the auction block. This recovery, in fact, exists within a larger global context. It extends to the Butler plantations and to the continent of Africa, where names and naming have historically held great significance. As such, names and naming are central to the recovery process for nuclear and extended families, but also for family lineages that extend back to the continent.

African Ancestral Names

In West and Central Africa, from where many of the Butler slaves and American slaves descended, the naming of a child was of supreme importance. There was great consideration of the nature of the birth: first-born, last-born, the day of the week of the birth, the ancestors of the child, and the period of time in which the child was born. The great King of Mali, Sundiata or Sundjata Keita Sogolon, had a royal name that said something about his ancestry as well as his future at the same time. In Malinke tradition, the mother's name is combined with the personal name. Sogolon was the name of the mother; *jata* means lion. And so, Sundiata became known as the lion king, who was heralded for solidifying and consolidating the ancient Kingdom of Mali as a major commercial and military center from 1217–1255. His name belied his past and his future all at the same time.[34]

When Africans became chattel and were branded like animals, their deeply meaningful ancestral names were almost lost. It was of little importance who they had been in their original homes. In fact, it would have been best for this identity to be lost or forgotten. Certainly, slave owners did much to stamp them out, yet many of these names were remembered, even if they were somewhat corrupted or changed from their original meaning and context.

Kofi became Cuffee. Kodjoe became Cudjo. But the practice of naming children after their forebears continued. They also did not completely forget the practice of recognizing unique circumstances of a child's birth. The difference was that they were now "Butler's Quashee" or "Couper's Cudjo." They were now more identified with their owners than with their culture and past. The plantation on which they worked now determined their fate. When sold to another plantation, the name of the new owner was now their new identity. Considering that the average slave could be sold six times in a lifetime, this situation easily led to a confused sense of identity.

During slavery, slaves were also given names that reflected their character or their jobs. In the auction catalog, Chattel no. 261 Lawyer Charles might have been a debater or one called in to settle disputes among the slaves. Cooper London, the preacher on the Butler plantation, was also a cooper who built and repaired wooden barrels and tubs.

As more and more African Americans converted to Christianity, many chose Biblical names. Moses, Elisahs, Israels, and Isaiahs abound. Indeed, the Old Testament prophets were very popular. But even more obscure Biblical names like Dorcas, a follower of Jesus known for her charity, or Shadrach, one of the three Hebrew boys who defied the orders of the King Nebuchadnezzar, were commonly used. Those who were Muslim also continued the tradition in naming their children Abel or Omar.[35]

As we have already noted, a number of slaves in America were Islamic. The story of Omar Ibn Said (1770–1864) is perhaps the most well-known. Born in the Muslim state of Futa Toro (modern-day Senegal), Omar was a scholar and trader who was captured and sold in Charleston, South Carolina and later sold to a plantation in North Carolina. He was given an Arabic Bible, which is preserved at Davidson College in North Carolina.[36]

When freedom came, a slave named Israel who was described as African and from the Couper plantation, which neighbored the Butler plantation, was described in a way that suggested he was likely Muslim:

Ole Israel he pray a lot wid a book he hab wut he hide, an he take a lill mat an he say he prayuhs on it. He pray wen duh sun go up an wen duh sun go down. Dey ain none but ole Israel wut pray on a mat. He hab he own mat. Now ole man Israel he hab shahp feechuh an a long pointed beahd, an he wuz bery tall. He alluz tie he head up in a wite clawt, an seem he keep a lot uh clawt on ban, fuh I membuh, yuh could see em hangin roun duh stable dryin.[37]

(Translation: Old Israel, he prayed a lot with a book he had but that he hid and he took a little mat and he said his prayers on it. He prays when the sun goes up and when the sun goes down. They say none but Old Israel could pray on the mat. He had his own mat. Now Old Man Israel he had sharp features and a long pointed beard and he was very tall. He always tied up his head with a white cloth and seemed to keep a lot of that cloth on hand, for I remember, you could see him hanging around the stable drying it.)

Slave names often reflected their strong religious identities. At the same time, they had to contend with the derogatory names that were randomly assigned them by owners, such as "Nigger," "Sambo," or "Jezebel." It was common for slaves to be called not by proper names, but by these terms that were intended to demean and devalue. These names carried a great burden – so great a burden that they are sadly still a part of our lexicon today. Given the importance of names in African heritage, names associated with negative stereotypes are very problematic. If names tell a story, the implication in the past is that story is a positive and productive one that is worth telling throughout the generations, not one that tears down or destroys.[38]

Names When Freedom Came

When freedom came, ex-slaves once again had choices. They could now choose their surnames, and, in so doing, made interesting choices. Some of the Butler freedmen like Bram and Joan (Chattel nos 43 and 44) kept the name of Butler. In fact, in the 1870 Census, we see at least six separate family groups that chose the name of Butler.[39] Others who had been sold elsewhere kept the names of their new masters. Annette Holmes' family initially took the name of Baird, since they had been sold in 1859 to the Baird plantation, and this name is seen on the 1870 Census for the family. But interestingly, by the 1880s they had changed their names back to

Butler, perhaps in recognition of the longstanding connection that they had with the Butlers and their plantation. And so even though the family stopped telling the story about their roots in Georgia, their name still told that story.[40]

Commodore Bob, the rice hand sold for $600 in 1859, who returned to the Butler plantation when freedom came, chose the last name Bob. Others chose names associated with important White families in Darien County: Goulding, Hazzard, Wylly, Cooper, Palmer, Young, Stoutenburg, Frazier, Waldburgh, and Bull.[41] Chattel nos 138–143 chose the name of Goulding to mark a real break with their slave past; they did not call themselves Butler. This name was nonetheless associated with one of the prominent White families in Darien County. Likewise, Chattel nos 72–75, Primus, Daphne, Dido, and their infant born on Valentine's Day a month before the 1859 auction, chose the name of Wilson. Chattel nos 127 and 128, Ned and Lena (also known as Scena), took the name of Bleach. Chattel nos 225–231, including Wiseman, chose the name of Ferguson. It made for an interesting mélange of names, but what is important was that, in most cases, these names were of their own choosing.

Even in contemporary times, African Americans and others of African descent have struggled with the importance of names and naming. Disconnected physically from their African past, some have attempted to make connections by naming their children with "Africanized names." Some of these names, like Aliya (which means trust in Swahili) come directly from the continent, but in truth, many of them are completely made up names *perceived* to be African, but in reality bearing little real connection to the African context. In these cases, the perception is almost as important as the reality, since for those parents who carefully considered conventional "American" names like Jill, Joan, and Carol, rejecting them in favor of Shaniqua, LaWanda, and Deneka may have been bridging the gap between Africa and America and restoring the breach.

Certainly, there were examples of this during and immediately after slavery, but never was this phenomenon more prominent than during the 1950s and 1960s, in the Second Civil Rights Movement. As Black people boycotted segregated buses and lunch counters, they also explored new opportunities and identities outside the confining boxes in which they had been placed by White society. One of these boxes was their surnames. Why carry what some called their "slave name" when they could take new names like Muhammad Ali did, who famously gave up his original name Cassius Clay for religious as well as historical reasons? New identities were sought by a number of Blacks who were wading into their complex past and digging out the bits they felt could point to a brighter future. Afros and colorful dashikis often accompanied new names, and for many were powerful symbols of the move from subservience and oppression to taking their rightful place as citizens in the United States of America. Many of these African Americans were also making connections with the several African independence movements that were taking place on the continent during the same period.

What is in a name? A lot, in the case of African Americans and others of African descent. Names tell a story of past and present and especially the future. In a history of displacement and loss, descendants of slaves on the auction block in 1859 started the process of recovery with their names. The auction represented the separation of families and a breach in their personal and collective histories. Their family members were reduced to numbers. It was and is now up to them to restore that breach. As they restore the breach in their personal lineage, they have paid homage to their African ancestors and an unknown lineage that extends back to the continent.

In the absence of ruins, they have only memory.[42] Thankfully, their story and the story of people of African descent did not end on the auction block. The auction was but a chapter, albeit a devastating chapter, in their long history extending backwards to the African continent. The auction block neither erased that history nor eradicated their future. The auction block that once represented a time of weeping can now represent a new era of recovery and restoration.

Notes

1   Auction Catalogue, Historical Society of Pennsylvania, March 2–3, 1859.
2   Ibid.
3   Interview with Ms. Annette Holmes.
4   Ibid.
5   Ibid.
6   Bell, p. 408.
7   Ibid., p. 407.
8   Interview with Annette Holmes.
9   Auction Catalogue, Historical Society of Pennsylvania.
10   Interview with Mabel T. Hewlin.
11   Ibid.
12   Ibid.

13 Interview with Tiffany Young.

14 Ibid.

15 Meetings and interview with Griffin Lotson.

16 1880 Census records.

17 Auction Catalogue, Historical Society of Pennsylvania.

18 National Archives, US Department of Commerce. Bureau of the Census, Manuscript Population Schedules for the 1870 and 1880 Census, District 483, Howard, Bibb County, GA; 1910 US Census, 1515th District, McIntosh County.

19 Walker Freedman's Records.

20 Auction Catalogue, Historical Society of Pennsylvania.

21 See also Darien Burial records on Bleach family.

22 1870 US Census: Darien, 271st District, McIntosh County, Georgia.

23 Auction Catalogue, Historical Society of Pennsylvania.

24 1880 US Census records, 271st District McIntosh County, Georgia.

25 1900 US Census records, 1515th District McIntosh County, Georgia.

26 1910 US Census records, 1515th District McIntosh County, Georgia.

27 See W. E. B. Dubois, *The Souls of Black Folk* (New York: Dover, 1994).

28 Auction catalogue, Historical Society of Pennsylvania.

29 National Archives, Military records of Thomas Baker, 21st Regiment, Company D, US Colored Troops.

30 National Archives, Military records of Noble Walker, 137th Infantry Regiment, US Colored Troops, and Civil War Pension Application file index, Widow Application no. 578592, Roll No. T288-494.

31 Death certificates of Broughton families and others, Georgia State Board of Health, Bureau of Vital Statistics.

32 Auction Catalogue, Historical Society of Pennsylvania.

33 Thomson, p. 15.

34 D. T. Niane, *Sundiata: An Epic of Old Mali* (Harlow, England: Pearson Longman, 2006).

35 See more in the important works of Michael Gomez and Sylvianne Diouf.

36 Patrick Horn, "Omar Ibn Said: African Muslim enslaved in the Carolinas," *Documenting the American South*, Accessed September 26, 2016 http://docsouth.unc.edu/highlights/omarsaid.html.

37 *Drums and Shadows*, p. 171.

38 Randall Kennedy, *Nigger: The Strange Career of a Troublesome Word* (New York: Pantheon Books, 2002).

39 Bell, p. 407.

40 1870 and 1880 US Census records.

41 Bell, p. 407.

42 See term and title of Orlando Patterson (1967), *An Absence of Ruins* (Peelpal Tree, 2012), James T. Haley's *Afro American Encyclopedia; Or the thoughts, Doings, and Sayings of the Race, Embracing lectures, Biographical sketches...and Women* (Nashville: Haley and Florica, 1895) in the thoughts, doings of the race in electronic edition in *Documenting the American South* p. 345–347. This is an account according the clerk of the sale but thus far not corroborated elsewhere.

Epilogue: History and the Democratization of Memory

This has been the story of the largest slave auction in US history. Before the outbreak of the Civil War, auctions were as common as modern stock trades, yet if most Americans were to be asked to name one significant auction, they would be hard-pressed to do so. Hopefully this book will change that and the memory of at least one auction and the people whose lives were changed forever will always be with us. In charting the paths of the slaves auctioned off by Pierce Butler in 1859 and the quests of their descendants to reconnect with their ancestors, we learn much about the enduring effects – traumatic, but also hopeful – that enslavement had on people of African descent and on the history of the African Diaspora. We also discover the equally profound impact that slavery had on the lives of owners, and in the case of the Butler family, the breaches it caused, reflecting the breaches in slave families. Throughout the book, we follow the course of one of America's most tumultuous and significant periods of history, which is actually still with us in the fragments of what we continue to remember and in the consequences of a tragic past with which we live every day.

The Butler auction has caused me to reflect deeply on the history, memory, and study of people of African descent, leading me to begin developing a taxonomy I call "The 7 Types of Remembering." My taxonomy, inspired by the Weeping Time auction, is informed by different periods of history, including World War II and the Holocaust, but has particular relevance for African Diaspora historical studies. Perhaps the word that sums up this taxonomy is *democratization* – the need for the democratization of memory.

My hope is that this brief and by no means conclusive discussion will encourage students and scholars of history to do further research on these and related issues. Though the taxonomy is my own, in the spirit of democracy and with respect to the academic tradition, I draw on my many influences, academic and otherwise. So many voices have already contributed honorably to this discussion and research effort, but so many more have yet to be heard.

The following types of remembering all point to a need to hear and respect *all* voices in history, including the voices of ordinary people caught up in extraordinary historical events. It is my hope that these seven types of remembering and the call for a democratization of historical memory will also allow history to fulfill one of its hallowed goals: to provide guidance and instruction to the issues we face in the present and not just to represent a narrative of the past.

Finally, I end this book in some ways similarly to how I ended my last book, *African Voices of the Atlantic Slave Trade*. Drawing on Toni Morrison's term, "rememory," I discussed the idea of reparations as rememory. At the time of writing, there is once again a call for slave reparations in both academic and activist circles. Building on a longstanding tradition, author Ta-Nehisi Coates has made a well-reasoned and passionate call for reparations in a much-quoted article in the June 2014 edition of *The Atlantic Monthly*. He wrote: "Two hundred fifty years of slavery. Ninety years of Jim Crow. Sixty years of separate but equal. Thirty-five years of racist housing policy. Until we reckon with our compounding moral debts, America will never be whole." It is my hope that historical memory will be deemed just as important as the call for other types of compensation like reparations. The following "rememberings" should be considered in this light.

Memory, Silence, and Its Companion, Denial

We began the book with a discussion of the forgotten auction experience in public American memory. The Weeping Time auction was the largest slave auction in US history, yet who remembers this story? Some 150 years later this story, like the story of the slaves' eventual emancipation in 1863, it is a distant memory. Some might say in many ways this memory and others like it have been silenced in American culture.

The year 2013 was the 150th anniversary of the Emancipation Proclamation. One hundred and fifty years is a major milestone, yet there was very little about this event in the national press and, more importantly, in the national consciousness. Some of the major news outlets published short pieces and reminded the public of the document's existence and the fact that the document was on tour across the country in museums and other venues. This hallowed document, where the phrase "forever free" was immortalized by Abraham Lincoln's pen, eventually returned to its Washington, DC home in the National Archives and was available for viewing by those who had heard about its arrival. Those fortunate few, one television program noted, queued up with eagerness to see the document that not only freed the slaves, but caused America to revisit the Declaration of Independence and the principles it holds dear.

Some radio programs also gave mention of the occasion and *Lincoln*, a major motion picture about the path toward the proclamation, was released, but in general the 150-year milestone was not seen as a major event. Ironically, even the Bicentennial of the Abolition of the Atlantic slave trade a few short years ago in 2007 seemed to have been given more attention with events and forums all across the globe. But the freedom of American slaves did not garner similar attention.

Given the enormous impact of the Emancipation Proclamation, one may wonder why such a momentous event would not be commemorated on a large scale on the occasion of its 150th anniversary. We may also wonder why it is not commemorated like a major national holiday each and every year.[1]

The United States of America was built on some of the highest ideals that man had ever espoused at any time in history. The Declaration of Independence's "All men are created equal" was a clarion call for freedom – but as it turns out, only freedom for some. The Republic was established with the aid of slave labor and with a blind eye to slavery.

The Emancipation Proclamation in so many ways reaches back to Jefferson's hallowed document and fills in the missing pieces. It at once represents an advance, but also a corrective: a 250-year-old wrong is corrected with one stroke of a pen. What that meant to African Americans, we have already discussed: freedom was the long and elusive goal, always at the center of hopes and prayers. Its delay made the reality of it all the more sweet, so it is no wonder that some African Americans, particularly in the South, still celebrate a service called Watchnight on New Year's eve. Watchnight is a church service in which they celebrate God's deliverance of them from slavery on that night 150 years ago. In this way, it is similar to Jewish Passover seder rituals.

But this event did not only change their lives, it changed the entire country. It would set America on the road towards equality and civil rights that it is still on today. It was not to be a straight line to full and total equality, for there would be setbacks and backlash, but a door had been opened that could not be easily shut. Inasmuch as that was the case, this Act was a monumental victory for all Americans. It has been said before that slavery was not unique to North America and the West. There are many historical examples, but surely what is unique in this case was the height of those tremendous ideals about freedom and equality – all men are created equal – and the fight to make those ideals a reality. They truly become a reality when the Emancipation Proclamation came into effect. The Emancipation Proclamation gave those words power and thus is worth commemorating not just on the 150th anniversary, but every year, as a reminder of great progress and even leadership in this area around the world.

Combatting Denial

The silence must also be broken because of its companion – denial. The other side of this silence is not just the downplaying or misunderstanding of this historical moment. It is the denial of the contribution of those who made history. The slaves whose innovation and labor contributed to the growth of the Georgia and South Carolina Low Country economy are easily erased or forgotten in a sea of silence. The skills that Africans such as the Butler slaves brought with them from hundreds of years of planting rice on the Rice Coast of Africa are downplayed or relegated to menial tasks. Their value, well known to Georgia and South Carolina planters, is simply a footnote of history.[2] But those sought-after skills made their owners so wealthy that it was said that, on the eve of the Civil War, the richest men in the country were from this area. Sea Island rice in antebellum America consistently fetched a good price in the US and abroad.

The discussion of slavery often does not include slave contribution to the building of America. Slaves and slavery are seen as a "problem" or a paradox of American life instead as part of the *backbone* of American life. Just as the founding fathers made no public acknowledgment of their dependence on the institution in part for the wealth they enjoyed, there is little acknowledgment of modernity's debt to these early builders of American society.

Furthermore, the phenomenon of denial also masks the heroes – the Frederick Douglasses and the Fanny Kembles – Black and White alike, who fought in their respective ways for slavery's end. Denial erases the contribution of the enslaved while at the same time erasing the contributors to slavery's demise.

One significant way in which some members of the Jewish community counters this type of denial is to remember each year every Holocaust survivor by calling out their names. As pointed out in an influential article by Cynthia Wroclawski,

Since its inception 60 years ago, one of Yad Vashem's central missions has been to recover the identity of each and every victim of the Holocaust. The Shoah Victim's Names Recovery Project realizes the moral imperative to remember each victim as a human being, with a name and a unique personal story. It's an extraordinarily complex endeavor, that requires sifting through archival material and postwar commemoration projects, working with Holocaust survivors to fill out Pages of Testimony, understanding many languages and the complexity of the etymology of names. Yet, to date, this ceaseless endeavor has identified an incredible 4.2 million names of Shoah victims, documented in Yad Vashem's Central Database of Shoah Victims' Names.[3]

In this way, the Holocaust cannot be denied but also those who died or the relatively few who lived to tell the tale cannot be denied. There was and is value to their lives and this poignant exercise in recovering their names brings this all into focus. This process is very similar to the annual reading of the 2,983 victims of the World Trade Center attacks on 9/11. Each year since then, relatives, friends and the general public have come together to mark the moments of the attacks and to remember those who lost their lives in this tragedy. It is a powerful ceremony which ensures that they will not be forgotten.

Memory and Power

According to an African (Ewe) proverb, "Until the lion has his or her own storyteller, the hunter will always have the best part of the story."

Gnatola ma no kpon sia, eyenabe adelan to kpo mi sena.
Ewe-mina (Benin, Ghana, and Togo) Proverb

This proverb captures one of the potential dangers of historical writing. As much as it is the historian's task to make an attempt at objectivity, there is a degree of subjectivity in the process. First, the historian is from a particular place and time. Second, he or she makes choices in terms of what to look at in the archive and beyond the archive, in part based on his or her interest and inclination. Historians are also heavily dependent on historiography – the history of the history of a topic. But what if that historiography is biased to begin with? What if that historiography, as Michel Rolph Trouillot showed in the case of some French historians writing in the colonial era about Haiti, was influenced by France's dismay at having lost its "jewel" in the Caribbean?[4] What if that historiography was influenced by two-time Prime Minister of France, Jules Ferry (1880–1885), and his belief in the inherent superiority of the French over what he called "inferior races?" As seen in the following quote, Ferry felt that colonial expansion was not just a right, it was a duty: "Gentlemen, we must speak more loudly and more honestly! We must say openly that indeed the higher races have a right over the lower races … I repeat, that the superior races have a right because they have a duty. They have the duty to civilize the inferior races."[5]

Would such views not influence the writing about Haiti and its legacy?

There is a power dynamic in the writing of history that cannot be denied, but one way it can be minimized is by an acknowledgment of the historian's potential biases or predilections in an effort to strike a balance between subjectivity and objectivity. For this reason, I initially discussed my own desire to know my origins in Africa and the West Indies. Another way that inherent power dynamics can be minimized is by seeking out multiple voices or points of view. This is a more democratic approach to history. Dependence on one set of views to the exclusion of others often leads to a one-sided view of history. This is why oral history or history from below is so important. The points of view of those who do not have access to conventional institutions are critical, but will never be heard if they are not sought out. Those not connected to the rich, the mighty, and the famous in history will not readily make our interview list unless we seek them out. The lion's voice does much to minimize the undue role of power in history. It is exactly for this reason that I sought to interview descendants of those sold on the auction block when preparing this book.

Contested Memories and Group Identity

One of the real stumbling blocks to remembering this past is its impact on individual and group identity. I find this to be the thorniest issue of all and admit to having no conclusive ideas as to how to overcome it but will put forward some potential solutions that can be considered. Memory scholar Paul Connerton, in his taxonomy "Seven Types of Forgetting," addressed the concept of "prescriptive forgetting,"[6] using the example of President Abraham Lincoln's speech at the end of the Civil War. Once the war was over, Lincoln made a decision not to gloat in victory. For the sake of the

Union, he suggested there were indeed no winners, for many lives on both sides had been lost. It was now up to both the North and the South to attempt to stitch together their fragile union. This kind of forgetting was state-sponsored. It was thought that there was a danger in remembering past wrongs that could have led to acts of revenge and retribution.

Unfortunately, Abraham Lincoln's speech did not have its intended consequence. It was not possible then or now to simply put the past behind him and behind the country and move forward. As said before, there was a cost in not dealing with the inhumanity of slavery and the fact that four million men, women, and children were left without adequate means to reconstruct their lives at the end of the war. They were like refugees after a brutal war, but there was no postwar Marshall Plan to help them build a new life; they were largely on their own. Some stayed close to home, as we have seen with some of the Butler slaves, for that was the only home they had ever known. But some others, also including Butler slaves, were on the move. As freedman Felix Haywood put it: "they seemed to want to get closer to freedom, so they'd know what it was – like it was a place or a city."[7]

While Lincoln did his best to handle what he saw as his political reality, the realities of the slaves on the ground had yet to be addressed. As Frederick Douglass said:

The nation, as a nation has sinned against the Negro. It robbed him of the rewards of his labor during more than two hundred years, and its repentance will not be genuine and complete till according to the measure of its ability, it shall have made restitution. It can never fully atone for the wrong done to the millions who have lived and died under the galling yoke of bondage, but it can, if it will, do justice and mercy to the living.[8]

Given his assassination in 1865, we will never know whether Lincoln would have tried to address the plight of former slaves more comprehensively. We do know that the lack of systematic attention to this population and how to permanently integrate them into American society had its cost. The most important stumbling block was the lack of public acknowledgment that slavery was a crime against humanity and, as such, there should be an atonement and then recompense.

But this very acknowledgment that it was a crime against humanity was by no means universally accepted. Black and White abolitionists on both sides of the Atlantic were very forthright and clear that it was. Lincoln himself, though initially ambivalent at the start of the war, was by the time of his drafting of the Emancipation Proclamation in 1862 ready to proclaim the slaves "forever free." But the South as a whole and even many Northerners who might have been sympathetic to the plight of slaves were not prepared to see slavery in such stark terms.[9]

After the war, they were not prepared to make an unequivocal statement that slavery was a wrong that had to be corrected. Instead, the North was ambivalent, and the South remained steadfast in its belief in the justness of its cause. When the elite ladies of Richmond, Virginia formed the group the Confederate Memorial Literary Society for the purpose of creating the Confederate Museum in 1896, they exemplified this thinking: "The Confederates were right, immortally right and that the conquerors were wrong, eternally wrong." The museum's founders further declared that the collection would demonstrate "striking object lessons ... of heroism and endurance."[10]

Such was the original mandate of the Confederate Museum: to be the preeminent repository of Lost Cause artifacts and in so doing make the case to the public of the rightness of the Confederate cause. Even now, panels in the museum emphasize that the Confederacy fought to preserve states' rights, not slavery as an institution. Furthermore, according to the museum's early documents, it was the South that fought to preserve the tenets of the American Revolution.[11]

In general, in the early decades of the museum's existence, slavery was portrayed as a benevolent institution; one that encouraged Christian values and preserved social order and stability. Slavery was not a central theme in the discussion and memory of the Confederacy. It was ancillary. And it was certainly not then or now categorically described as a crime against humanity. It is instead subordinate to what are thought to be higher and nobler themes of "military valor and sacrifice."[12] Such was the lack of the moral unpacking of the institution of slavery. This neglect had real costs, including the issue of contested memories. Whites and Blacks, North and South, remember this period in different ways.

How do some Southern Whites view the war today? For an answer to this question, scholars Lori Holyfield and Clifford Beachman's study of major Civil War memorials points out these differences: the changing landscape and the politics of memory. The Articles of Secession state clearly that a principle cause of war was the dispute over slavery.[13] From that institutional standpoint, the Confederacy did not hide its aims, yet since the end of the war and persistent in some circles, we see that a debate rages on.

Holyfield and Beachman show how this debate plays out at major National Park Service sites. With the exception of Chickamauga-Chatanooga, these sites have obscured the issue of slavery as a cause of the

Civil War and largely neglect to portray the extent of the service of Black soldiers. This is the case in spite of the 1999 Congressional mandate that slavery be discussed as a cause of the war in National Park Service sites. Some of those who work on these issues and are involved in the public portrayal of American history at these sites are still wary of this more inclusive approach. A number of the roughly eleven million visitors who come to these sites are even more uncomfortable with this approach if the petitions of some groups, including the Daughters of the Confederacy, are to be taken at face value.[14]

Still, change is occurring, and more is on its way. "Multivocal sites"– sites that tell a more inclusive history of Black and White participation in the war – are appearing with greater regularity. The creation of the African American Civil War memorial, as well as the New American Civil War Center in Richmond, are good examples. The latter aims to tell "three sides to the story" in order to "promote racial healing and a sense of shared national heritage." This includes identifying multiple causes for the war, including slavery, and illuminating the role of Black soldiers. These are positive developments yet we still do not have overwhelming consensus on the cause of the Civil War.[15]

How did the North view the war? Notwithstanding Lincoln's attempt at diplomacy in his Second Inaugural speech, Northerners were in some quarters blatantly triumphalist for a long time after the Civil War. This triumphalism also silenced the truth of their connection to the institution of slavery, as well as their ambivalent attitudes toward Blacks in general. Their early colonial experience with slavery, economic dependence on slave by-products to fuel Northern industries, and their promulgation of scientific racism in institutions of higher learning were simply left out of the historical record. As victors, they could profess to have long held noble aims of emancipation. They could pretend that had it not been for reluctant Southerners, they would have long abolished slavery across the nation and promoted the equality of the Black race. In reality, there were too many examples to the contrary not the least of these was the Northern creation of the American Colonization Society, whose sole purpose was to send American Blacks back to Africa.

And what about Blacks? What was and is their memory of the Civil War and its legacy? As we discussed in Chapter 7, many made their views known with their feet. When thousands of slaves walked off the Butler and other plantations and either joined Union lines or formed semi-autonomous communities like those on St. Simon's Island, they spoke volumes about what they understood to be the cause of the war. They did not need historians or public memorials to tell them what this war was about. They knew it was about their present and future status. As W. E. B. Dubois was to later to say in his seminal 1906 book, *The Souls of Black Folk*:

However much they who marched South and North in 1861 may have fixed on the technical points of union and local autonomy as a shibboleth, all nevertheless knew, as we know now, that the question of Negro slavery was the real cause of the conflict.[16]

Historian David Blight gives us a window into the Black response to the war for the first fifty years after its end. He notes that there were three distinct visions of Civil War memory: 1) reconciliationist vision, 2) white supremacist vision, and 3) emancipationist vision. African Americans tended strongly to favor the latter, whereas Whites in those sample fifty years after the war followed Lincoln's impulse to emphasize reunion and reconciliation.[17] This reconciliation often came at the expense of a focus on the continuing challenges that Blacks faced in the postwar period.

At the fiftieth anniversary of the war, the Governor of Virginia, W. Hodges, captured this sentiment well: "We are not here to discuss what caused the war of 1861–65, but to talk over the events of the battle here as man to man." This type of unity made "remembering safe."[18] This also helps to explain the great and persistent interest in reenactments of the various battles of the war. Such remembering tended effectively to silence the memory of slavery and emancipation toward which Blacks gravitated. Blacks during this period were critical of this omission of the cause and consequences of the war. At the same time, emancipation celebrations by Blacks took place in the context of the notion of progress as an upward march, or "up from slavery," as the formidable Black leader Booker T. Washington entitled his autobiography.

The twentieth anniversary of Emancipation Proclamation was a major cause for celebration in the Black community. On New Year's Day, January 1, 1883, a major banquet was held in honor of Frederick Douglass, to which important Black leaders were invited.[19] He was to repeat themes he had touched on for years; they were a people reborn, despite the persistence of numerous challenges.

Today, there are more varied responses in the Black community. As discussed, Watchnight services still take place across the country, particularly in the South. Others have chosen to focus more on Juneteenth celebrations that extend the period of emancipation. Juneteenth refers to June 19, 1865 – the day that slaves in Texas officially received news of their freedom. This was a full two-and-a-half years after Lincoln's Emancipation Proclamation. Many different reasons have been given for this delay, but since that time, a number of African Americans have been celebrating this day as Emancipation Day. It is a commemoration that is growing in popularity with its 150th anniversary having taken place in June, 2015, with Dr. Ronald Myers, a physician and preacher, at the forefront of the movement to promote Juneteenth as a national holiday.[20]

One thing that is apparent is that these issues are all connected to themes of group identity. As Holyfield and Beachman point out, the average visitor (in addition to schoolchildren on field trips) to the National Park sites that commemorate the Civil War is a White Southern male. Most come to trace the paths of their forebears in various battles and sites.[21] Given this fact, how should a White Southerner feel about an ancestor who fought for the Confederate cause? With the ever-changing environment of public memorials, some may experience what people of African descent and others have long since felt: a sense of a fragmented past, if not fragmented identity. That shift for some can be disquieting.

But is it possible to honor an ancestor's valor but disagree with that which gave rise to that valor? Or as scholars Robin Wagner-Pacifici and Barry Schwartz suggest, that we adhere to a platform that shifts the focus from causes to "commitments and sacrifices that would be considered heroic in the service of *other* ends."[22] Might it one day be possible to honor the service of one's Confederate ancestors while at the same time clearly acknowledge that, on the question of slavery, they were wrong? And while we cannot apologize for these acts, we can as a nation offer a solid apology upon which true reconciliation can be built. Today it appears that silence covers these issues perhaps out of a perceived sense of shame. "But unacknowledged shame interferes with the ability to experience reconciliation," explains Scheff, "it paralyses both the ability and desire to reach a compromise."[23] And finally, apology, "the most concentrated path to the repair of bonds, is not possible when shame is denied."[24]

As it turns out, Southern White males may be able to draw on an important resource as the terrain is shifting beneath them: Christianity. Many identify themselves as Christians and see themselves as connected to their Southern forebears by a strong Christian heritage. Often religion is cited as a divider (and it was certainly used as such during slavery), but, in this case, given the characteristics of this population, is it possible that Christianity could help to heal this history?

The theme of repentance for wrongdoing is at the heart of the Bible and Christian ideology. The Augustinian view holds that humans are not good; neither are they pure. Hence, Augustine's famous quote: "Lord makes me pure ... but not yet."[25] Repentance is a constant theme in Christianity and is said to be the beginning of true freedom. Could this heritage, thus perceived, aid in the acknowledgment of the wrongs of slavery and further aid in mending fences that a war that took 620,000 lives did not?

Other suggestions come from authors like philosopher, Linda Martin Alcoff, who as a product of a biracial union has been able to see both sides from a unique perspective. In her article, "What should white people do?" she talks about the invisibility of White privilege and tries to support those theorists, activists, and others who are trying to carve out a more positive way forward. She recommends tearing down the strict binaries of Black and White.

"Should we not move beyond race categories?" she asks. "I doubt that this can be done anytime soon. The weight of too much history is sedimented in these marked bodies with inscriptions that are very deep. Rather than attempting to erase these inscriptions as a first step, we need a period of reinscription to redescribe and reunderstand what we see when we see race." In the end, she proffers what she calls a White version of Dubois's famous "double consciousness." Dubois coined the term to refer to the dual identity that characterized Black life.

It is a peculiar sensation, this double-consciousness, this sense of always looking at one's self through the eyes of others, of measuring one's soul by the tape of a world that looks on in amused contempt and pity. One ever feels his two-ness, – an American, a Negro; two souls, two thoughts, two unreconciled strivings; two warring ideals in one dark body, whose dogged strength alone keeps it from being torn asunder.[26]

This would require a conscious acknowledgment of a dual historical legacy. On the one hand, there is the "persistent structures of inequality and exploitation," and on the other, there is a "newly awakened memory of the many white traitors to white privilege who have struggled to contribute to the building of an inclusive human community."[27]

These white "traitors" are indeed heroic. They include the Fanny Kembles of the world and her descendants: White college students who rode the buses in Freedom Summer and other civil rights activists who fought alongside Black students for the ideals of freedom and equality. These "traitors" to outmoded and mythical ideas of race are, in a word, heroes. A dual legacy with both positive and negative aspects is more representative of the truth. Furthermore, this dual approach allows for true liberation from old racial ideologies. As Booker T. Washington, said, "You can't hold a man down without staying down with him."[28]

Finally, this dual approach leans towards the positive because those positive examples of the past are great role models for the future. They open up the vast potential that is there for individuals and eventually institutions to change and to more accurately reflect America's ideals of freedom and equality.

Memory and Homelessness

Where is home? Is home a physical place or an idea? Is it the place you live now? Is it the home of your ancestors? Is it your adopted home? The history of the African Diaspora since the fifteenth-century European encounter with the African continent can be characterized in part as a history of displacement. The forced migration of Africans through the Atlantic slave trade to the Americas, the frequent and routine separations of families on the auction block, as well as the internal and external migrations after the end of slavery suggest a kind of rootlessness or homelessness that has been experienced by many in the Diaspora.

The auction block in particular represents this homelessness and displacement. But even in freedom, there was that sense of rootlessness. There has been a longing for home – a longing for a place of belonging. Beyond the notion of citizenship, there has been a search for that which is familiar and at the same time comforting and accepting.

That concept of home has meant different things to different people. Home, in the case of the Butler slaves and others after the war, was about people. It was about finding and recovering family members split apart on the auction block. For others in African American history, home has been about reconnecting to the African past in a very concrete way. It has been about the return to Liberia or Sierra Leone or pilgrimages in the modern day to the African continent. For still others, that pilgrimage was not physical but metaphysical. Literary movements like the Harlem Renaissance or Negritude movements of the early decades of the twentieth century created avenues for Blacks on both sides of the Atlantic to take pride in their history and to reconnect with the African continent on a philosophical level.

In these myriad ways of searching for home, there has been a strong search for identity. As historian Henry Weincek says in his book on George Washington:

The history of slavery is in large part the history of families; and the recovery of that history has become today most powerfully the work of white and black families trying to piece together their history and understand themselves.[29]

And in this sometimes painful process, there is hope. The hope is in the recovery of self and recovery of identity. This kind of recovery process need not be an attempt to romanticize the past or to live in the past. The past is dredged up neither to glorify some, nor to punish others. It is dredged up for the purpose of liberation from old racial ideologies. The challenge is to expose the roots of this history of inequality for the purpose of upending them and recreating new modes of thinking, new modes of behavior – in effect, new identities. In a word, the more we understand how we got here, the more we have the potential to overcome that past.

In a sea of forgetfulness, many of African descent have only had fragments of the past with which to work. There have been no convenient linear histories available to them. For the Butler slaves on the auction block and their descendants, the recovery process has been about piecing together this history like a patchwork quilt. It has been about preserving the memories of their ancestors and their language, food, music, and other folkways that were so greatly influenced by the African continent. But for them and others whose voices are often silenced in history, the recovery process also includes the creation of new memories in the present. It gives those who seek a foundation upon which to reinvent themselves – taking the good and the bad from the past and using it as a springboard. For those in this process, there is power even in the powerlessness of the past. There is power in knowledge of roots. There is power in the knowledge of ancestors' contributions to the global economy and world history. There is power in memory. Yet the recovery process for some, certainly for the Butler descendants and the residents of the Sea Islands, is not some distant or academic endeavor for they live and breathe African ancestral memories in the day-to-day expressions of their culture.

Reverend Griffin Lotson, resident of Darien County, and the other Commissioners of the Gullah-Geechee Cultural Heritage Corridor, are doing just that. Created by a Congressional Act of 2006, the Gullah-Geechee culture areas located in four states (Georgia, North Carolina, South Carolina, and Florida) are now designated as National Heritage areas. The Commission is actively bringing awareness to the area to ensure its cultural preservation and reconnecting people with roots in the region.

Memory, History, and Contemporary Relevance

The democratization of memory means giving equal time to the period of slavery and its legacy worldwide. Dealing with past issues with respect to race may help us to deal with current race matters in the United States and around the world. This history is also relevant to many contemporary issues, such as immigration and modern-day slavery.

Both sides of the political aisle say that America's immigration system is broken. But how do we address this brokenness and can the past give us any assistance in addressing these issues? First, it is important to acknowledge that today's immigrants – regardless of origin – owe a great deal to the Black American struggle for freedom and equality. That struggle culminated in the major milestones of the 1950s and 1960s on which important immigration legislation was built.

The 1965 Immigration Act, which opened the floodgates to immigrants from Asia, Africa, and the Caribbean, to name but a few populations, came on the heels of the groundbreaking 1964 Civil Rights Act fought for by the Reverend Dr. Martin Luther King Jr. and his coalition. In this way, all subsequent immigrant populations have been able to benefit from a struggle centuries old and not of their making. This struggle for freedom did not begin in the 1950s and 1960s. It began when the first African was kidnapped off the African coast. Resistance in the period of slavery soon followed, and it is this legacy that is the foundation of all the great legislative accomplishments of the civil rights movement, from which many immigrant populations now benefit.

So immigrants like myself may have a great debt to pay to the Black American struggle. This fact alone might help to address racial and ethnic fissures as well as build coalitions around common causes. But other issues remain, such as assimilation. "There are so many people with one foot in this country and one foot in another country," an interviewee told Charlie Rose on his show of July 2, 2014. This is a condition and circumstance that African-descended peoples in America and elsewhere know well.

How do immigrant populations move between their two worlds? The African American past and the gift of resilience of Black families in the present may be instructive or at least important to note. For white Americans, many of whom are the product of previous mass migrations to the United States, this history may help them to look at the current immigration crisis as part of an evolving American saga. Knee-jerk xenophobic responses to immigration may give way to more thoughtful reactions to history in the making. This is not to say that all who have strong opinions about immigration, particularly immigration from Mexico and Central America, are expressing racist views because the issues are not always about race. On the same Charlie Rose program, a Southern White male named Doug stood on his porch looking wistfully at the American flag perched above: "People's loyalties will change," he lamented. Doug seemed to believe the unproven notion that immigrants may be less loyal to America since they were born elsewhere.[30]

But what if Doug and others like him shared the view of American history developed in this book and realized that it was never only Black and White? American history is made and experienced by those that migrate to, live in, and migrate out of its borders and eras. With the benefit of distance and memory, we can hopefully embrace our shared history – a history of linked fates. We cannot change the past, but when confronted with similar issues of integration, we can choose to take advantage of lessons learned.

Memory and the Gift of Resilience

We have seen in the retelling of the Butler auction how family life was a casualty of slavery for Black and White alike. Family life has been a motif throughout this book. On a micro level, we have seen the brave attempts of Black families to stay together and to restore their ties in spite of a history of displacement, loss, and dislocation caused by the auction block in particular and slavery in general. Other books about the African Diaspora have made the point directly or indirectly that the history of African-descended peoples since the advent of the Atlantic slave trade is a history of migrations.[31] Even in freedom and sometimes especially in freedom, Blacks were on the move, best exemplified by the masses of Black American Southerners who moved north in the first few decades of the twentieth century during the Great Migration in search of freedom and better opportunities. Caribbean populations also have experienced this phenomenon. Jamaicans, for example, have not only a history of migrating to the US, Canada, and Britain, but also to Panama, Cuba, and elsewhere in the region. Maintaining family ties then was not just a challenge during slavery but also in freedom.

The story of the men, women, and babies sold on the auction block in 1859 and their descendants is a testament to how far these Black families have been willing to go to maintain their family ties. In the face of this history, there is no death knell on Black families. They face great challenges today, but have endured much worse and survived. If they have a gift that has seen them through this fraught and fractured history, it is the gift of resilience.

As we saw in the previous chapter, the Butler slave descendants and many other Black families have drawn increasingly on reunions to reestablish and maintain bonds. "They are empowering; they symbolize the resilience of our families and the black family," said Dr. Jacqueline Copeland-Carson and her cousin, Ms. Antoinette Stanley, when I interviewed them about Black family reunions. The women hail from the Gullah-Geechee region and have staged multiple reunions since 1984. "I like to know what people are doing," said Antoinette. "It has been a great learning experience and a way to encourage each other."[32]

Both Jacqueline and Antoinette have lived in Philadelphia, New Jersey, and California but their family calls Allendale, South Carolina home. At their first reunion in Allendale, they went to the church that their family helped start in the 1800s and shared a meal with relatives still living in the area. This was the high point of their trip to see what their family had built in the face of tremendous odds. But they also saw the other side in their visit to the Aiken plantation, which, like a number of similar sites in the South, now holds tours. "For some of the older folk, it was emotionally difficult," said Jackie, but at the same time there was this sense that they had come full-circle and come out of this experience whole. It was an experience that they could now impart to the youngest in the family while also sharing it with the oldest members.[33]

For Jackie, it was particularly bittersweet. An anthropologist with a Ph.D. from the University of Pennsylvania, she is an embodiment of what her grandmother, born and bred in the Low Country, wanted her to be. Her grandmother, Grandma Aiken, spoke the Gullah language and so had the strongest connection to their African forebears. But she was born in an era where it was not typical to be proud of Gullah heritage. Still, she passed onto her granddaughter and other relatives such wisdom that that granddaughter could give voice to her life and countless other previously invisible voices in her work as an anthropologist. That granddaughter could do her part of democratizing memory – starting with her very own family and heritage.[34]

In spite of seemingly endless challenges, Black families have a strain of resilience and enduring power that a sea of statistics on obstacles to their strength cannot erase. The Black family reunions bear out this resilience; not only are they growing in numbers but many families are also professionalizing the process. They record the reunions for history and form organizations akin to NGOs complete with by-laws and subcommittees to work on every aspect of the reunion. They wear their family name on brightly emblazoned tee shirts with pride, telling the world in their small way that many Black families are alive and well and here to stay.

Memory and Science

In the first chapter, I mentioned the fact that new and pioneering DNA research can aid people in the African Diaspora in restoring links to their African past. It also reveals how linked they are to other groups around the world. In fact, where the history is silent, the field of genetics is not. Many African American and Caribbean communities, for example, share DNA with Europeans and other groups. There seems to be little question about the linked fate of these groups genetically, and hopefully, as we have shown here, historically.

But science has even more to offer in the field of history and memory. My conversations with Jamaican neuroscientist Dr. Yasmin Hurd revealed that the fields of psychology, psychiatry, and neuroscience can potentially open up new and exciting avenues to explore. These fields may provide answers to some of our most challenging questions. One of the key questions is whether historical trauma can be inherited, or as scholar Nathan Kellerman asks in his article, "Can Nightmares be Inherited?" Or, put a bit differently: if historical traumas can be inherited, how can they be healed? Breaking the silence on historical trauma is not just an end in and of itself, it is a catalyst for recovery and change. Both psychologists and neuroscientists have found research on Holocaust survivors and their descendants as well as on animals illuminating. Comparative work has yet to be done on African-descended peoples of the Diaspora, but it would be a good follow-up to this book.[35]

Kellerman asks: "How can a repressed memory be passed from one person to another? Can a child really 'inherit' the unconscious mind of a parent? Is it possible for a child to remember what a parent has forgotten?" Scientists are interested in hard data such as an MRI scan or a blood specimen that could show just that.[36] Neuroscientist Dr. Hurd, for example, is confident that this breakthrough may be around the corner as animal studies on the epigenetic memory of rats show that there are changes in their brains and the brains of their children when subjected to intense stress.

In the case of Holocaust survivors and their descendants, psychologist Felix De Mendelssohn has already determined that such transmission does take place.

"The central point of these formulations is that traumatic experiences of the one generation can be transmitted *unconsciously* to the second, and often third generation in some fashion, such that these children and grandchildren find themselves living out in their private and professional lives certain aspects of the original trauma in a way that they cannot recognize or understand because the origins are *hidden*. (Author emphasis.)[37]

The origins are often hidden because the silence of the first generation becomes like an undetected tumor quietly causing damage and injury.

Mendelssohn's family history is a case in point. According to his mother, a Jewish native of Germany, the family fled Germany in the 1930s ostensibly because of intellectual differences with the Nazi government, not out of fear they would be exterminated in Hitler's death camps. It was only decades later upon his mother's death that Mendelssohn learned through perusal of her private papers that her grandmother had indeed been sent to the concentration camp Terezin and killed there. He had never been told about her death and how she died. There was, as is the case with many families who have experienced historical trauma, a blanket of silence about this pivotal and tragic event in their family history. The Holocaust was real, but it was something that happened to other people, not their family. Yet this was not true. Now Mendelssohn had to grapple with this important discovery as well as how he himself had previously disassociated himself from Jews, Judaism, and Jewish causes.[38]

The psychologist asks: what is the role of environmental factors in the inheritance of trauma? The neuroscientist asks: What is the role of genetics? Is there a way to map historical trauma on the brains of the descendants of relatives that have suffered trauma? Finally, what is the way forward to heal such trauma? Studies on rats by researchers Fabiola Zucchi, Youli Yao, and Gerlinde Metz, and others reveal that future generations inherit certain environmental stresses akin to historical trauma, demonstrating that transgenerational stress is real, and it manifests itself in identifiable physical ways.[39]

Science and the Road to Recovery

Science may have valuable lessons to share with the fields of social science, particularly in the search for healing and recovery. Much work remains to be done, but what has been done is very exciting. Multiple animal and human studies show that life experience can modify these stress imprints and thus reduce the risks for disease. As Zucchi, Yao, and Metz confirm: "Positive experiences such as education, physical activity, and social environment can ameliorate maladaptive programming and disease vulnerability."[40] As such, enriched environments have been shown to reverse the negative effects of inherited stress.

Studies have also shown that, in a number of cases, there is a silver lining to this historical and physically encoded stress. Hurd's "improved coping skills," which I call the "gift of resilience," are present in future generations. Again, much more work needs to be done here, particularly with African-descended populations in the Diaspora, to see what factors are present that encourage and bring about resilience in some and not in others. Hurd's take on this literature and its application to African Americans and others who share the legacy of slavery is that it is quite possible that those who do not "make it" – as in they do not succeed by society's standards – are in a fight or flight mode. Dropping out in a perceived adverse environment may be a survival mechanism learned by way of environmental and genetic mechanisms. This promising research may have real applications to questions in the social sciences and may also influence public policy that attempts to heal the wounds of the past.[41]

To recap, we have seven types of remembering:

1) Memory, Silence, and its Companion, Denial;
2) Memory and Power;
3) Contested Memories and Group Identities;
4) Memory and Homelessness;
5) Memory, History, and Contemporary Relevance;
6) Memory and the Gift of Resilience; and
7) Memory and Science.

Yet questions remain. Does memory matter? If yes, why does it matter? In a word, if racial reconciliation matters, then memory matters. If honoring your dead matters, then memory matters. If the voices of the past can empower those in the present, then memory matters.

Memory Matters

Memory matters because, as Civil War historian James McPherson says: "the war is still with us." It is not only the great academic works that have looked at the War from every angle that demonstrate this continued interest, it is also the Lincoln Associations, the Civil War Round Tables, and the hundreds of reenactors who meet regularly throughout the year to reenact battle scenes of bygone days.[42] In short, memory matters because the past is hardly past, as Faulkner would say. It lingers around the contours of our minds and hearts as any unresolved issue tends to do.

And unresolved it remains, according to historians Lois Horton and the late James Horton. From the earliest days of the establishment of American colonies, the following may be said to have been true:

> Slavery provided a racial floor below which no white person could fall. All whites regardless of social and economic standing, were encouraged to feel a common racial bond. Each had a vital interest in maintaining an orderly society that could control the slaves. Under these circumstances, the rich seemed to have less to fear from unruly masses at the bottom of white society so long as the presence of black slavery emphasized their common commitment to white supremacy.[43]

Racial slavery, then, is at the core of the American experience and its legacy looms large, or, as historian Ira Berlin asserts, "slavery is the ground zero of race relations."[44] There is no getting around it or avoiding it. Although there has been much progress, the dream of a post-racial society is just that: a dream. Ironically, it may in fact be the deepest desire of many in American society, but we still have a long way to go. Memory matters because without it we are left with a shadowy lens of the past, which is a dangerous obstacle to racial reconciliation. As the Gullah proverb reminds us: "Mustekcyear a de root fa heal de tree." (You need to take care of the root in order to heal the tree.) Ultimately, memory matters because racial reconciliation matters.

Memory also matters because west and central African societies – the origin of most slave populations in the Americas – had and still have a great reverence for the sacred. Honoring the dead is not taken lightly. The original slave burial ground on the Butler estate in Darien has almost washed away because of the gradual erosion of the banks of the Altamaha River. On a boat tour given by a descendant of the Butler estates, Tiffany Young, who we met in Chapter 9, one can still see the faded wooden markers sticking out of the water representing graves of those who worked and built that estate. With our new understandings of equality and freedom, how do we honor in death those who were not honored in life? Can we honor them today as their ancestors would have wanted?

As descendants of these and the other former estates in the Low Country region seek to honor their dead, so too they honor the living. Memory is not just past; it is also the present. It keeps alive the sparks of the past, and in this case, helps to give voice to the living. Gullah-Geechee communities are rediscovering their voices as the preservation commission they advocated for has been established on the federal level. But they are also participating in a number of other organizations committed to cultural and land preservation. From the historic Penn Center in South Carolina to the St. Simon's African American Heritage Coalition and the Sapelo Island Cultural and Revitalization Society, Gullah-Geechee residents of the Low Country are making themselves heard. They are coming out of the shadows of history and telling their vitally important stories.[45]

Like the rest of the local White population, in addition to some farming and fishing, they are involved in a variety of fields. Ultimately, according to a National Park Service study, they seek to "adapt and thrive in the 21st century in new ways, but without exploitation, without gentrification or commodification and without the intrusion of a New Plantation economy."[46] They are honoring the rich heritage of their ancestors and sharing this heritage with the world, or as the Darien Ring Shouters, the local musical group including descendants of the Butler plantation that we learned about in Chapter 6, say after a stirring retelling of the Weeping Time auction: "Hatred is not what we teach. Heritage is what we preach." In the end, that is why memory matters. Implicit in these words is a call for much-needed healing.

Recovery and the Democratization of Memory

The Weeping Time auction not only represented a breach in the family lineages of those people of color who were sold on the auction block, but a breach in world history. For there was a time when peoples of the world did not see themselves in terms of race. Ethnic groups, language groups, or the physical boundaries of their communities or nations, yes, but not by race. The poisonous codification of race and its amplification during the era of the transatlantic slave trade and slavery created a significant breach in our understanding of ourselves and our potential links to one another.[47] The next 500 years since the abolition in the nineteenth century could be about recovery and restoration of that breach.

That restoration depends in significant part on the democratization of memory: the acknowledging of all voices in history and breaking the silence of those voices previously muted or unheard. It may then be possible for more of us to live lives informed by the past but not burdened by it. It may also be possible for us to live lives more conscious of our linked past, present, and future and more committed to the ideals of freedom we hold dear.

THE END

Notes

1   A notable exception was the United Nations Presentation "Forever Free," in observance of the International Day of Remembrance of the Victims of Slavery and the Transatlantic Slave trade, March 18, 2013, webtv.un.org/meetings-events/watch/forever-free:-celebrating-emancipation-dpingo-briefing/2235556987001, accessed October 29, 2016.

2   As noted previously in Littlefield, *Rice and Slaves,* and Judith Carney, *Black Rice,* and Charles Joyner, *Down by the Riverside: A South Carolina Slave Community.*

3   Cynthia Wroclawski, "Death did not kill their names: Yad Vashem's quest to identify Holocaust victims," *Haaretz,* April 8, 2013, www.haaretz.com/opinion/death-did-not-kill-their-names-yad-vashem-s-quest-to-identify-holocaust-victims.premium-1.514204, accessed September 26, 2016.

4   Michel-Rolph Trouillot, *Silencing the Past: Power and the Production of History* (Boston: Beacon Press, 1995).

5   "Modern History Sourcebook: Jules Ferry (1832–1893) On French Colonial Expansion," Fordham University, www.fordham.edu/halsall/mod/1884ferry.asp, accessed February 24, 2017.

6   Paul Connerton, "Seven Types of Forgetting," *Memory Studies,* Sage Publications, 2008; 1:59, Accessed online October 4, 2016 http:mss.sagepub.com/cgi/content/abstract/1/1/59, p. 61– 65.

7   Diouf, *Dreams of Alabama,* p. 128.

8   Ibid., p. 202.

9   See Eric Foner, *The Fiery Trial: Abraham Lincoln and American Slavery* (New York: W.W. Norton and Co., 2010) for more.

10 *The Confederate Museum Yearbook,* 1912, in Reiko Hilyer, "Relics of Reconciliation: The Confederate Museum and Civil War Memory in the New South," *The Public Historian,* Vol. 33, No. 4 (November 2011) p. 43.

11 Ibid., p. 17.

12 Ibid., p. 4.

13 "Articles of Secession," http://avalon.law.yale.edu/19th_century/csa_scarsec.asp, accessed October 29, 2016.

14 Lori Holyfield and Clifford Beacham, "Memory Brokers, Shameful Pasts and Civil War Commemoration," *Journal of Black Studies,* Vol. 42 no. 3 (2011 04 01): pp. 436–456.

15 Ibid., p. 451.

16 Dubois, *Souls of Black Folk,* p. 15.

17 David Blight, *Race and Reunion: The Civil War in American memory* (Cambridge, MA: Belknap Press of Harvard University Press, 2001) p. 2.

18 Ibid., p. 3.

19 Ibid., p. 303.

20 "National Juneteenth Observance Foundation," http://www.nationaljune teenth.com/Founder.html, accessed September 26, 2016.

21 Holyfield and Beachman, p. 444.

22 Ibid., p. 440

23 T. J. Scheff, *Bloody Revenge: Emotions, Nationalism and War* (Boulder: Westview, 1994) pp. 54 and 113 in Holyfield and Beachman, p. 452.

24 Ibid.

25 *The Confessions of St. Augustine* (London: Sheed & Ward, 1984, 1944).

26 W. E. B. Dubois, "Of our Spiritual Strivings," *The Souls of Black Folk, Chapter 1.*

27 Linda Martin Alcoff, "*History is A Weapon: What should White people do,*" www.historyisaweapon.com/defcon1/alcoffwhitepeople.html, accessed October 29, 2016.

28 Booker T. Washington, as quoted in George Seldes, ed., *The Great Quotations,* (New York: Pocket Books, 1972) p. 641.

29 Henry Wiencek, *An Imperfect God: George Washington, His Slaves and the Creation of America* (New York: Farrar, Straus and Giroux, 2003) p. 281.

30 Charlie Rose program on Immigration, July 2, 2014.

31 See Ira Berlin, *The Making of African America: The Four Great Migrations* (New York: Viking, 2010), and Isabel Wilkerson, *The Warmth of Other Suns: The Epic Story of America's Great Migration* (New York: Random House, 2010).

32 Interview with Dr. Jacqueline Copeland Carson and Antoinette Stanley.

33 Ibid.

34 http://books.google.com.jm/books?id=Dzm15gG7NUwC&pg=PR9&lpg= PR9&vq=preface&dq=creating+africa+in+america&output=html_text& redir_esc=y, accessed September 26, 2016.

35 Interviews with Dr. Yasmin Hurd and Nathan Kellerman, "Epigenetic Transmission of Holocaust Trauma: Can Nightmares be Inherited," *Israel Journal of Psychiatry and Related sciences,* the official publication of the Israel Psychiatric Association, Vol. 50, No. 1 (2013), pp. 33–37.

36 Ibid., p. 33.

37 Felix de Mendelssohn, "Transfer, Transmission of Trauma: Guilt, Shame and the Heroic Dilemma," *International Journal of Group Psychotherapy*, Vol. 58 no. 3 (2008), p. 390.

38 Ibid., pp. 394–395.

39 Fabiola C. R. Zucchi, Youli Yao and Gerlinde A. Metz, "The Secret Language of Destiny: Stress Imprinting and Transgenerational Origins of Disease," *Frontiers in Genetics* Vol. 3 (June, 2012), Article 96.

40 Wirdefeldt et al. 2005, Carlson et al. 2008, James et al. 2011, in Zucchi, Yao, and Metz, p. 6.

41 Interview with Dr. Yasmin Hurd.

42 McPherson, *Battle Cry of Freedom*, pp. viii–ix.

43 James O. Horton and Lois E. Horton, *Slavery and Public History: The tough stuff of American History* (New York: New Press, 2006) p. 5. See also Edmund Morgan, *American Slavery American Freedom* (New York: Norton, 1975).

44 Ira Berlin in Horton, p. 13

45 See also Ron and Natalie Daise's TV show, "Gullah Gullah Island," and Cornelia Baker, *God, Dr. Buzzard and the Boleto Man* (New York: Anchor Books, 2000).

46 Pinsky 1983, 1992 in National Park Service book.

47 See also Stephen Jay Gould, *The Mismeasure of Man* (New York: Norton, 1981.)

Appendix

Butler Descendants of Slaves Bram & Joan Butler

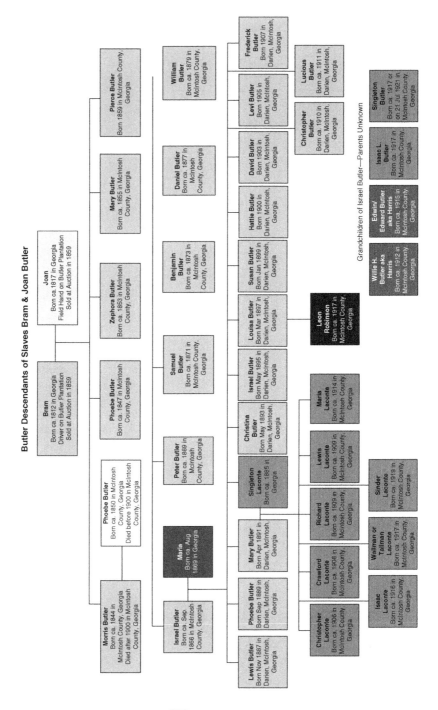

Genealogical chart.

Top level:
- Bram — Born ca. 1812 in Georgia, Driver on Butler Plantation, Sold at Auction in 1859
- Joan — Born ca. 1817 in Georgia, Field Hand on Butler Plantation, Sold at Auction in 1859

Children of Bram & Joan:
- Phoebe Butler — Born ca. 1850 in McIntosh County, Georgia, Died before 1900 in McIntosh County, Georgia
- Phoebe Butler — Born ca. 1847 in McIntosh County, Georgia
- Zephora Butler — Born ca. 1850 in McIntosh County, Georgia
- Mary Butler — Born ca. 1855 in McIntosh County, Georgia
- Pierce Butler — Born ca. 1859 in McIntosh County, Georgia

- Morris Butler — Born ca. 1844 in McIntosh County, Georgia, Died after 1900 in McIntosh County, Georgia
- Peter Butler — Born ca. 1869 in McIntosh County, Georgia
- Samuel Butler — Born ca. 1871 in McIntosh County, Georgia
- Benjamin Butler — Born ca. 1873 in McIntosh County, Georgia
- William Butler — Born ca. 1879 in McIntosh County, Georgia
- Daniel Butler — Born ca. 1877 in McIntosh County, Georgia

Descendants:
- Israel Butler — Born ca. Sep. 1866 in McIntosh County, Georgia
- Maria — Born ca. Aug. 1869 in Georgia
- Lewis Butler — Born Nov 1887 in Darien, McIntosh, Georgia
- Phoebe Butler — Born Sep 1889 in Darien, McIntosh, Georgia
- Mary Butler — Born Apr 1891 in Darien, McIntosh, Georgia
- Christina Butler — Born May 1893 in Darien, McIntosh, Georgia
- Israel Butler — Born May 1895 in Darien, McIntosh, Georgia
- Louisa Butler — Born Mar 1897 in Darien, McIntosh, Georgia
- Susan Butler — Born Jan 1899 in Darien, McIntosh, Georgia
- Hattie Butler — Born 1900 in Darien, McIntosh, Georgia
- David Butler — Born 1903 in Darien, McIntosh, Georgia
- Levi Butler — Born 1905 in Darien, McIntosh, Georgia
- Frederick Butler — Born 1907 in Darien, McIntosh, Georgia
- Christopher Butler — Born ca. 1910 in Darien, McIntosh, Georgia
- Lucious Butler — Born ca. 1911 in Darien, McIntosh, Georgia

- Singleton Laconte — Born ca. 1885 in Georgia
- Christopher Laconte — Born ca. 1906 in McIntosh County, Georgia
- Crawford Laconte — Born ca. 1908 in McIntosh County, Georgia
- Richard Laconte — Born ca. 1909 in McIntosh County, Georgia
- Lewis Laconte — Born ca. 1909 in McIntosh County, Georgia
- Maria Laconte — Born ca. 1914 in McIntosh County, Georgia
- Isaac Laconte — Born ca. 1916 in McIntosh County, Georgia
- Wallman or Tallman Laconte — Born ca. 1917 in McIntosh County, Georgia
- Sinder Laconte — Born ca. 1919 in McIntosh County, Georgia
- Leon Robinson — Born ca. 1917 in McIntosh County, Georgia

Grandchildren of Israel Butler—Parents Unknown:
- Willie H. Butler aka Harris — Born ca. 1912 in McIntosh County, Georgia
- Edwin/Edward Butler aka Harris — Born ca. 1915 in McIntosh County, Georgia
- Isaac L. Butler — Born ca. 1917 in McIntosh County, Georgia
- Singleton Butler — Born ca. 1917 or on 21 Jul 1921 in McIntosh County, Georgia

Grandchildren of Israel Butler—Parents Unknown

A Note on Sources and Bibliography

African American history in this period, as I say in the beginning of the book, is a patchwork quilt, with some pieces clearly missing from the known historical record. This history is at once intriguing and frustrating because of the paucity of sources from the enslaved themselves. As such, this has been the story of the Butler slaves before, during, and after the auction event of 1859, as sources permit.

There were several leads that I followed with great enthusiasm and effort, which then led ... nowhere. For example, I found a short written contemporary account that seemed to suggest that one owner bought almost half of the slaves on auction! He was reportedly from Vicksburg, Mississippi. I did as much tracking as I could do but, to date, have not found a record of this possible slaveowner (who might have been an agent, not an owner) or the slaves he supposedly bought. So, in the end, I had to work with the individual stories of descendants as well as other important primary sources like the diaries or journals of some of the Butler family members.

I am thankful, however, for being able to find fifteen percent of the slaves in the records after the auction, detailing the trends and patterns of their lives in Chapter 9. Altogether, ten families and fifty men, women, and children from the original 436 on the auction catalogue have been found in the historical record. Census records and Freedman's Bank records were critical to telling this part of the story. In the end, however, this story could not have been told without multiple visits to Savannah, Darien, Butler, and St. Simon's Island, as well as visits to significant public history sites around the country over a ten-year period. These include visits to George Washington's Mt. Vernon estate as well as to Colonial Williamsburg, trips that were both educational and inspiring.

I do hope to continue to pursue this research and suspect that other records may turn up or that other scholars may join me in building on this work. As we have already discussed, a number of the descendants, like ace investigative sleuths, are continuing to do some excellent work identifying their ancestors. This work, when properly crosschecked with other sources, will add greatly to the telling of the Weeping Time event and beyond.

Archival Sources

Library of Congress
Georgia Slave Narratives and selective narratives from other Southern states, *Born into Slavery: Slave Narratives from the Federal Writers' Project 1936–38.*

National Archives
United States Department of Commerce. Bureau of the Census; Census Records for the following years: 1870, 1880, 1900, 1910, 1920

Freedman's Bank Records
The United States Colored Troops
The Civil War Pension Application Files
Freedom and Southern Society Project

Yale University Avalon Project
Secession Acts of the Thirteen Confederate States
Burial Records, Darien Cemetery
Chatham County Superior Court House records, Savannah, Georgia
Georgia Historical Society Savannah newspapers

Historical Society of Pennsylvania
The Auction Catalogue
Cadwalader papers
Wister family collection
Butler Plantation Papers, 1744–1822

Other Primary Sources

Butler Leigh, Frances. *Ten Years on a Georgia Plantation Since the War*. London: Richard Bentley and Son, 1883.

Butler, Pierce. *Mr. Butler's Statement*. Philadelphia: JC Clark, 1851.

Dubois, Sylvia. *A Biography of Sylvia Dubois, the Slave Who Whipt Her Mistress and Ganed Her Freedom* (1883). Edited by C. W. Larison and Jared C. Lobdell. New York: Oxford University Press, 1988.

Haley, James T. *Afro American Encyclopedia; Or the Thoughts, Doings, and Sayings of the Race, Embracing Lectures, Biographical Skeches ... and Women*. Nashville: Haley and Florica, 1895.

Kemble, Fanny. *Journal of a Residence on a Georgia Plantation 1838–39*. Athens: University of Georgia Press, 1863.

King, Roswell. "On the Management of the Butler Estate," *Southern Agriculturalist* (December 1828).

Legacies of British Slave Ownership project, www.ucl.ac.uk/lbs/project/.

Moynihan, Daniel Patrick. "The Negro Family: The Case for National Action." 1965. Office of Policy Planning and Research, US Department of Labor.

Taylor, Susie King. *Reminiscences of My Life in Camp: An African American Woman's Civil War Memoir*. New York: Arno Press, New York Times, 1968.

Thomson, Mortimer. "What Became of the Slaves on a Georgia Plantation," *African American Perspectives: Pamphlets from Daniel A. P. Murray Collection* (1818–1907), Library of Congress.

Wainwright, Nicholas B., ed., *A Philadelphia Perspective: The Diary of Sidney George Fisher Covering the Years, 1834–1871*. Philadelphia: Historical Society of Pennsylvania, 1967.

Secondary Sources

Books and Articles

Acs, Gregory, Kenneth Braswell, and Elaine Sorensen. *Moynihan Report Revisited*. Washington, DC: Urban Institute, June 13, 2013.

Araujo, Ana Lucia. *Public Memory of Slavery: Victims and Perpetrators in the South Atlantic*. Amherst, NY: Cambria Press, 2010.

Armstrong, Julie Buckner, Susan Hult Edwards, Houston Bryan Roberson, and Rhonda Y. Williams. *Teaching the American Civil Rights movement: Freedom's Bittersweet Song*. London: Routledge, 2002.

Augustine, Bishop of St. Hippo. *The Confessions of St. Augustine*. London: Sheed & Ward, 1984, 1944.

Bacon, Margaret Hope. *The Quiet Rebels: The Story of the Quakers in America*. New York: Basic Books, 1969.

Bailey, Anne. *African Voices of the Atlantic Slave Trade*. Boston: Beacon Press, 2005.

Ball, Edward. *Slaves in the Family*. New York: Ballantine Books, 1998.

Baptist, Edward E. *The Half Has Never Been Told: Slavery and the Making of American Capitalism*. New York: Basic Books, 2014.

Baptist, Edward E. and Stephanie Camp. *New Studies in the History of American Slavery*. Athens, GA: University of Georgia Press, 2006.

Bahadur, Gaiutra. *Coolie Woman, The Odyssey of Indenture*. Chicago: University of Chicago Press, 2014.

Bancroft, Frederic. *Slave Trading in the Old South*. New York: Frederick Ungar Publishing, 1959.

Bell, Malcolm. *Major Butler's Legacy: Five Generations of a Slaveowning family.* Athens, GA: University of Georgia Press, 1987.

Beckert, Sven and Seth Rothman eds. *Slavery's Capitalism: A New History of American Economic Development.* Philadelphia: University of Pennsylvania Press, 2017.

Beckles, Hilary and Verene Shepherd. *Caribbean Freedom: Economy and Society from Emancipation to the Present.* Princeton, NJ: Markus Wiener Publishers, 1996.

Berlin, Ira. *The Making of African America: The Four Great Migrations.* New York: Viking, 2010.

Berry, Diana Ramey. *The Price of Their Pound of Flesh: The Value of the Enslaved from Womb to Grave in the Building of the Nation.* Boston: Beacon Press, 2017.

Berry, Mary Frances. *The Long Memory: The Black Experience in America* (1982).

 My Face Is Black Is True: Callie House and the Struggle for Ex-Slave Reparations. New York: Vintage Books, 2009.

Blassingame, John. *The Slave Community: Plantation Life in the Antebellum South.* New York: Oxford University Press, 1979.

Blight, David. *Race and Reunion.* Cambridge, MA: Belknap Press of Harvard University Press, 2001.

 Beyond the Battlefield: Race, Memory and the American Civil War. Amherst: University of Massachusetts Press, 2002.

 Frederick Douglass' Civil War: Keeping Faith in Jubilee. Baton Rouge, LA: Louisiana State University Press, 1989.

Boney, F. N. *Rebel Georgia.* Macon, GA: Mercer University Press, 1997.

Bordin, Elisa and Anna Scacchi. *Transatlantic memories of the Slavery: Reimagining the Past, Changing the Future.* New York: Cambria Press, 2015.

Carney, Judith. *Black Rice.* Cambridge: Harvard University Press, 2001.

 "Rice Milling, Gender and Slave Labour in Colonial South Carolina," *Past & Present*, No. 153 (1996).

Chireau, Yvonee P. *Black Magic: Religion and the African American Conjuring Tradition.* Berkeley, CA: University of California Press, 2003.

Clinton, Catherine. *Harriet Tubman: The Road to Freedom.* Boston, MA: Little, Brown, 2004.

 Tara Revisited: Women War and the Plantation Legend. New York: Abbeville Press, 1997.

 Fanny Kemble's Civil Wars. New York: Simon and Schuster, 2000.

Coates, Ta-Nehisi. "The Case for Reparations," *The Atlantic Monthly* (June 2014).

Connerton, Paul. "Seven Types of Forgetting," *Memory Studies* (2008), Sage Publications. Accessed October 4, 2016, http:mss.sagepub.com/cgi/content/abstract/1/1/59.

Cross, Wilbur. *Gullah Culture in America.* Winston–Salem: John F. Blair Publisher, 2012.

David, James Corbett. *Dunmore's New World: The Extraordinary Life of a Royal Governor in Revolutionary America.* Charlottesville, VA: University of Virginia Press, 2013.

Davidson, Basil. *African Civilization Revisited*. Trenton, NJ: Africa World Press, 1991.

DeGraft-Hanson, Kwesi. "Unearthing the Weeping Time: Savannah's Ten Broeck Race Course and 1859 Slave Sale," *Southern Spaces* (2010).

de Mendelssohn, Felix. "Transfer, Transmission of Trauma: Guilt, Shame and the Heroic Dilemma," *International Journal of Group Psychotherapy*, Vol. 58, No. 3 (2008).

Diouf, Sylviane. *Dreams of Africa in Alabama: The Slave Ship Clotilda and the story of the Last Africans brought to America*. New York: Oxford University Press, 2007.

Dusinberre, William. *Them Dark Days: Slavery in the American Rice Swamps*. New York: Oxford University Press, 1996.

Farrand, Max. *The Framing of the Constitution*. New Haven, CT: Yale University Press, 1913.

Faust, Drew Gilpin. *This Republic of Suffering: Death and Dying and the American Civil War*. New York: Knopf, 2008.

Fields, Edda. *Deep Roots: Rice Farmers in West Africa and in the African Diaspora*. Bloomington, IN: Indiana University Press, 2008.

Foner, Eric. *Forever Free: The Story of Emancipation and Reconstruction*. New York: Penguin Random House, 2005.

 Voices of Freedom: A Documentary History. New York: W.W. Norton and Co., 2005.

 The Fiery Trial: Abraham Lincoln and American Slavery. New York: W.W. Norton and Co., 2010.

 Gateway to Freedom: The Hidden History of the Underground Railroad. New York: W.W. Norton and Co., 2015.

Foster, Thomas A. "The Sexual Abuse of Black Men under slavery," *Journal of the History of Sexuality*, Vol. 20, No. 3, web (September 3, 2011): 445–464.

Fox-Genovese, Elizabeth. *Within the Plantation Household: Black and White Women of the Old South*. Chapel Hill, NC: UNC Press, 1998.

Franklin, John Hope. *The Militant South 1800–1861*. Cambridge: Harvard University Press, 1956.

Fraser, Walter. *Savannah in the Old South*. Athens, GA: University of Georgia Press, 2003.

Frazier, Franklin E. *The Negro Family in the United States*. Chicago: University of Chicago, 1939.

Gandi, Lakshmi. "A History of Indentured Labor gives 'Coolie' its sting." Accessed October 26, 2016, www.npr.org/blogs/codeswitch/2013/11/25/247166284/a-history-of-indentured-labor-gives-coolie-its-sting.

Golden, Leon and O. B. Hardison Jr. *Horace for Students of Literature: The Ars Poetica and its Tradition*. Florida: University of Florida Press, 1995.

Gomez, Michael. *Black Crescent: The Experience and Legacy of African Muslims in the Americas*. New York: Cambridge University Press, 2005.

 Exchanging Our Country Marks: The Transformation of African Identities in the Colonial and Antebellum South. Chapel Hill, NC: University of North Carolina Press, 1998.

Gordon-Reed, Annette. *Thomas Jefferson and Sally Hemings: An American Controversy.* Charlottesville, VA: University Press of Virginia, 1999.
    The Hemingses of Monticello: An American Family. New York: W.W. Norton and Co., 2008.
Gould, Stephen J. *The Mismeasure of Man.* New York: Norton, 1981.
Guelzo, Allen C. *Fateful Lightning: A New History of the Civil War and Reconstruction.* New York: Oxford University Press, 2012.
Gutman, Herbert. *The Black Family in Slavery and in Freedom, 1750–1925.* New York: Pantheon, 1976.
Hacker, David. "Disunion: Recounting the Dead." September 20, 2011. Accessed October 24, 2016, opinionator.blogs.nytimes.com/2011/09/20/recounting-the-dead/#more-105317.
Haley, Alex. *Roots.* Garden City, NY: Doubleday, 1976.
Hendrick, Willene and George Hendrick, eds. *Fleeing for Freedom: Stories of the Underground Railroad as told by Levi Coffin and William Still.* Chicago: Ivan R. Dee Publishers, 2004.
Hess, Karen. *The Carolina Rice Kitchen: The African Connection.* Columbia, SC: University of South Carolina Press, 1998.
Higgenbotham, Evelyn and John Hope Franklin. *From Slavery to Freedom Vol.1.* New York: McGraw Hill, 2010.
Hilyer, Reiko. "Relics of Reconciliation: The Confederate Museum and Civil War Memory in the New South," *The Public Historian.* Vol. 33, No. 4 (November 2011).
Holyfield, L. and C. Beacham, "Memory Brokers, Shameful Pasts and Civil War Commemoration," *Journal of Black Studies,* Vol. 42, No. 3 (2011): 436–456.
Holzer, Harold, Edna Greene Medford, and Frank J. Williams. *The Emancipation Proclamation: Three Views.* Baton Rouge, LA: Louisiana State University Press, 2006.
Horn, Patrick. "Omar Ibn Said: African Muslim enslaved in the Carolinas," *Documenting the American South.* Accessed September 26, 2016 docsouth .unc.edu/highlights/omarsaid.html.
Horton, James O. and Lois E. *Slavery and Public History: the Tough Stuff Of American History.* New York: New Press, 2006.
Hymowitz, Kay. "The Black Family: 40 years of lies," *City Journal* (Summer 2005). Accessed November 2, 2016, www.city-journal.org/html/15_3_black_family.html.
Jacobs, Harriet, Lydia M. Child, and Jean Fagan Yellin. *Incidents in the Life of a Slave Girl written by herself.* Cambridge, MA: Harvard University Press, 1987.
Johnson, Walter. *Soul by Soul: Life inside the Antebellum Slave Market.* Cambridge, MA: Harvard University Press, 1999.
Jones, Jacqueline. *Labor of Love, Labor of Sorrow: Black Women, Labor and Family from slavery to the present.* New York: Basic Books, 2010.
Jung, Moon-Ho. *Coolies and Cane: Race, Labor and Sugar in the age of Emancipation.* Baltimore, MD: Johns Hopkins University Press, 2006.
Jones, Charles E. *Georgia in the War, 1861–65.* Augusta, GA: C.E. Jones, 1909.

Jones, Jacqueline. *Saving Savannah: The City and the Civil War*. New York: Alfred A. Knopf, 2008.

Kellerman, Nathan. "Epigenetic Transmission of Holocaust Trauma: Can Nightmares be Inherited," *Israel Journal of Psychiatry and Related sciences*. Vol. 50, No. 1 (2013).

Kelsey, Harry. *Sir John Hawkins: Queen Elizabeth's Slavetrader*. New Haven, CT: Yale University Press, 2003.

Kennedy, Randall. *Nigger: The Strange Career of a Troublesome Word*. New York: Pantheon Books, 2002.

Kleber, Martha. *Georgia Historical Society marker application program*. March 1, 2007.

Lincoln C. Eric and Lawrence H. Mamiya. *The Black Church in the African American Experience*. Durham, NC: Duke University Press, 1990.

Littlefield, Daniel. *Rice and Slaves*. Baton Rouge, LA: Louisiana State University Press, 1981.

Lovett, Bobby L. *The African-American History of Nashville, Tennessee, 1780–1930*. Fayetteville, AR: University of Arkansas Press, 1999.

Mair, Lucy. *The Rebel Woman*. Jamaica: Institute of Jamaica Publications Ltd., 1975.

McPherson, James Allan. "Going Up to Atlanta." Accessed on August 16, 2016, http://www. almostisland.com.

McPherson, James M. *For Cause and Comrades: Why Men Fought in the Civil War*. New York: Oxford University Press, 1997.

Ordeal By Fire: The Civil War and Reconstruction. New York: Alfred Knopf, 1982.

Miller, Robert. "American Indians and the US Constitution," *Native America Discovered and Conquered*. Accessed November 2, 2016, www.flashpointmag .com/amindus.htm.

Morgan, Edmund. *American Slavery American Freedom: The Ordeal of Colonial Virginia*. New York: Norton, 1975.

Nash, Gary B. *Race and Revolution*. Madison, WI: Madison House, 1990.

Niane, D.T. *Sundiata: An Epic of Old Mali*. Harlow, England: Pearson Longman, 2006.

Northrup, Solomon. *Twelve Years a Slave, A Narrative of Solomon Northrup*. Auburn, NY: Derby and Miller, 1853.

Patterson, Orlando. *An Absence of Ruins*. Leeds, UK: Peelpal Tree, 2012.

Quarles, Benjamin. "Lord Dunmore as Liberator," *The William and Mary Quarterly*, Vol. 15, No. 4 (October 1958).

Regosin, Elizabeth Ann and Donald Robert Shaffer. *Voices of Emancipation: Understanding Slavery, the Civil War and Reconstruction through the U.S. Pension files*. New York: New York University Press, 2008.

Rivoli, Pietra. *The Travels of a T shirt in a Global economy: An Economist examines the markets, power and politics of world trade*. New Jersey: John Wiley and Sons, 2009.

Rodney, Walter. *How Europe Underdeveloped Africa*. London: Bogle L'Ouverture Pub., 1972.

Rose, P. K. *Black Dispatches: Black American Contribution to Union Intelligence During the Civil War*. Washington, DC:Center for the Study of Intelligence, Central Intelligence Agency 1999.

Scheff, T.J. *Bloody Revenge: Emotions, Nationalism and War*. Boulder, CO: Westview, 1994.

Seldes, George, ed. *The Great Quotations*. New York: Pocket Books, 1972.

Selig, Robert. "The Revolution's Black Soldiers," Accessed November 3, 2016, www.americanrevolution.org/blk.html.

Southern, Eileen and Josephine Wright. *African American Traditions in Song, Sermon, Tale and Dance, 1600's-1920*. Westport, CT: Greenwood Pub. Group, 1990.

Stampp, Kenneth. *The Peculiar Institution*. New York: Knopf, 1984.

Sullivan, Buddy. *Memories of McIntosh: A Brief History of McIntosh Island, Darien and Sapelo*. Darien, GA: Darien News, 1990

Tibbetts, John. "African Roots Carolina Gold," *Coastal Heritage*, Vol. 21, No. 1 (Summer 2006), South Carolina Sea Grant Consortium.

Trouillot, Michel-Rolph. *Silencing the Past: Power and the Production of History*. Boston, MA: Beacon Press, 1995.

Walker, Sheila S., ed. *African Roots American Cultures: Africa in the Creation of the Americas*. Lanham, MD: Rowman and Littlefield, 2001.

West, Jean. "King Cotton: The Fiber of Slavery," *Slavery in America*. Accessed October 29, 2016, cuwhist.files.wordpress.com/2012/07/king-cotton-the-fiber-of-slavery.pdf.

White, Deborah Gray. *Arn't I A Woman: Female Slaves in the Plantation South*. New York: Norton, 1999.

White, Shane and Graham White. *The Sounds of Slavery: Discovering African American History Through Songs, Sermons and Speech*. Boston, MA: Beacon Press, 2005.

Wiencek, Henry. *The Hairstons: An American Family in Black and White*. New York: St. Martin's Griffin, 1999.

Wilkerson, Isabel. *The Warmth of Other Suns: The Epic Story of America's Great Migration*. New York: Random House, 2010.

Wilson, William Julius. *Truly Disadvantaged*. Chicago: University of Chicago Press, 1987.

Williams, Eric. *Capitalism and Slavery*. New York: Capricorn, 1966.

Williams, Rhonda and Julie Buckner Armstrong, Susan Hult Edwards, Houston Bryan Roberson, eds. *Teaching the Civil Rights Movement*. UK: Routledge Press, 2012.

Woodward, C. Vann. *Reunion, and Reaction: The Compromise of 1877 and the End of Reconstruction*. New York; Oxford: Oxford University Press, 1991.

Zucchi, Fabiola C. R., Youli Yao and Gerlinde A. Metz. "The Secret Language of Destiny: Stress Imprinting and Transgenerational Origins of Disease," *Frontiers in Genetics*, Vol. 3, Article 96 (June 2012).

Zuczek, Richard. *Encyclopedia of the Reconstruction Era*. Westport, CT: Greenwood Press, 2006.

Index